Islamic Monetary Economics

The existence of fiat currencies has long been cited as one of the major contributing factors to the challenges facing contemporary economies, and the current monetary system is not only a key source of exorable increases in interest rates but also a principal cause of inflation and decline in the value of money in many countries. The editors argue that an Islamic monetary system, with its specific money concepts, interest-free financial institutions, and monetary policy embedded in real growth, provides a solution to this conundrum.

Contributions from many world-renowned experts consider a wide array of topics, ranging from the theoretical concepts of money and banking in conventional and Islamic economics to the historical journey of money from precious metals to plastic money and digital currency today. The book outlines the problems that sprout from interest-based banking and multiple debt structures. It then mirrors the Islamic concepts of money as well as idiosyncrasies of its monetary policy. Supported with meticulous research and empirical evidence, the book demonstrates the efficacy of Islamic monetary system in delivering real growth along with equitable distribution of wealth and prosperity in the economy. It additionally acquaints the readers with juristic debates about money and monetary policy.

This is essential reading for both students and researchers in Islamic economics, banking, and finance, expertly promoting a fair and just economic system that emerges as a result of interest-free banking and monetary policy based on Islamic principles.

Taha Eğri, PhD, is currently a research fellow at Kırklareli University, Turkey. He completed his BA at Bogazici University, Turkey, and obtained his MA and PhD degrees at Istanbul University, Turkey. He was a visiting scholar at George Mason University, USA, between 2014 and 2016. His primary research areas are institutional economics and International political economy. He is currently focusing on MENA countries' economic policies, military-economic relations and Islamic economics. He is Director of the Research Center for Islamic Economics (IKAM), Istanbul, and the editor of two peer-reviewed journals.

Zeyneb Hafsa Orhan, PhD, received her undergraduate degree on economics from Bahcesehir University, Turkey, and her master's degree on international and European relations from Linköpings University, Sweden. Finally, she obtained her PhD degree on economics (with a thesis specializing in Islamic banks) from the International University of Sarajevo, Bosnia. After over eight years of international experience, she has been working at Istanbul Sabahattin Zaim University since the beginning of 2015. Currently she is an assistant professor in the Islamic Economics and Finance Department. Her current research areas include Islamic economics and finance, finance, and banking.

Islamic Business and Finance Series
Series Editor: Ishaq Bhatti

There is an increasing need for western politicians, financiers, bankers, and indeed the western business community in general to have access to high quality and authoritative texts on Islamic financial and business practices. Drawing on expertise from across the Islamic world, this new series will provide carefully chosen and focused monographs and collections, each authored/edited by an expert in their respective field all over the world.

The series will be pitched at a level to appeal to middle and senior management in both the western and the Islamic business communities. For the manager with a western background the series will provide detailed and up-to-date briefings on important topics; for the academics, postgraduates, business communities, manager with western and an Islamic background the series will provide a guide to best practice in business in Islamic communities around the world, including Muslim minorities in the west and majorities in the rest of the world.

A History of Interest and Debt
Ancient Civilizations
Edited by Murat Ustaoğlu and Ahmet İncekara

Awqaf-led Islamic Social Finance
Innovative Solutions to Modern Applications
Edited by Mohd Ma'Sum Billah

The Evolution of Interest and Debt
From Middle Ages to Modern Times
Edited by Murat Ustaoğlu and Ahmet İncekara

Growth of Islamic Banking in Indonesia
Theory and Practice
Sigit Pramono and Yasushi Suzuki

Islamic Monetary Economics
Finance and Banking in Contemporary Muslim Economies
Edited by Taha Eğri and Zeyneb Hafsa Orhan

For more information about this series, please visit: www.routledge.com/Islamic-Business-and-Finance-Series/book-series/ISLAMICFINANCE

Islamic Monetary Economics

Finance and Banking in Contemporary Muslim Economies

Edited by Taha Eğri and Zeyneb Hafsa Orhan

Routledge
Taylor & Francis Group
LONDON AND NEW YORK

First published 2021
by Routledge
2 Park Square, Milton Park, Abingdon, Oxon OX14 4RN

and by Routledge
52 Vanderbilt Avenue, New York, NY 10017

Routledge is an imprint of the Taylor & Francis Group, an informa business

British Library Cataloguing-in-Publication Data
A catalogue record for this book is available from the British Library

Library of Congress Cataloging-in-Publication Data
Names: Eğri, Taha, editor. | Orhan, Zeyneb Hafsa, editor.
Title: Islamic monetary economics: finance and banking in contemporary Muslim economies/edited by Taha Eğri and Zeyneb Hafsa Orhan.
Description: Abingdon, Oxon; New York, NY: Routledge, 2021. | Series: Islamic business and finance series | Includes bibliographical references and index.
Identifiers: LCCN 2020031873 (print) | LCCN 2020031874 (ebook) | ISBN 9780367457730 (hardback) | ISBN 9781003025191 (ebook)
Subjects: LCSH: Finance—Islamic countries. | Finance—Religious aspects—Islam. | Banks and banking—Islamic countries. | Banks and banking—Religious aspects—Islam. | Monetary policy—Islamic countries.
Classification: LCC HG187.4.I83656 2021 (print) | LCC HG187.4 (ebook) | DDC 332.0917/67—dc23
LC record available at https://lccn.loc.gov/2020031873
LC ebook record available at https://lccn.loc.gov/2020031874

ISBN: 978-0-367-45773-0 (hbk)
ISBN: 978-1-003-02519-1 (ebk)

Typeset in Times New Roman
by Apex CoVantage, LLC

Contents

Figures

Tables

Contributors

Editors' biographies

Taha Eğri

Dr Taha Egri is currently a research fellow at Kırklareli University, Turkey. He completed his BA at Bogazici University, Turkey, and obtained his MA and PhD degrees at Istanbul University, Turkey. He was a visiting scholar at George Mason University, USA, between 2014 and 2016. His primary research areas are institutional economics and international political economy. He is currently focusing on MENA countries' economic policies, military-economic relations, and Islamic economics. He is Director of Research Center for Islamic Economics (IKAM), Istanbul, and the editor of two peer-reviewed journals: *The Journal of Humanity and Society* and the *Turkish Journal of Islamic Economics* (*TUJISE*).

Zeyneb Hafsa Orhan

Zeyneb Hafsa Orhan got her undergraduate degree on economics from Bahcesehir University, Turkey. Then she got her master's degree on international and European relations from Linköpings University, Sweden. Finally, she got her PhD degree on economics (with a thesis specialized on Islamic banks) from International University of Sarajevo, Bosnia. After having more than eight years of international experience, she has been working at Istanbul Sabahattin Zaim University since the beginning of 2015. Currently she is an assistant professor of the Islamic Economics and Finance Department. Her current research areas include Islamic economics and finance, finance, and banking.

Authors' biographies

Abdul Rashid

Dr Abdul Rashid is currently working as Associate Professor/Chairman of Research at the International Institute of Islamic Economics (IIIE), International Islamic University Islamabad, Pakistan. He possesses vast experience of research, teaching, and project leadership in economics, finance, and Islamic banking and finance. He carries a wealth of published research (more than 120 papers), earning an impact factor of greater than 15. Having received PhD in economics from the

University of Sheffield, UK, in 2012, Dr Rashid is actively involved in research in applied econometrics, international finance, corporate finance, and Islamic finance and related disciplines. He has published his work in *Economic Inquiry*, *Empirical Economics*, *Small Business Economics*, *Energy*, *Energy Policy*, *Risk Management*, *Baltic Journal of Economics*, *Emerging Market Finance and Trade*, *Managerial Finance*, *Journal of Economic Studies*, *Management Decision*, *Romanian Journal of Economic Forecasting*, *Research in International Business and Finance*, *Journal of Islamic Business and Management*, *Pakistan Development Review*, and several other well-reputed national and international journals.

Adam Abdullah

Adam Abdullah holds a PhD in (Islamic) economics. He is currently an associate professor at the College of Economics and Management, Al-Qasimia University, UAE, and was the former Deputy Dean (Research & Publications) at IIUM's Institute of Islamic Banking and Finance (IIiBF). He specializes in Islamic economics, finance, and investment, and has published over 65 articles and books. Dr Adam has written extensively on an Islamic monetary economics, publishing *The Islamic Currency* (2016), which included an analysis of monetary performance over 1,300 years involving gold, silver, and commodity price data in Egypt, Ottoman-Turkey, England, America, and Malaysia. He has presented at a number of international conferences, including as guest speaker. He has also taught various subjects at both undergraduate and postgraduate levels and has supervised a number of PhD and master's students in Islamic economics, finance, and banking.

Ahsan Shafiq

Ahsan Shafiq graduated from the Department of Economics, University of Hertfordshire, UK, in 2010. He later attained his master's degree in 2012 from the Economics and Finance Department at the University of Leeds, UK. In 2013, he started his professional career as a faculty member at National University of Science & Technology (NUST), Pakistan. He left NUST for further studies in 2015 and is currently pursuing his doctoral degree at Marmara University in Turkey. He has authored several academic articles and chapters in several books and has represented his works at various conferences. Ahsan is Senior Researcher and the Coordinator of the Research Center for Islamic Economics (IKAM), Istanbul as well as Associate-Editor of its indexed journal, *Turkish Journal of Islamic Economics* (*TUJISE*).

Hüseyin Burgazoğlu

He graduated from the Business Administration Department of Bogazici University in 2007. He received his master's degree from Istanbul University, Department of Numerical Methods. Between 2009 and 2014, he worked as a research assistant at the Faculty of Economics and Administrative Sciences, Kirklareli University. He continues the doctorate programme at Istanbul University, Department of Numerical Methods. He is working as a research assistant at Sakarya University,

Faculty of Business Administration. He has several studies published in national and international journals in the field of business and economics.

M. Fahim Khan

Dr Fahim Khan is currently an emeritus professor of economics. He served 12 years in senior positions in work related to macroeconomic frameworks and policies for five-year plans. He served as Director of Research at the Islamic Development Bank, focusing on policies relating to development finance in Muslim countries. In between he served as the Director of the School of Economics at the International Islamic University, Islamabad, and for one year served as advisor to the governor of the State Bank of Pakistan when the Supreme Court of Pakistan asked the central bank of the country to form a high-level commission to transform the financial system of the country and to conform to shariah. His current work is about developing a research-based policy framework for achieving those UN sustainable development goals that require priority in the country in view of the current social and cultural environment in the country. His research includes how to enhance financial inclusion by transferring non-bank financial activities based on cultural and religious activities to formal financial institutions.

M. Kabir Hassan

Professor Dr M. Kabir Hassan is Professor of Finance in the Department of Economics and Finance in the University of New Orleans. He currently holds two endowed Chairs—Hibernia Professor of Economics and Finance and Bank One Professor in Business—at the University of New Orleans. Professor Hassan is the winner of the 2016 IDB Prize in Islamic Banking and Finance. Professor Hassan received his BA in economics and mathematics from Gustavus Adolphus College, Minnesota, USA, and MA in economics and PhD in finance from the University of Nebraska-Lincoln, USA.

Mabid Ali Al-Jarhi

Dr Mabid Ali Al-Jarhi is Professor of Economics and Finance as well as Coordinator of International Center of Islamic Economics & Finance at Ankara Sosyal Bilimler University. He has previously served at INCEIF, Malaysia, and Hamad Bin Khalifa University, Qatar, as a senior faculty member. He earned his PhD from University of South California, USA, in 1975. Since then he has worked at several academic and professional positions. He was Director of Economic and Policy Planning at Islamic Development Bank (IsDB) from 1976 to 1978 and was Director General of IRTI from 1996 to 2003. He has won several awards, including Islamic Development Bank 2019 prize in Islamic economics, banking, and finance. Mabid does research in macroeconomics, monetary economics, and financial economics from an Islamic perspective.

Maryam Soleimani Movahed

Maryam Soleimani Movahed is Assistant Professor at Iran University of Medical Sciences. She has received her PhD in economics from Alzahra University, Tehran, Iran, in 2016.

Mehmet Saraç

Professor Mehmet Saraç received his undergraduate degree from Istanbul University, Faculty of Business Administration, in 1990. He completed the master's program at the same faculty in accounting and auditing in 1992 and also received a master's degree in accounting and taxation from George Washington University in 1997. After graduation, he worked for the Financial Regulation Project for the Washington, DC, government. In 1988 he started his PhD in finance in Boğaziçi University, where he worked as an RA until the completion of his PhD studies in 2004. He also advised the private sector during that period. He taught at Mersin University for a short period and was assigned to Sakarya University as Assistant Professor in 2007. He became Associate Professor of finance in 2012. He played a key role in establishing the Islamic Economics and Finance Department at Sakarya University and launching the first interdisciplinary master's program in this field in Turkey and chaired for the department for a year. In 2014 he became affiliated with Istanbul University and helped to establish and develop Islamic economics and finance programs there too. In 2016, he contributed to establishing the Center for Islamic Economics and Finance at Istanbul University and has been appointed as the first director through 2019. He currently teaches corporate finance, Islamic finance, capital markets and institutions and other related courses. His recent publications concentrated in Islamic economics and finance. He is also a member of advisory boards at several institutions, including Türkiye Emlak Participation Bank, the International Council of Islamic Finance Educators (ICIFE), and the Research Center for Islamic Economics (IKAM).

Mücahit Özdemir

Mücahit Özdemir is a vice director at the Research Center for Islamic Economics and Finance (İSEFAM) in Sakarya University. He graduated from Boğaziçi University with a bachelor's degree in economics in 2009. After graduation, he worked at the investor relations department in Albaraka Türk Participation Bank from 2010 to 2014. After five years of professional life in the Islamic banking sector, Özdemir returned to the academy in the Department of Islamic Economics and Finance at Sakarya University in 2014. He earned an MA degree in banking at Marmara University in 2013 and an MSc degree in the Islamic Finance and Management Program of Durham University in 2017. He earned his PhD at the Department of Islamic Economics and Finance at Sakarya University in 2018, with his thesis on Islamic microfinance. Özdemir is also serving as a chairman in the Foundation of Research and Praxis for Islamic Economics (İKSAR), which is the first Islamic microfinance institution in Turkey, with its *qard al hassan*-based model.

Ömer Faruk Tekdoğan

Dr Omer Faruk Tekdogan is Head of the Department at the Ministry of Treasury and Finance—DG Economic Programs and Research. He worked as team leader in the Public Finance Transformation Office of the Ministry and as senior specialist for the Undersecretariat of Treasury. He was a policy analyst in the Development Co-Operation Directorate in the Organisation for Economic Co-Operation and Development, where his main research areas were official development finance for infrastructure, investment, private sector development, and regional connectivity. He received his PhD in Islamic economics and finance from İstanbul University, and he holds a master's in economics from North Carolina State University. He is a visiting lecturer in the Ankara Yildirim Beyazit University Faculty of Political Sciences. His past and present research fields cover Islamic economics and finance, monetary economics, banking, financial economics, and agent-based modelling.

Sajjad Zaheer
Dr Sajjad Zaheer holds a PhD in economics and business from the University of Amsterdam. His PhD research focuses on the salient features of Islamic banking and finance, Islamic banking products, monetary policy, financial stability and capital structure of Islamic banks, and distress resolution mechanisms in *sukuk*. He worked with the IMF and European Central Bank on different projects. Currently, he is working as an economist in the Monetary Policy Department, State Bank of Pakistan. He has contributed to the implementation of Shariah governance framework for Islamic banking industry in Pakistan. His research work is very well received, which is evident from his publications in quality outlets like the *International Journal of Central Banking* and the IMF Working Paper Series and his winning a research award from Central Bank of Turkey for his article "Transmission of Monetary Policy Through Conventional and Islamic Channels".

Salman Ahmed Shaikh
Dr Salman Ahmed Shaikh is Assistant Professor of Management Sciences at SZABIST Karachi. He holds a PhD in economics from National University of Malaysia. He also received a BBA in finance from Bahria University, an MS in finance from SZABIST Karachi, and a master's in economics from the Institute of Business Administration, Karachi. He has published several research papers on Islamic economics and finance in Scopus and Web of Science indexed journals as well as chapters in books published by Web of Science publishers. He has presented in international conferences in Turkey, Indonesia, Malaysia, Brunei, and Pakistan. He was the recipient of two Emerald Highly Commended Paper Awards in 2018.

Syed Muhammad Abdul Rehman Shah
Syed Muhammad Abdul Rehman Shah is a PhD scholar and is serving as a lecturer at the Department of Basic Sciences and Humanities in the University of Engineering and Technology (UET) Taxila, Pakistan. He is also a part-time faculty member at several other universities. His subjects are Islamic law of business contracts; Islamic professional ethics; Islamic theology, regulation, supervision, and control of Islamic financial institutions (IFIs); Islamic banking and finance; financial management; and engineering economics.

Zahra Afshari
Zahra Afshari is Professor of Economics at Alzahra University in Iran. She has received her PhD in Economics from Indiana University, Bloomington, Indiana,

USA. She teaches macroeconomics and monetary economics at the PhD level. She is the author of many research papers in the field of monetary economics, development economics, and gender economics.

Zohra Jabeen

Dr Zohra Jabeen is an assistant professor at the Institute of Management Sciences, Peshawar. She has a PhD in finance from Mohammad Ali Jinnah University, Islamabad, and an MS in international banking and finance from the University of Southampton, UK. She is a former banker and has specialized in banking and financial regulations as well as *sukuk* in combination with AAOIFI Shariah Standards and Basel Regulations. Her recent involvement is in monetary economics from an Islamic perspective and waqf-based economy in collaboration with her mentors and peers.

Preface

Money has been used in various ways as a tool that organized trade relations between people at different times in history and allowed them the accumulation of wealth and prosperity. It has been involved in economic activities in many forms, from seashells to precious metals and from gold and silver to paper notes. As it has been for centuries, it still maintains its importance in the centre of life and economy. Based on this importance, it has been discussed from different angles at various times and on multiple grounds. The subject of money has a wide place in the history of economic thought. Mercantilists accepted gold and silver as the only source of wealth, while in the classical thought it was considered to be only a medium of exchange. However, in the first half of the twentieth century, the meaning attributed by Keynesian thought to money carried the economic theory to an advanced level in a macro sense. The Chicago school, which later emerged as a "monetarist" school, focused on the effect of money on inflation and macro variables and put monetary policy at the centre of the economy.

In the historical development of money, it has changed from a metal system to fiat money and has taken its present form. However, this dynamic structure is still ongoing, and with the advent of "crypto currencies", its evolution still continues, albeit in another dimension. In this context, while the problem of debasement was the centre of debates in the past, the future of digital currencies is under discussion today; hence. monetary issues continue to occupy the agenda.

In the field of Islamic economics, discussions are increasing in a practical and theoretical sense. Some of these problems are based on questions like how Muslim countries could protect their economic wealth, the independence of national monetary systems and the strengthening of international competitiveness, as well as succeed in their pursuit of transition from interest-based practices of the conventional system to an interest-free monetary system. The search for a monetary policy in line with the aims of maintaining price stability, ensuring economic growth, ensuring full employment and economic welfare, and promoting justice in income distribution is on the agenda of Islamic economic studies.

This book contains a comprehensive range of topics from the history of Islamic economics to the monetary policies in accordance with Islam in today's central banks and from the debates of fiat currency to the Islamic point of view on digital money.

For their help in the process of creating the book, we would like to thank all the authors for their contributions.

Taha Eğri—Zeyneb Hafsa Orhan
Kirklareli-Istanbul 2020

Money from the viewpoint of Islam, history of Islam and Islamic economics

Zeyneb Hafsa Orhan

Introduction

Money is one of the most widely discussed concepts on a micro and macro scale today, and in practice, it is at the center of all relational network. Has this always been the case throughout history? And if not, what are the reasons for this being the case today? Although questions like this are crucial to answer, it is beyond the scope of this chapter. The aim of this chapter is to examine the Islamic point of view about money taking Islamic (economics) history and modern Islamic economics into consideration. It is also intended to be the introductory article of this book, which is a collection of the papers presented at the 7th Islamic Economics Workshop, organized by IKAM (Research Center for Islamic Economics) in 2019. Therefore, it also aims to review these papers, now chapters, in a systematic way.

This chapter is based on a qualitative method, in accordance with the nature of its subject. We have searched and examined the literature that could provide direct or indirect information about the aforementioned purpose and reached some conclusions.

What makes this chapter noteworthy is the need for an introductory framework for modern Muslims, which could also be used as a guideline to evaluate these concepts and issues. Although this chapter does not claim to present the general framework in question, it does, together with the other articles in the book, provide an effort and example for this.

The chapter is organized as follows: the second section discusses the history of money, then in the third section, money in Islamic history and Islam is examined. The fourth will be devoted to money in the context of Islamic economics. The last section will be a summary and conclusion of the main topics covered in the chapter. On a side note, there is not a separate chapter for a literature review, because the related literature will be discussed in each section. The methodology has also already briefly been mentioned, and no separate section has been allocated to it.

Money in history

Before discussing the basic purpose of this chapter, it is worth mentioning the history of money in brief. Once Muslims came onto the stage of history, they faced an existing monetary structure, and hence their views on money were shaped on the basis of this structure.

Although there is no standard explanation for when and how money emerged and developed in the sense of a medium of exchange for a goods or services, the most commonly accepted definition by the students of classical economics is as follows: People used to trade (barter) at first, but because of bartering's limitations in various aspects, the coin was invented as a standard and universally accepted medium of exchange. This was followed by paper money/nominal money in parallel with the state's authority to print money and then virtual money in parallel with technological developments. Although this presumption generally persists, Polanyi (2001), quoting Melitz, claims that it is because of classical economists that the creation of money in the "primitive era" is attributed to the inadequacies of the barter system, while Melitz (ibid.) actually bases this opinion on Aristotle's writings. A remarkable study that questioned this issue and reached a negative conclusion was published in 2011. American anthropologist Graeber (2015), in his work titled *Debt: The First 5000 years*, criticizes the idea that money emerged after the barter economy in the chapter titled "The Myth of the Barter": "The problem is there is no evidence that it ever happened, an enormous amount of suggesting that it did not. For centuries now, explorers have been trying to find this fabled land of barter—none with success." According to Graeber, the true version of the previously mentioned standard narrative that follows the chain of barter → money → credit chain is actually the exact opposite, that is, virtual money → coin, with barter as a by-product.

Regardless of which theory is accepted, as we understand it today, the first manufactured coin as a standard medium of exchange that is not a commodity money, such as barley or a cowry shell, etc., appeared in the kingdom of Lydia in Asia Minor somewhere around the seventh century BC. It was made of an alloy of gold and silver called electrum. Since the coin, which has been used for a long time throughout the history of mankind, is identified with the money itself, the word money in different languages today comes from *monoi*, the ancient French word for "coin."

Although paper or nominal money, which is widely used today, became popular in seventeenth-century Europe, it is recorded that the first paper money known in history was invented and used by the Chinese in the seventh century. But the Chinese had stopped using this kind of money since the fifteenth century—albeit only for a while—due to their negative experiences with it.

The developments mentioned in the last two paragraphs are critical because they are also closely related to one of the controversial issues in Islamic economics; that is the question of whether money should be based on something of self-worth, such as gold or silver, or whether paper/nominal money, which derives its origin from an authority such as the government, can also be considered as money. The details of this matter will be discussed next.

The debates today about the issue of money goes even beyond these two definitions, because especially with the development of technology, quasi types of money have emerged other paper money; cryptocurrency (bitcoin, ethereum, iota, etc.), electronic money and so on. Although we will not go into the details of these types of money, it must be stated that further studies are needed to address this issue, especially in the context of Islamic economics.

The ontological meaning, content, and development of money—especially in Western literature—as well as how money emerged and in which forms it was used in the history, have been subject of various studies. These studies also coincide with the literature, which is sometimes referred to as theory of money in classical economics. Although we will not go into the details of this theory here, the ontological debates about money will be discussed later, since it is more related to the main topic of this chapter.

According to Innes (1914), who advocates the so-called credit theory of money, there is no such thing as a medium of exchange. Buying and selling something simply means its exchange for credit. Therefore, money's function is solely as an exclusive credit.

Searle (1995), a contemporary researcher who asks questions about what money is and why it exists, states that some parts of real life and the objective realities in this world are only real because of the agreement between people. According to him, money is one of the objective realities developed by inter-human contract. There is also criticism against this view. For example, according to Smit, Buekens and du Plessis (2011), the collective intention (which Searle explains with the word "contract"), which is defined as one of the fundamental characteristics of institutional realities such as money, is not a necessary condition for the existence of institutional realities. Therefore, institutional realities can be reduced to natural realities, contrary to Searle's claim. According to these authors, what lies behind objects such as money is the need for encouragement. Indeed, nominal money, like the electronic money used today, is backed by people's preferences. This is also an answer to the claims that there is nothing that supports nominal money. Kocherlakota (1998) points out the importance of incentive and refers to its relationship with memory, and ultimately defines money as a primitive type of memory. What is meant by the term memory here is a historical record that informs to any representative, at any time of the history, the past of all the actors with whom he has directly or indirectly contacted (ibid). Accordingly, money has no intrinsic value, and is useless in this sense.

In the Preface to Polanyi's (2001) *Great Transformation*, Fred Block summarizes Polanyi's view on money as follows: "According to Polanyi, the definition of commodity is something produced for sale in the market. By this definition, land, labor and money are fictitious goods because they are not actually produced for sale in the market." But Polanyi was criticized by Melitz (1970) because he points to multifaceted money as one of the most important pillars of the great transformation in the nineteenth century. Melitz (ibid.) claims that today's money is not multifaceted, but rather it has a special function similar to the one in the "primitive periods." Accordingly, there are not tremendous differences and a break between the monetary structure in modern and ancient times. Melitz's (ibid.) other criticism of Polanyi and his supporters is that they see monetary development in a progressive and straight line.

Ozel (2019), one of the authors writing on the relationship between Islam and economics in Turkey, argues that there are three fictions (i.e., imaginary frameworks, or in other words nominal elements): Paper money, nations, and novels. According to him, "capitalism would not have existed if there was no paper money." Of course, such a claim should be backed by concrete reasons and data, but what matters here is the emphasis on the close relationship between paper/nominal money, modernism, and capitalism, which was also discussed by Polanyi.

Money in the history of Islam and Islam

Islam is a religion that in essence could be traced to Adam, the first man and prophet. Uslu (2014) from this point of view writes as follows regarding the relationship between Adam and money: God Almighty, who taught Adam the names of all things and created him as the caliph on earth, also taught money and money-related terms and words and guided him in this regard. Although it is not possible to present direct evidence for this claim, we can deduce that: Adam was taught the names of all things → money and related concepts are also names → then Adam was informed about them. In addition, Uslu quotes Makrizi's (1364–1442) argument that the one who first used dinar and dirham was Adam. However, as far as we know, there is no anthropological or archaeological evidence for this claim.

Uslu (ibid.) also presents following examples about the prophets' relationships with money and money-related issues until the era of Muhammad (pbuh): Musa (pbuh) worked for Shuaib (pbuh) for a wage; prophets did not expect any wage from their community; and Yusuf was sold into slavery in return for a small amount. In the first two examples, the word "wage" is used for money, while in the last example direct terms, a low amount and a few dirhams, are mentioned. "Dirham" in Islamic law is used both as a generic name and for a certain currency and a unit of measure (ibid.).

There were two types of coins used in Arabia when the religion of Islam emerged: Byzantine gold dinars and Sassanid silver. Muslims used them for a certain period. Although there were unofficial local coins minted during the reigns of four caliphs (Uslu, ibid.) the first official money issued by Muslims themselves was the gold and silver coins minted by the Umayyads in the seventh century.

As mentioned earlier, societies minted and used their own coins for a long time throughout the history of Islam. For example, the Ottoman state had used coins until the first paper money, *kaime*, was printed in 1840. For other Muslim societies, this process went in parallel with colonialism. According to Kahf (2019), gold and silver coins used in Syria and Lebanon since the Ottoman period were replaced by paper money under the French occupation (1920–1945) .

The use of coins for such a long time has led to the discussions about money in classical Islamic jurisprudence to revolve around gold and silver coins. Let us begin our discussion on money in *fiqh* literature with the etymology of the word money in Arabic, which is "mal." The plural of this word is *amwal*, and it covers everything that is possessed, as it is also used in Turkish today. Therefore, it has a broader meaning than what we understand from the word "money" today.

Accordingly, money is simply one of the types of goods possessed. Today, the direct word used for money in Arabic is "naqd." The difference between *mal* and *naqd* is that the former is capable of meeting the needs and wants directly, whereas the latter can meet them indirectly. For example, Ibn Qayyim (Aybakan, 2006) states that money should be considered as a means of accessing the goods. Otherwise, the social order would be destroyed if it is seen and treated as an end in itself.

Khan and Jabeen (2019), who made a presentation in the workshop and contributed to this book with a chapter (Chapter 2), state that there had not been a well-established monetary theory until Islamic economics was developed. However, "An important subject in the Islamic legal thought has been how money affects economic relations" (Siegfried, 2001, 2011). In this regard, we can list the main issues related to money discussed in Islamic law as follows:

First, the provisions for the retention of raw gold and silver are clearly defined. The most known embodiments of this are in the hadith, referred to as the hadith of six commodities. This hadith also presents an important guide about the types of interest. The summary of it is shown in Table 0.1.

Looking at the intersection of fields, the exchange of a commodity with itself diagonal part, the exchange of a commodity with itself should be in equal quantities and on spot. The exchange of other commodities with gold and silver is allowed either on spot or on deferred payment. The exchange of four commodities other than gold and silver must be on spot. Different schools of *fiqh* have different opinions on the meaning of the rule of "in equal quantities"; that is, it is either by

Table 0.1 The content of the hadith of six commodities, including provisions on the exchange of gold and silver

	Gold	*Silver*	*Dates*	*Salt*	*Barley*	*Wheat*
Gold	In equal quantities and on spot	On spot	All types	All types	All types	All types
Silver	On spot	In equal quantities and on spot	All types	All types	All types	All types
Dates	All types	All types	In equal quantities and on spot	On spot	On spot	On spot
Salt	All types	All types	On spot	In equal quantities and on spot	On spot	On spot
Barley	All types	All types	On spot	On spot	In equal quantities and on spot	On spot
Wheat	All types	All types	On spot	On spot	On spot	In equal quantities and on spot

Source: Tabulated by the author

weight or volume. In addition, there is also a disagreement in determining which type of commodity gold, silver, and other items belong to. In this context, there is a lot of controversy about gold and silver being non-commodities, which are self-denominated. Siegfried (ibid.) reports that the earliest written document where gold and silver were mentioned as a conventional medium of exchange was found in the H. 4 century. However, the source remains unknown.

Second, the question of debate in the following periods became debasement of precious metals, including *fels* (copper and bronze coins). Historically, *fels* can be classified as the first example of traditional money, as it reflects in a way the value that is not by itself. The debasement policy in the Ottoman Empire began in the late 1500s (Erdem, 2006).

Third, the exchange rate between gold and silver is another matter of debate among *fiqh* scholars. This rate is of importance in terms of the punishment of cutting off hands for theft or determining the amount of capital contribution of each party to the partnership.

Fourth, a development that led to the discussion of paper money-like things other than *fels* in classical *fiqh* was the use of the *suftaja* in long-distance trade in the Middle Ages. *Suftaja* is "a commercial paper, or the transaction itself, for an unconditional payment order of the loaned amount by the debtor to the creditor or a third party (the creditor's representative, partner, agent, proxy or debtor) in another geographical location" (Kallek, 2010).

Eventually, although there is no direct discussion of paper money in classical Islamic law, based on the information already described, this issue can be discussed through analogy (Siegfried, ibid.):

1 Paper money can be seen as a gold and silver indexed instrument.
2 It is based on *suftaja*.
3 In classical legal thought, paper money can be given the same legal position as the *fulus* (plural of *fels*).
4 Money can be presented like a simple commodity.
5 It can be seen as a medium of exchange for many things.

Among these, Siegfried (ibid.) opts for the last one.

Keles (1998), who carried out one of the most detailed studies on the discussion of money in Islamic law in Turkish, shares the following information in his unpublished PhD thesis: Muslim scholars divided money into two categories once different types of money other than coins began to be used: money by nature (such as gold and silver) and money that is technically money (such as paper money). This distinction does not depend on the function of money but on its substance. In addition, Keles (ibid) makes the following observation, which is one of the central claims of his thesis: The definition of money in Islamic *fiqh* is not based on *nass* (an explicit statement in the Quran or hadith) but is influenced by the conditions of the day. In his view, it is therefore unnecessary to discuss whether gold or silver is money. Nevertheless, this discussion is important, as will be seen in the next section, and must be analyzed carefully.

Money in Islamic economics

Islamic economics emerged at the beginning of the twentieth century with the attempts of Muslim societies that lost their independence after the First World War to gain independence and establish a proper economic structure for themselves. Then it developed as an academic discipline through the accumulation of scientific and systematic knowledge. Any economic issue that could be examined from the Islamic point of view is of interest to Islamic economics today, including money and related subjects. Based on our survey about the money-related discussions in Islamic economics during the last decades, basic topics can be listed as follows:

1 Whether money should only be made of gold and silver and the question of representative or nominal money
2 The relationship between nominal money and money creation
3 Money-bank, central banking and monetary policy instruments in Islamic economics
4 Public finance
5 Other matters related to money (interest, cash waqf, time value of money, etc.)

Each topic will be discussed below.

Gold-silver coin vs. nominal money

Asadov (2017) provides a good summary of the first question. In his view, Islamic economists have two basic positions toward money: (1) Those who confine the definition of money to gold and silver and (2) those who do not limit it and accept representative money. Analyzing these two groups, Asadov includes Hosein, Meera and Larbani, and Vadillo in the first group and Zubair Hasan and Murat Cizakca in the second. As an example for the opinions of the first group, the author quotes Vadillo (2006): "Gold and silver have not become money by any choice, or order. On the other hand, paper money has been imposed on people." By contrast, the second group believes that this situation emphasizes the importance of the social contract in accepting money as money.

Another writer that can be included in the first of these two groups is Adam Abdullah, who has also contributed to this book with his chapter. Based on his empirical investigation of Ottoman Empire (1469–2009) and Malaysia (1970–2014), Abdullah (Chapter 4) discovered that prices expressed in pure gold and silver were stable over the long term, while under the fiat standard prices have increased exponentially. His findings also show that aggregate interest on deposits and loans are the primary determinants of the growth in money supply under the fiat standard. Therefore, Abdullah emphasizes the importance of a gold and/or silver backed medium of exchange over the money created by banks through interest-based credit and nominal money.

As a result, although it is difficult to say that there is a consensus in Islamic economics regarding the issue of nominal money in relation to gold and silver, it can be said that nominal money is mostly regarded as money, too.

Money creation through nominal money

In connection with the previous issue, one of the matters discussed in Islamic economics regarding money is fractional reserve banking, which is known as the money-creation mechanism of banks. Fractional reserve banking, in the simplest term, involves the process of the bank keeping some of the money deposited in demand deposits as reserves with the central bank (the official ratio for required reserve is generally around 10 percent), while the remaining amount is issued as loans, and this cycle being maintained by other banks in the market. This process eventually leads to credit/money creation. Debates on fractional reserve in Islamic economics began in the 1990s. As in the previous discussion, we can define two main groups: (1) Those who argue that fractional reserve banking is not illicit and that this structure is also found in the Islamic banking system and (2) those who assert that fractional reserve banking leads to macro problems and claim that this structure is unfavorable in the Islamic banking system. The former group base their arguments on research by Western economists. The business cycle theory by Austrian School and the Chicago Plan can be named as two examples. Siddiqi and Hasan are in the first group whereas Ariff, Choudhury and Al-Jarhi can be grouped under the latter. Those in the second group recommend 100% reserve banking instead of fractional reserve banking. But so far, no concrete steps have been taken in this regard.

In our opinion, the fractional reserve system is an underestimated problem in Islamic economics and finance. The following steps can be taken in this regard: First of all, empirical studies should be conducted in order to find out in what ways fractional reserve banking is a problem. In fact, in the 7th Islamic Economics Workshop, Tekdoğan and Saraç (Chapter 6) attempted to reveal the problems of fractional reserve banking using agent-based simulation modelling. Second, an alternative model should be proposed to be replaced by fractional reserve banking. However, such a proposal should be backed by different scientific methods, and the results should be provable.

Money-bank-central banking and monetary policy instruments

Al-Jarhi, mentioned earlier, also participated in the 7th Islamic Economics Workshop and contributes to the book. He has authored several articles on monetary policies and central banking in the context of Islamic finance and has written a chapter on how to apply the Islamic macroeconomic model (Chapter 1). Money creation process and management of money supply are some of the issues discussed in his macroeconomic framework. Al-Jarhi lists 11 steps in order to apply an Islamic macroeconomic structure.

Sajjad Zaheer, who has been associated with the State Bank of Pakistan, made a presentation on a similar topic in the workshop. Zaheer (2019, Chapter 7) first systematically makes mention of monetary policy instruments and then examines examples of non-interest monetary policy implementation. Finally, he offers solutions to potential or existing problems. As is known, monetary policy is carried out by central banks, and most of the monetary policy instruments are based on interest. Therefore, even if they do not function in a full interest-free economic and financial system, such studies are vital for central banks who want to use interest-free monetary policy instruments.

Shah and Rashid (Chapter 8) also examine money-bank-monetary policy issues and make an empirical analysis of how monetary policy affects the credit supply in Islamic banks in the cases of Pakistan and Malaysia. They conclude that there is strong evidence for the existence of the credit supply channel of monetary policy for both countries.

On the other hand, Shaikh and Hassan (Chapter 3) analyze the consequences of the asset market in an interest-free economy and compares it with the current system. They empirically prove that in the full reserve banking system, or the system where there is only asset-backed financing and a greater capital buffer, the distribution effects are expected to be more egalitarian.

Public finance

Another topic that is also studied by Shaikh with regard to money in Islamic economics is the issue of public finance. In this context, Shaikh (2010) examines the tools of public finance in Islamic economics. As might be expected, zakat is the leading one among these tools.

Other studies on public finance similarly focus on *zakat*. For example, Ahmad (1989) mentions *zakat* under the title of income and public expenditures in an early work on Islamic economics.

Although many studies have emphasized the importance of *zakat* in terms of public finance, the main issue to be discussed in Islamic economics is how to collect and distribute *zakat* in a systematic and efficient way.

Other matters related to money

Other matters related to money in Islamic economics can be summarized as follows; interest, time value of money, money waqfs and less-debated topics. Among these, interest constitutes a complete field of study, so we will not go into the details. In fact, the 5th Islamic Economics Workshop organized by IKAM in 2016 was devoted exclusively to this topic.

The principle of time value of money, which is also related to the issue of interest, is another matter to be discussed, because time value of money in modern economic theory explains why interest exists. Time value of money principle, in its simplest terms, states that today's 100 TL has more value than tomorrow's 100 TL. This is due to three facts: risk, inflation, and interest. As it will be noticed, interest is both cause and effect of this principle. Discussion of time value of money in Islamic economics began especially in the context of project valuation and discounting in the 1990s. M. F. Khan (1991), cited earlier, states that, considering the *bai-salam* and *bai-muajjal* contracts, the difference between the present and future prices of something is not only dependent on time but also on supply and demand at different times. What is not allowed in Islam is a predetermined time value of money. In his article in response to Khan, Kahf (1994) underlines that intertemporal choice depends on an investment rather than consumption. Therefore, the prohibition of interest in Islam does not mean that money has no time value. The main difference here is that the compensation of the person who earns revenue should be after investment. As it can be seen from these two different opinions, the main matter of debate in Islamic economics is whether money has any time value, and if yes, under which conditions. However, it is also crucial to carry out empirical studies on this subject.

Another topic that has been discussed with regard to money in Islamic economics is cash waqfs. Waqfs, which could be traced back to the period of the Prophet (pbuh), became an important source of social expenditures such as education and health, which were not undertaken by the government, especially during the Ottoman period. Cash waqfs, which are based on endowment of movables, became widespread in the Ottoman society after the fifteenth century (Gunay, 2012). As a matter of fact, there were many debates on the practices of cash waqfs in the Ottoman period among the scholars of *fiqh*. Studies on current practices of the cash waqfs in different Muslim societies, and suggestions for their development are carried through today. One of the proposals is to merge cash waqfs with cooperatives or microfinance institutions, although, these institutions are not found in present-day Turkey.

In our opinion, empirical studies and mathematical modeling on money-related subjects in Islamic economics are not sufficient. Although their effectiveness and reliability are controversial, they have the potential to be a guide for practical applications of different theoretical frameworks provided that scope and limitations of the tools such as general equilibrium models, econometric models, system dynamics, agent-based modelling, and neural networks are taken into consideration. The 7th Islamic Economics Workshop also contributed in this sense, because in addition to the previously mentioned agent-based modeling (Tekdoğan and Saraç, Chapter 6), Iranian researchers Afshari and Movahed (Chapter 5) attempted to establish a general equilibrium model within an Islamic framework. One of the actors in the model is the monetary authorities.

Another unexplored area in my view is the ontological and philosophical issues. Since money is closely related to interest, monetary policy, and bank theories, practices and suggestions on these are affected by the way money is seen. As mentioned earlier, the research on the view of money in the Western literature has reached a certain level, even if a consensus is not reached. At this point, it is perhaps not enough to say that the view of money simply affects other related subjects, because various factors can also form the view of money. Especially, it can be said that the last two centuries with the industrial revolution and the rise of capitalism reshaped the view of money. In order to be able to understand this interaction and to answer the questions such as the definition of money in Islam, how money should be perceived, and how and to what extent changes can be made toward this perception today, there is a need for an extensive study of the ontology and philosophy of money.

Conclusion

This chapter has been written as an introduction for this book, which is a collection of papers presented at the 7th Islamic Economics Workshop on money. In this context, the main aim of this chapter is to present an outline on the subject.

To this aim, a qualitative research method based on a detailed literature review and evaluation is followed, and as a result, the subject is examined under the following headings; history of money, money in Islamic history and law, and money in Islamic economics. Furthermore, the papers, now chapters, presented in the workshop are listed under the headings listed here.

References

Afshari, Z. and Movahed, M. S. (2019). Designing a simple DSGE model in an Islamic framework. *7. İslam İktisadı Atolyesi,* İstanbul.

Ahmad, Z. (1989). Public Finance in Islam. *IMF Calışma Makalesi,* WP/89/68.

Aybakan, B. (2006). Nakit, *TDV İslam Encyclopedia*, Vol. 32, pp. 324–326.

Asadov, A. (2017). *Money in Islam: A Social Perspective*, Ten Makales, INCEIF, Malaysia.

Erdem, E. (2006). Osmanlı Para Sistemi ve Tağşiş Politikası: Dönemsel bir Analiz, *Bankacılar Dergisi*, Vol. 56, pp. 10–28.

Graeber, D. (2015). *Borç: İlk 5000 Yıl*, Everest Yay., İstanbul.

Gunay, H. M. (2012). Vakıf. *TDV İslam Ansiklopedisi,* 42. Cilt, s. 475-79.

Innes, A. M. (1914). The Credit Theory of Money, *The Banking Law Journal*, Vol. 31, Dec./Jan., pp. 151–168.

Kahf, M. (2019). *İslam İktisadının Temelleri: Kurumlar ve Kuramlar*, İktisat Yay., İstanbul.

Kahf, M. (1994). Time Value of Money and Discounting in Islamic Perspective: Re-Visited, *Review of Islamic Economics*, Vol. 3, No. 2, pp. 31–38.

Keleş, A. (1998). İslam'a Gore Para Kavramı (*Tarihi, Tanımı ve Fonksiyonları*).Unpublished doctoral dissertation, Uludağ University, Institute of Social Sciences, Bursa.

Kallek, C. (2010). Süftece, *TDV İslam Encyclopedia*, Vol. 38, pp. 19–21.

Khan, M. F. (1991). Time Value of Money and Discounting in Islamic Perspective, *Review of Islamic Economics*, Vol. 1, No. 2, pp. 35–45.

Khan, M. F. and Jabeen, Z. (2019). Monetary Economics and Monetary Policy in Islamic Perspective: Focus on Contemporary Muslim Economies Aiming at Making their Economies Islamic, *7th Islamic Economics Workshop, April 2019,* IKAM, İstanbul.

Kocherlakota, N. R. (1998). Money Is Memory, *Journal of Economics Theory*, Vol. 81, No. 2, pp. 232–251.

Melitz, J. (1970). The Polanyi School of Antrophology on Money: An Economist's View, *American Antropologist*, pp. 1021–1040.

Ozel, M. (2019). Roman mert, *sosyal bilimler namert kurgu*, Karar Gazetesi, Retrieved 21 January 2020 from https://www.karar.com/hayat-haberleri/roman-mert-sosyal-bilimler-namert-kurgu-1209735

Polanyi, K. (2001). *The Great Transformation: The Political and Economic Origins of Our Time*, Beacon Press, Boston.

Searle, J. (1995). *The Construction of Social Reality*, Penguin Books, London.

Shah, S. M. A. R. and Rashid, A. (2019). Impacts of Monetary Policy on Credit Supply of Islamic Banks: An Empirical Study of Pakistan *versus* Malaysia, *7. İslam İktisadı Atolyesi,* İstanbul.

Shaikh, S. A. (2010). *Sources of Public Finance in an Islamic Economy*, MPRA Working Paper, No. 22998.
Siegfried, N. A. (2001, 2011). İslam Hukuk Düşüncesinde Kâğıt Para Kavramı, Trans. M. T. Kılıç, *Dicle Üniversitesi İlahiyat Fakültesi Dergisi*, Vol. 13, No. 1, pp. 271–294.
Smit, J. P., Buekens, F., and Du Plessis, S. (2011). What Is Money? An Alternative to Searle's Institutional Facts, *Economics and Philosophy*, Vol. 27, pp. 1–22.
Tekdoğan, O. F., and Sarac, M. (2019). The Problems With Fractional Reserve Banking and Proposing A Shariah Compliant Full Reserve Banking Model, 7th Islamic economics workshop, Istanbul.
Uslu, R. (2014). İslam Hukukunda Para Birimleri, *Journal of Islamic Research*, Vol. 25, No. 1, pp. 28–38.
Vadillo, U.I., 2006. Fatwa on Banking: *And the Use of Interest Received on Bank Deposits*, Available at: www.tauhid.net/FatwaOnBanking.pdf
Zaheer, S. (2019). Monetary Policy and Islamic Banking: Key Challenges. *7. İslam İktisadı Atolyesi,* İstanbul.

Online sources

Online Etymology Dictionary, Money (Para), https://www.etymonline.com/word/money
The British Museum, Money: The Origins of Coinage (Para: Madeni Paranın Kökenleri), https://www.britishmuseum.org/explore/themes/money/the_origins_of_coinage.aspx
Time, Top 10 Things You Didn't Know About Money: The First Paper Money (Para Hakkında Bilmediğiniz En Önemli 10 Şey: İlk Kâğıt Para), http://content.time.com/time/specials/packages/article/0,28804,1914560_1914558_1914593,00.html#

1 The Islamic macroeconomic model

How to apply it

Mabid Ali Al-Jarhi

Introduction

Islamic economic macro models can be broadly divided into two categories. Both categories ignore the neoclassical microfoundations based on the utility-maximizing individual, the profit-maximizing firm, the typical macroeconomic agent and the different versions of strict rationality attached to an all-knowing decision-making unit. Both approaches give due attention to the importance of equity and the role of *Zakah* and *Awqaf* in providing a significant share of public services.

The first category was inspired by Mannan (1970), Siddiqi (1981, 2006) and Chapra (1985, 1996) and elaborated by Khan and Mirakhor (1994) and Iqbal and Mirakhor (2011), in addition to Mirakhor and Zaidi (2007). This profit and loss sharing (PLS) approach implicitly assumes a pure equity-based system and draws important conclusions about its efficiency, equilibrium, and stability. Meanwhile, it ignores the institutional details of the monetary and financial structure. When discussing monetary policy, the traditional policy tools are usually listed, with the exception of those that use the rate of interest. The neoclassical straightjacketing into a stable equilibrium remains.

The second category proposes a detailed institutional structure of the monetary or financial sector of an Islamic economic system. This structure has distinctive features with respect to the money creation and finance allocation. In addition, the money market contains the necessary instruments for the anchor and conduct of monetary policy. In other words, the rules of Shari'ah with regard to economic behaviour have been translated into a behavioural structure attached to an institutional framework. This category has been offered by Al-Jarhi (1981, 1983) with several consequent modifications and improvements.[1] Most importantly, it started with a Hicksian IS-LM structure, which is neoclassical in essence, with some recent attempts to switch to a disequilibrium structure.[2]

This chapter provides a description of the Islamic macroeconomic model according to Al-Jarhi's approach. It provides recommendations on applying this model to the macroeconomy for economic development and stabilization purposes. In this regard, the chapter considers gradualism and institutional competition as the two driving forces behind implementation. As to the latter, the legal and regulatory environment is continuously modified to provide both conventional and Islamic economic institutions working side by side to have an equal opportunity to operate, leaving competition to have the final say for the public to judge the usefulness of each.

How money is created

Issuing money

In the conventional monetary model, money is created in the form of credit balances to be lent to the treasury as well as banks. The treasury uses those balances to cover the deficit in government budget. Banks use the balances as reserves to cover their (interest-based) lending to the public.

Under the fractional reserve system, the neoclassicists claim that fractional reserves create a multiple of reserves initially issued by the central bank in the form of the monetary base. Banks allegedly issue multiple reserves in the form of derivative deposits through lending to the public. The maximum amount of money issued would be equal to the monetary base multiplied by the money multiplier, which would be equal to the reciprocal of the required reserve ratio.

Some theorists, however, argue that banks do not wait for the central banks to issue the monetary base. They instead take the initiative to make loans and create derivative deposits, then rush to the central bank to cover their reserve positions. The central bank finds itself, at least in the short run, forced to oblige (Basil Moore, 2001). This opinion later found convincing empirical support (Kydland and Prescott, 1990). This means that the concept of the money multiplier has been a myth, with no factual support. At any rate, money in a conventional economy is issued on a lending basis. What then is the basis for issuing money in an Islamic economic system?

Before we answer this question, it is important to note that the misunderstanding regarding the money multiplier has led to theories that assume the exogeneity of money, which ends up claiming that money is only a veil, as changes in its rate of growth would only affect prices, leaving real variables unchanged.

In addition, the application of fractional reserves has weakened the grip of the central bank on the money supply, as most of the money supply would be issued by banks as multiple of the monetary base. It also allowed banks to gain wealth at the expense of the public as they lend money to the public at a rate of interest, while the public is the only party that can be credited with giving the quality of moneyness to money, through bestowing on it their general acceptance. Moreover, the use of the required reserve ratio as a tool of monetary policy appears to be counterproductive, as any change in the ratio would produce multiple changes in the money supply, threatening to make monetary policy a source of instability.

Based on these three reasons, Al-Jarhi's model (Al-Jarhi, 1981, 1983) insists on the application of total reserves in order to provide the central bank with absolute power to control the money supply, to prevent the wealth redistribution in favour of banks' shareholders, and to do away with a tool of monetary policy that mostly led to instability.

In Al-Jarhi's model, money is created as credit balances to be credited to the central bank investment accounts with banks under the name of central bank deposits or central deposits, CDs for short. They are placed in Islamic banks based on the *Mudaraba* contract. The newly issued money would be allocated to Islamic banks according to their record of profitability and safety. Issuing and retiring new money by adding or subtracting from CDs would be the first and utmost tool to manage the money supply

In order to assist in managing and fine-tuning the rate of monetary expansion, the central bank issues monetary instruments called central deposit certificates, CDCs, which would be offered to banks, financial institutions, and the public. Their proceeds are added to CDs and allocated among banks in a similar fashion.

The CDCs represent an undivided common share in the *Mudaraba* pool of assets created by banks through their financing provided to the household and business sectors, using Islamic finance products. Such products are based on Islamic finance contracts that range from partnership in product, partnership in profit, investment agency, and *Ijarah*, as well as sale finance that includes deferred-payment sale and deferred delivery sale.

The CDCs stand to compete with other investments, like shares, fund certificates and *sukuk*. However, it is distinguished by being the lowest-risk monetary asset, thanks to the automatic diversification by the central bank, who knows the most about its member banks.[3] Therefore, on the liquidity scale, it stands as the nearest asset to money in liquidity, while it pays a rate of return that is equal to the average of returns on all assets included in the *Mudaraba* pools of all banks in the economy.[4]

Estimating the real rate of growth: why?

We start with a relatively stable state of (disequilibrium) prices, where pressures of excess demands or supplies are in state of moderation, that is, with moderate pressure on prices towards upward and downward movements to their nearest disequilibrium values. Meanwhile, markets would be characterized with a degree of monopolistic competition, where markets are generally fragmented by brand names, geographic locations, and related price-searching tactics on the sides of both buyers and sellers.

Prices in such an environment vary with the degree of price differentiation related to promotion and advertisement activities and the related services provided by sellers. Traders, meanwhile, stay busy with price searching in a way that makes it impossible for any market to reach a stable equilibrium, due to the interactions (emerging or strategic behaviour) between traders in addition to information-cost differential between markets. This, we argue, is the realistic state that is far removed from the neoclassical attachment to stable equilibria, which increasingly appears as a fanciful idea.

In this disequilibrium mode, the movement towards or away from equilibrium would become vigorous or weaker depending on the extent of excess demands and supplies in markets and the degree of awareness among traders with these excesses as well as their expectations with regard to their effects. Some would expect price increases and therefore continue buying. Some others would expect price declines and therefore go for selling. In such an environment of uncertainty, expectations are mostly disappointed. Prices would thus continue to approach or go further from equilibrium, which continues to give rise to traders' interaction or emergent behaviour.

In this economy, a higher rate of monetary expansion is followed by excess demands for all commodities to varying degrees. This leads firms to seek financing in order to provide more supplies. The fact that banks, using Islamic modes of finance without resorting to ruses, provide finance either to suppliers alone or demanders and suppliers together would closely connect the finance sector with the real sector, which are mostly disconnected in a market economy. It would attenuate price rises and allow the finance sector to positively influence the speed of adjustments in commodity markets.

Excess supplies would tend to go down, depending on the extent of monetary expansion and the responsiveness of supply to an increased availability of financing. What stands between the economy and equilibrium is the state of uncertainty, which caused producers to raise their supplied by an amount that is always significantly or slightly below or above what is needed to reach equilibrium.

Let us remember that we have started with an economy in disequilibrium, and then the emergent behaviour got hotter with the increase in monetary expansion. Because of the initial and following conditions, the relationship between monetary expansion and price stability remains central. To the extent that monetary expansion remains within the limits of economic growth, excess supplies dominate the scene, keeping disequilibrium prices calm. Once monetary expansion exceeds the limits of economic growth, excess demands dominate, forcing prices out of control. Therefore, the monetary authority must monitor the relationship between monetary expansion and economic growth for the benefit of reaching price stability.

If the increase in monetary expansion is far below economic growth, excess demand would be modest, and so would their effect on the speeds of adjustment and price levels. The opposite is also true. If the increase in monetary expansion exceeds economic growth, excess demands would be proportionately higher and the increase in prices would be larger.

While we make no claims to a perfect or competitive asset market, we can nonetheless claim that there would be some reasonable degree of *general awareness* among investors regarding the trade-offs between different investments (stocks, *sukuk*, fund shares, investment deposits in different banks, and direct investment).

We would not, therefore, indulge in making assumptions parallel to those made by the "efficient market hypothesis". Some of those assumptions can be mentioned here as examples. First, the collective expectations of stock market investors are accurate predictions of companies' future prospects. Second, share prices fully reflect all information pertinent to the future prospects of traded companies. Third, changes in share prices are due to changes in information relevant to future prospects. Such assumptions would make all knowledgeable prophets out of investors and provide baseless rationalization for a theory that claims that financial markets are stable and not subject to fluctuations, which is contrary to reality (Keen, 2011).

Such general awareness would motivate investors to take the existence of the trade-offs as much as possible in their investment decision. This implies no claim to their considering all possible alternatives or being rational in the calculative sense.

Due to extremely curtailed speculations, which will be explained later, the absence of hoarding puts more steam in increasing the commodity supplies. However, this process will continue to work, as long as monetary expansion stays within the requirements of real growth.

The continuous interaction among investors, based on bounded rationality, supported by a state of limited awareness of trade-offs between assets, will lead the rate of return on CDCs or registered CDC (RCDC) to approach the average rate of return on national wealth. The difference would be the market assessment of the risk premium that CDCs enjoy, due to the nature of their issuer and the high diversification of the issuer's portfolio.[5]

The central bank would therefore have two options with regard to anchoring monetary policy. The first is to use RCDC as a presumed approximation of the real rate of growth. The second is to attempt to estimate the real rate of growth using the RCDC. With either option, the central bank has to monitor inflation, as it would deliver the final say on whether the rate of monetary growth is overshooting or undershooting real growth requirements.

How the real rate of growth would be estimated, based on the RCDC, is the next step. Being aware of the risk premium, the central bank can estimate the rate of growth of the economy as equal to the RCDC plus an estimated risk premium that changes from time to time, depending upon the state of expectations about

- i the performance of the real sector,
- ii its fundamentals, and
- iii the attitude of traders in the financial market.

Notably, the financial market here has a much smaller amount of speculative trading, defined as trading based on price expectations rather than the rate of return of the financial instrument. The reason is that financial-market trading cannot be financed. Admittedly, this would not remove all speculative trading but would reduce it much below what is familiar in contemporary financial markets. Based on this, the real rate of growth would be equal to the RCDC plus some nonlinear function of the difference between the rate of return on shares (possibly estimated by the rate of growth in some stock market index) and the RCDC.

Monetary management

Islamic finance reform

Islamic finance has succumbed to the use of ruses to mimic conventional finance. While Islamic finance is costly to document and implement, conventional finance is simpler and less costly. The benefits of Islamic finance are significant, but they tend to be external macroeconomic benefits that cannot be internalized by a single bank. Naturally, in the absence of regulatory discipline, due to the disinterest of monetary authorities, Islamic finance has spent much effort in structuring products that have the Islamic garb while being conventional in essence. No economy can therefore benefit from adopting an Islamic finance camouflage for conventional finance. Reform must be done head on before the economy can make use of the benefits of Islamic finance.

The RCDC and the rate of real growth

The rate of return on CDCs or the RCDC is a market-determined measure of investment profitability (or the rate of growth of wealth) in a large section of the economy. This makes it rather useful in estimating an approximation of the real rate of growth for the whole economy. Once the central bank has a money-market determined indicator that can be used to estimate the real rate of growth, the latter would become an ideal anchor for monetary policy. Whether the supply of money should be changed and by how much can be figured out through comparing the RCDC and the rate of inflation. As inflation (as well as deflation) is known to have serious efficiency and redistributional drawbacks, the monetary authority must seek absolute price stability. Initially, the central bank would anchor the rate of growth of money to the RCDC. To the extent that there is no inflation, such policy should be judged successful.

Our assertion is that the real rate of growth is a function of the RCDC, particularly in the case of no inflation. However, this must be subject to some reservations. First, the CDC trading in the money market would produce a series of disequilibrium prices over time. Traders would be uncertain about prices. They would take the present as a guide to the future, in the way Keynes introduced uncertainty into his model. In contrast with Keynes model, in an Islamic economy, those who would wish to speculate at a wider scale would not be financed for this purpose, as the financing of trading in financial instruments would be prohibited. The tendency of trying to predict where the trading herd is heading would not find the financing support to make it profitable to seasoned traders. The mere reliance on current conditions and on the information regarding economic fundamentals would settle the trading price of CDCs, and consequently its rate of return, close to but never at its equilibrium level.

This provides the central bank some guidance to the state of economic growth that can be sharpened by looking at the inflation rate. The extent to which inflation is close to zero indicates how closely the central bank estimate of the rate of growth, based on the RCDC, approximates its actual value. Such comparisons should help the central bank fine-tune the rate of monetary expansion to reach two objectives: (i) provide the monetary requirements for growth and (ii) maintain price stability.

It is therefore important that Islamic banks do not provide any finance to speculators.[6] This would increase the usefulness of the RCDC to be used in estimating an approximate rate of growth. Moreover, it facilitates monetary management through monitoring the rate of inflation in order to gauge monetary expansion to price stability.

We have argued that the RCDC can be a base for estimating real growth, provided that financing of trading in the financial market is not available. The value of the RCDC will not be exactly the same as the value of the real rate of growth, except under very restrictive assumptions. The central bank has therefore two options. The first is use the RCDC as the only guide to monetary policy, while monitoring the rate of inflation. If it exceeded zero, the central bank would have overshot the rate of monetary expansion that is commensurate with the target of price stability. It therefore has to reduce monetary expansion, using the excess of inflation above zero as a guide.

In reverse, if the rate of inflation drops below zero, a similar but upward adjustment process would be required in monetary expansion. The hunch is that the RCDC would be a useful guide of monetary policy in the short run, which is the most relevant time span for stability.

Alternatively, the central bank can make its own estimate of the real rate of growth, based on the RCDC. However, it has keep monitoring the rate of inflation for fine-tuning. It appears a much easier task to rely solely on the RCDC, without attempting to estimate the rate of growth and while monitoring the rate of inflation, to be the better guide to monetary policy.

Summary of the estimation method

In an environment of highly subdued speculation, the difference between the real rate of growth and the RCDC would depend upon the state of expectations under uncertainty. Therefore, we can postulate that (real rate of growth, g − RCDC) would be a nonlinear function of the rates of growth of investment and consumption and the financial market trend, measured by the rate of growth of the general market index, as a proxy variable for short term expectations under uncertainty. The market index should include stocks and *sukuk*.

In other words:

$$g - \text{RCDC} = f\left(\dot{I},\ \dot{S},\ \theta\right) \qquad \text{(Equation 1)}$$

Where:

- $\dot{I}$ is the rate of growth of investment.
- $\dot{S}$ is the rate of growth of consumption.
- θ is the rate of growth of the financial market general price index.
- The estimated real rate of growth (g) for the current RCDC is used as an anchor to monetary policy.
- Monetary expansion would be equated to (g),

While monitoring the rate of inflation,

If inflation > zero, reduce the rate of monetary expansion; if inflation < zero, increase the rate of monetary expansion.

Table 1.1 Monetary survey in an Islamic economy

Assets	*Liabilities*
CASH IN VAULT	Money
NET FOREIGN ASSETS	Money in Circulation
DOMESTIC LIQUIDITY	Demand Deposits
Finance to households & businesses	Investment Accounts
Finance to central & local governments	Households investment accounts
Finance to nonbanking financial institutions	Business Sector
Central Deposit Certificates	Investment
	Central Deposits

Through this process, the central bank may arrive at the conclusion that it should change the rate of monetary expansion. If the desired change in the money supply is large, a change in the volume of CDs would be in order. If the change is not so large, the money supply can be fine-tuned through open market operations in CDCs (Table 1.1).

Monetary management in mixed systems

In the case of mixed finance systems, where Islamic and conventional finance are practiced side by side, the management of the money supply would be more complicated, unless the financial market authority absolutely prohibits financing speculation, and particularly through trading at the margin. In addition, Islamic banks must be prohibited from financing the purchase of stocks and other financial instruments for short-term acquisition. This step of financial reform would facilitate monetary management a great deal. Otherwise, the central bank use of the RCDC to estimate an approximation of the real rate of growth would result in a distant approximation. Gauging monetary expansion to a distant approximation of the real rate of growth would not help approach price stability.

If the prohibition of financing speculation were not an available option, the CDC market would become a part of the financial markets' gambling casino. CDC prices and rates of return would not be useful in calculating a good approximation of the rate of growth. As disequilibrium prices, they would stand at a much larger and less certain distance of their (presumed but imaginary) equilibrium level.

In such case, the monetary authority must decide whether to continue using its monetary management approach, particularly inflation targeting, or move to a higher and perhaps easier level of monetary management under the rules of Islamic finance.

How finance is allocated

Under Islamic finance, money would be used by banks to provide financing of economic activities (public and private investment and private consumption) carried out by the government, firms and the public. Financing would be provided in three major categories: permanent and/or diminishing partnership in profit and product (several forms of *Musharaka*),[7] fixed or diminishing, restricted and unrestricted profit and loss sharing, or PLS (*Mudaraba*), restricted and unrestricted investment agency, or *Wakala*, deferred-payment sale finance (*Bai' Bethaman Ajel* and *Murabaha*), and deferred delivery sale finance (*Salam* and *Istisna'*).

There are many regulatory rules and safeguards that the monetary authority must put into force in order to ensure that Islamic finance is properly working within its own paradigm (Al-Jarhi, 2016). For the purpose of insuring proper allocation of finance, the central bank is advised to apply the rules listed in the appendix.

Government budget finance

In our macroeconomic model, the government is barred from using borrowing from the central bank to finance its budget deficits. Its activities can be divided into two main categories. The first is its pure public goods, which cannot be subject to the exclusion principle.[8] For this category of goods, the government must use the political process through which it can obtain tax revenues to finance their production. The second category is quasi-public goods. Their production and distribution can be designed to be amenable to the exclusion principle. Examples include speedways, bridges, water passages, and the like. They can be designed with turnpikes or gates to exclude non-payers. They can therefore be financed through offering bids through build, operate, and transfer (BOT). The government itself or bid-winners can apply for financing for such ventures through Islamic banks. In either case, banks must decide such cases based on feasibility alone.

Islamic finance is also amenable to crowdfunding. The government can finance some of its social services through *sukuk* (equity-based financial instruments), which, when properly structured, can be effective in mobilizing large amounts of resources to finance economic activities.[9]

Awqaf and public services

Public services, like health, education, garbage collection and recycling, sustainable energy, and many other types can be at least partially provided through *Awqaf*. Such public services can be financed through waqf funds. Such funds can be placed with banks as investment accounts whose earnings are earmarked for a particular use. They can also be used to finance income earning assets whose returns can be perpetually earmarked to support certain activities. This latter method would be more effective if direct investment brings in higher returns than investment accounts with banks. Similar arrangements can be developed to provide students' scholarships, teachers' supplementary salaries, support of research institutions, and so on.

In other words, *Awqaf* can be used at the widest possible scale to provide a good share of public services so as to relieve the government and, consequently, taxpayers from financial burden. A decided advantage of finance through *Awqaf* is that it could provide independence to educators and researchers from government and business influence. Such arrangements can be extended to institutions that require independence, like the judiciary, the election supervisory institutions, and so on.

Zakah and public services

Based on economic reasoning, equity is a valuable social service. Economic reasoning is based on labour productivity. One of the reasons for poverty is that the poor may have lower productivity on the account of lack of human capital (in the form of education, training) as well as lack of physical productive assets. Once both elements are provided, the poor become more productive. National GDP, employment and growth would be positively influenced. Therefore, equity leads to improvements in productivity, which in turn would assist in economic development.

From an Islamic vantage point, all citizens must be capable of fulfilling their basic needs, including food, clothing, and shelter, as a minimum. When the society is sufficiently rich, merit wants must also be added, like education, transport, communications, marriage, and employment. If we excluded the level of income that is sufficient to provide for basic needs as well as merit wants,[10] any income or wealth over and above such level must be subjected to a levy called *al-Zakah*. *Zakah* is levied on all assets and/or their returns (rental, profit, etc.). There are those who prefer to narrow down the list of zakatable assets, but we prefer to join those who make it all inclusive.

Zakah is earmarked for certain uses, the most important of which is redistribution aiming at enriching the poor. Enrichment here is taken to mean that the poor become capable of covering their basic needs and merit wants during their lifetime. Such a redistributive process must be conducted yearly in order to reach wealth (human and physical) maintenance for the poor, that is, a level of wealth that is sufficient to produce an income to cover both needs and wants.

The ideal method which we have repeatedly proposed is to make Islamic banks custodians of collected *Zakah* and allow them to invest the same temporarily until they are used. Meanwhile, Islamic banks would use such proceeds to establish microprojects whose titles would be transferred to the qualified poor. Each project would produce enough income to support the needs and wants of a poor family. Meanwhile, since this process of redistribution would be time consuming, the poor would be provided income maintenance until each family possesses a suitable microproject of its own. Title transfer would also include education and training to make the family capable of managing their project. The sale of projects after their possession by the poor should be restricted and closely monitored to make sure that such a sale would not return them to poverty.

Financial markets

Financial markets have failed to some extent to provide sufficient fund mobilization for economic development. They have mostly turned into gambling casinos with an open gate to hot money that has been a source of instability and contagion. The reason behind this gambling tendency is the gambling contracts that allow for transactions based on fictitious sales and betting on future prices as well as interest rates. It was clearly pointed out by some that common use of such contracts was an important element behind the latest Great Recession of 2007–2012 (Keen, 2011). However, no country so far has come forward to make their use illegal.

Since such contracts are strictly prohibited under the system of Islamic finance, financial markets would be a good candidate to play an important role in mobilizing resources for growing economic activities. However, care must be taken to prevent the financing of short-term trading in the financial market. This would serve as a backdoor for gambling activities.

Provided that such safeguards are effectively implemented, an Islamic financial market would become an effective tool for obtaining finance. Financial instruments that would be available include corporate shares, fund shares, and *sukuk*. In addition, Islamic banks may issue their certificates of investment accounts to circulate together with CDs. They would all be equity based, that is, giving their holders common undivided shares in firms or assets.

The formation of such markets would not come automatically, especially when moving from conventional to Islamic finance systems. The financial market authority must start with allowing each financial market in the country to start an Islamic financial market in which all instruments would conform to the rules of Islamic finance. It should follow this with setting standards for the shares, *sukuk*, funds, and hedging that must be followed before allowing such instruments to be listed in an Islamic market as an Islamic financial instrument. Gradually, some Islamic financial markets would become able to function side by side with conventional financial markets. This would facilitate subjecting all financial markets to the rules of Islamic finance.

Monetary policy

Once the Islamic finance part of the monetary and financial system is established, the central bank can exercise Islamic monetary policies with vigour. The total supply of money would be augmented or reduced through adding to or subtracting from CDs. The fine-tuning of the rate of monetary expansion can easily be accomplished by open market operations in CDCs.

A question arises regarding monetary policy in a mixed economic system. Let us assume that a country starts with a fully conventional monetary and financial system. As commonly practiced, some Islamic banks and nonbanking financial institutions may be in operation, but they are totally uninvolved in monetary policy. In order to have a viable Islamic finance sector, we suggest the following:

1 The practices of Islamic banks in operations must be streamlined to remove all finance products that camouflage interest-based finance, like *Tawarruq*, debt trading, and risk trading. This would lead to a significant increase in Islamic banks' profitability, raising the profits distributed to the holders of

investment accounts. Obviously, there would be a gradual shift of funds from conventional to Islamic banks.

2 All Islamic finance windows would be considered as a first step to move from conventional to Islamic finance within a certain number of years. Then all branches would be closed as they are replaced by full-fledged Islamic banks.
3 Holders of investment accounts in Islamic banks must be treated as shareholders. They should be allowed to take a share in management that is commensurate with their share in the resources invested by the bank. That would lead to a new type of banking institution that is predominantly managed by investment account holders. It would also remove the information asymmetry associated with the *Mudaraba* contract, upon which investment accounts are based.
4 A percentage of the money supply equal to the market share of the Islamic banking assets in total assets can be placed as CDs with Islamic banks. The percentage would be adjusted with the change in the market share of Islamic finance. Similarly, the remaining part of the money stock can be placed as time deposits in conventional banks. Such procedure would go hand in hand with the application of the system of total reserves.
5 The system of total reserves would be introduced gradually, raising the required reserve ratio while increasing CDs with Islamic banks and central bank time deposits with conventional banks.
6 CDs would grow at the expense of government time deposits with conventional banks. The use of CDs and CDCs would become increasingly more influential in monetary policy.
7 Within a period of two to four years, Islamic banks should dominate the scene, and monetary policy would depend more exclusively on CDs and open market operations in CDCs. the economy would start enjoying a higher level of price stability and higher growth. Investment account holders would enjoy rates of profits that are comparable with the rate of return on equity, after adjusting for the risk differential.

Development policies

Once the Islamic monetary and financial system is established, the central bank finds itself with much more economic influence than is usually perceived for central banks. First, it would have much more power in controlling the money supply, with the application of total reserves. Second, it has the power to allocate a good part of the financial resources (the total money supply) for banks towards investment. This opens the door for designing and implementing an investment policy by the central bank, which would ultimately become a policy for economic development.

The central bank, jointly with the relevant ministry (of economy, treasury, planning, etc.) can set some development priorities with regard to the sectors and regions to be targeted for higher rates of investment. The profit share, which should be clearly defined in the investment-account contract, can be subject to central bank control as a policy variable. Restricted PLS deposits can be allowed with higher profit shares to customers in order to encourage the financing of certain types of investments and in certain types of sectors or geographic locations. The profit share can be one of the tools of influencing the size of credit money in the economy being directed sectorally or geographically. The central bank is well advised to gauge and monitor profit shares without directly interfering in the investment process.

Fiscal policy

Fiscal policy would focus on reducing the tax burden through good governance and supervising the institutions of *Zakah* and *Awqaf* to insure their viability in bearing a good share of providing public services and establishing equitable distribution of wealth.

Trade and exchange policies

Once the Islamic finance program is implemented, the economy will have a rate of inflation that will narrowly oscillate around zero. This would place the currency of the country at an impeccable position *vis-à-vis* other currency. The stability of the exchange rate attracts more investment, especially through shares, fund shares, and *sukuk*. The country would enjoy significant improvement in trade competitiveness. The country would also enjoy investment inflows that would be an additional factor in strengthening its currency and improving its current account balance.

Dealing with crises

Will our economy after reform become an ideal economy in the neoclassical sense, meaning that it would enjoy a stable equilibrium with no crises? Of course not. The neoclassical utopia does not exist. The economy will have prices moving towards ever-changing equilibria but never reaching equilibrium. Crises can happen, either because of policy errors, laxity in the application of rules, natural disasters, or imported shocks, especially if an economy is modest in size with great interdependencies on several trading partners.

However, when an economic crisis takes place, policies to confront it should be radically different from the policies used to confront, for example, the last Great Recession.

Let us assume some form of a crisis and see how it would be dealt with. If a large group of farmers obtain financing to build their homes through *Ijarah Muntahia Bettamleek*, their leased homes are securitized by *Ijarah sukuk*, through which *sukuk* holders own the leased part of the homes (which is declining over time) and get paid their share of principal and rent. *Sukuk* are also traded in the financial market.

The onset of the crisis could be a crop failure. Farmers find themselves unable to pay their *Ijarah* instalments. *Sukuk* holders will get no lease payments. If all behaved like the American administration during the international financial crisis, homeowners would be kicked out of their homes and declared bankrupt. The part they own of their houses would be sold under duress for negligible prices. *Sukuk* values would decline to almost nothing. Farmers would not be able to purchase their basic needs. Aggregate demand would significantly decline, and the economy would enter into a recession.

The government would allocate huge amounts of taxpayers' money to bail out banks in order to prevent a bank run. Banks get more resources but avoid lending, which perpetuates the crises getting worse over time. They instead place their money in government debt instruments.

In an Islamic economic system, the handling of the crisis is very different. First, homeowners, as debtors suffering from temporary insolvency, receive from banks free rescheduling with no increase in their debt. The central banks increase the volume of their CDs with banks in order to allow them to provide rescheduling while keeping their volume of investment growing. Since farmers will not be bankrupt and will obtain free rescheduling, they can obtain bridge assistance from *Zakah* and *Awqaf* institutions to maintain their purchases of necessities. They can also obtain financing for cultivating their next crop from banks. In total, aggregate demand will not significantly decline, and hence there is no reason for a recession.

Sukuk holders may not be able to get the same level of payments on their *sukuk*, but they are assured of continued payments in the future, as farmers' finances are still sound. There would be no sudden dip in *sukuk* prices. *Sukuk* prices will suffer only to the extent that this year's payments are partly reduced and partly pushed forward to the following periods.

Most importantly, no taxpayers' money has been spent to bail out banks. Meanwhile, no bank failure would be recorded.

How can we make use of Islamic macroeconomics?

An Islamic macroeconomic arrangement can push such an economy to a take-off stage where growth would reach unprecedented levels. In order to apply the macroeconomic model, a country can take the following steps that gradually add an Islamic macroeconomic structure to its economy, with all the expected benefits. The steps are ordered in a time sequence as a game plan.

1 Streamlining the Islamic finance sector through the following steps:

   1.1 Issue an Islamic-finance product handbook and establish a training program for the employees of participating banks in order to learn the subtle secrets of Islamic finance and how to implement it.
   1.2 Adjust the banking law to include specific rules that enable participating banks to operate at a higher level of compliance and to improve their governance process.
   1.3 Convene a meeting of entrepreneurs, Islamic bankers and some academicians to discuss how businesses and participating banks can

cooperate to improve the Islamic finance sector on the one hand and provide more resources to businesses on the other.

2 Set new rules for participating banking windows and branches to make them a temporary step towards full-fledged Islamic banking.
3 Adjust the rules regarding governance to allow for more involvement of investment account holders and better Shari'ah governance.
4 Start to implement the system of total reserves gradually, perhaps within 2–5 years. As the required reserve ratio is raised, the central bank would provide more time deposits to conventional banks and CDs to participating banks.
5 Establish *Awqaf* funds whose proceeds would be invested in participating banks until they are placed into suitable industrial, agricultural, or commercial investments. Income gained from investing would be directed for the following purposes:

   5.1 An education waqf to spend on the education sector, with the intention to include all the young in elementary and high school education and all high school graduates into university education. In addition, the waqf would encourage specializations that are lacking in some economic sectors. The waqf would also finance basic research in strategic fields with the cooperation of the business sector.
   5.2 A health waqf to spend on improving and augmenting health services in Turkish hospitals, with donations to improve hospital equipment and provide supplementary salaries and financial incentives to professors in medical schools and doctors in hospitals.
   5.3 An infrastructure waqf that supports planting the barren parts of the land with fruit and timber trees, establishing energy production from sustainable sources like solar energy, improving the transportation network, and modernizing the communication network.

6 Any reduction in government expenditures that results from using these waqf funds should be used to reduce the tax burden on the poor.
7 Establishment of two *Zakah* funds, one to be spent on making microprojects whose titles would be transferred to the qualifying poor, with a view towards their wealth maintenance. The other would be used for income maintenance of the qualifying poor until they can have a title to a microproject.
8 Establish an Islamic financial market in Bursa Istanbul with standards for shares, *sukuk*, and funds, and relevant listing and trading rules.
9 Establish *sukuk* funds for the following purposes:

   9.1 Finance of agricultural cropping, produce distribution locally, and exports of produce. This would include the development of animal wealth and the promotion of meat, poultry, and fish production and trade.
   9.2 Finance of industrial projects, especially those that have a higher technology content, like electronics, computers, and mobile phones.
   9.3 Finance of Turkish domestic and international trade.

9.4 Provide extra finance to Turkish firms to enable each to substitute their domestic and international debt with domestic Islamic finance.

9.5 All *sukuk* would be marketed at the retail level so that individuals can purchase and hold *sukuk* easily. In addition, they should be marketed domestically and internationally. *Sukuk* funds would be established to provide investors with bundles of *sukuk* with more variety in combinations of return and risk.

10 Start apportioning the money supply as time deposits and investment deposits in conventional and Islamic banks, respectively.

11 Once Islamic finance reaches 25 percent of the total financial assets, monetary policy based on CDs, CDCs and absolute price stability should be gradually introduced.

Appendix

Regulatory rule for finance

The use of these finance contracts or modes is subject to the following (regulatory) rules:

- Contracts can be mixed and matched to form financial products that fulfil the banks' business objectives of return and safety and customers' objectives of finance requirements.
- Contracts are well defined. They cannot be mixed and matched to provide ruses to camouflage selling present for future money or interest-based finance, as in the cases of *'Eina* sale and *Tawarruq*. Unlawful products must be included in the bank regulations to insure enforcement.
- In the cases of PLS finance, safeguards must be provided to reduce information asymmetry including mixing with *Musharaka* and placing the burden of proof on the *Mudareb*, requiring good bookkeeping and feasibility studies.
- Islamic banks must be equipped with capabilities to make and review feasibility studies and participate in management of the firms they finance.
- The central bank must insure balanced use of finance modes. If left alone, Islamic banks would focus on *Murabaha*, because of its close but incomplete similarity with the classical loan contract. It is also amenable to ruses that allow for mimicking conventional finance through the use of agency (*Wakala*) contract.
- Debt sale must be prohibited, except at its nominal value.
- Risk trade must be prohibited. No finance should be provided to financial market speculation, sometimes named as Ponzi schemes (Keen, 2011).[11]

Notes

1 Al-Jarhi's (2017) forthcoming book, "Economic Analysis: an Islamic Perspective," offers an integration of the second category.

2 Hicks (1937) claimed that his IS-LM analysis was an interpretation of Keynes. He later admitted (Hicks 1980) that it was his own neoclassical ideas. My recent attempt to avoid the neoclassical straight jacket is still under preparation.

3 Despite the fact that the *Mudaraba* contract suffers from information asymmetry, the central bank supervisory role over banks enables it to monitor banks continuously, which renders information asymmetry nil.

4 Such would be a weighted average.
5 Central deposits are invested in all areas of the real sector, corporate and noncorporate, listed and unlisted. Therefore, they carry a degree of diversification that has a wider range than placing funds in the portfolio of a financial market index or any other combination of listed companies.
6 Financing speculators in the financial market is considered as some sort of a Ponzi scheme (Keen, 2011).
7 *Musharaka*, *Muzara'a*, *Mugharassa*, and *Mussaqah*.
8 The exclusion principle is to make commodities available only to those who pay their prices. Others would be excluded. There would be no chance for taking a free ride. This can be done with private goods and semi-public goods. Pure public goods, once provided, become available to all, and none can be excluded. They must therefore be financed through taxation.
9 The relative effectiveness of *Sukuk* in resource mobilization is directly related to being common undivided shares in income earning assets, not in debt. They can earn higher rates of return that would attract investors of all types.
10 This level is an interpretation of the concept of *Nissab*. Some prefer to use its measure in grams of gold used at the time of the Prophet. Others prefer to define it by the cost of obtaining basic needs and merit wants, which would vary from time to time and from society to society.
11 An example of Ponzi transactions under the guise of Islamic finance is shares *Murabaha*, which commonly exercised by Islamic banks everywhere.

References

Al-Jarhi, Mabid (1981), Towards an Islamic Monetary and Financial System: Structure and Implementation, the Arabic Publications Series (5), June, King Abdulaziz University, Jeddah, KSA. http://iei.kau.edu.sa/Files/121/Files/149853_48-Al-Jarhi.pdf

Al-Jarhi, Mabid (1983), A Monetary and Financial Structure for an Interest-Free Monetary Economy: Institutions, Mechanism and Policy", presented to Seminar on Monetary and Fiscal Economics, Islamabad, January, 1981, in Z. Ahmad, M. Iqbal and M.F. Khan (eds.), *Money and Banking in Islam, Center for Research in Islamic Economics, Jeddah, and the Institute of Policy Studies*, Islamabad. https://mpra.ub.uni-muenchen.de/66741/1/MPRA_paper_66741.pdf

Al-Jarhi, Mabid (2016), An Economic Theory of Islamic Finance Regulation, *Islamic Economic Studies*, Vol. 24, No. 2, December, 1–44.

Al-Jarhi, Mabid (2017), Economic Analysis: An Islamic Perspective, forthcoming. https://ulifam.asbu.edu.tr/sites/digerleri/ulifam.asbu.edu.tr/files/inline-files/Economic%20Analysis%2C%20An%20Islamic%20Perspective%20Volumel%20I_0.pdf

Chapra, M. Umer (1985), *Towards a Just Monetary System*, Leicester: The Islamic Foundation, 1985/1405 A.H.

Chapra, M. Umer (1996), Monetary Management in an Islamic Economy, *Islamic Economic Studies*, Vol. 4, No. 1, December.

Hicks, J.R. (1937), Mr. Keynes and the "Classics": A Suggested Interpretation, *Econometrica*, Vol. 5, No. 2, 147–59.

Hicks, J.R. (1980), IS-LM: An explanation, *Journal of Post Keynesian Economics*, Vol. 3, No. 2, 139–54.

Iqbal, Zamir and Abbas Mirakhor (2011), *An Introduction to Islamic Finance Theory and Practice*, 2nd Ed., Singapore: John Wiley & Sons (Asia) Pte. Ltd.

Khan, Mohsin S. and Abbas Mirakhor (1994), Monetary Management in an Islamic Economy, *Journal of King Abdulaziz University: Islamic Economics*, Vol. 6, No. 1. SSRN: https://ssrn.com/abstract=3075074

Keen, Steve (2011), *Debunking Economics: The Naked Emperor Dethroned*, Revised and Expanded Ed., London and New York: Zed Books.

Keynes, John Maynard (1930), *Treatise on Money*, London: Macmillan.

Kydland, F.E. and E.C. Prescott (1990), Business Cycles: Real Facts and a Monetary Myth, *Federal Reserve Bank of Minneapolis Quarterly Review*, Vol. 14, No. 2, 3–18.

Mannan, M.A. (1970), *Islamic Economics-Theory and Practice*, Lahore: Muhammad Ashraf, 386p.

Mirakhor, Abbas and I. Zaidi (2007), Profit-and-Loss Sharing Contracts in Islamic Finance, in Ch. 4, *Handbook of Islamic Banking*, Cheltenham: Edward Elgar Publishing, pp. 49–63.

Moore, B.J. (2001), Some Reflections on Endogenous Money, in L.-P. Rochon and M. Vernengo (eds.), *Credit, Interest Rates and the Open Economy: Essays on Horizontalism*, Cheltenham: Edward Elgar, pp. 11–30.

Siddiqi, Mohammad Nejatullah (1981), *Muslim Economic Thinking*, Leicester: The Islamic Foundation.

Siddiqi, Mohammad Nejatullah (2006), Islamic Banking and Finance in Theory and Practice: A Survey of State of the Art, *Islamic Economic Studies*, Vol. 13, No. 2, February.

2 Monetary economics and monetary policy in Islamic perspective

Focus on contemporary Muslim economies aiming at making their economies Islamic[1]

M. Fahim Khan and Zohra Jabeen

Introduction

Monetary policy and hence monetary economics has never been a subject in the economies of the Muslim world until the eighteenth century, when they lost their economic power and independence. This was the period when Adam Smith developed the so-called science that is known as economics. This is perhaps the only science that was developed without a basis derived from the knowledge developed in Islamic history. Because neither economics nor monetary economics were a subject in Islamic economic history in the past, that history does not give a clue about how to talk about monetary policy and even economics and economic policy. In Islamic society, economics and social matters were taken in combination, such as *ilm ul Iqtasaadiaat*.

Monetary economics is a subject of macroeconomics. Both occurred as a result of rejection of the classical theory of economics that resulted from Adam Smith's *The Wealth of Nations*. The classical theory of economics that emerged in the eighteenth century was not very enthusiastic about monetary economics and macroeconomics. Their concern was the real aspect of the economy, and money did not matter in economic behaviour. Monetary economics and macroeconomics emerged only during and after the so-called Great Depression of the 1930s, when John Maynard Keynes' book *The General Theory of Employment, Interest and Money* appeared in 1936. The book described macroeconomic concepts in explaining the fluctuations in market in the real sector due money market depending on demand for money and supply of money. With Keynes' aforementioned book, the idea of understanding macroeconomic policy emerged. This included monetary policy, which required role of central bank in credit creation by banks' interest-based borrowing and lending in managing growth and stability of the economy at a macro level. This was the period when almost the entire Muslim world was under colonial rule and their economy could not create any development from an Islamic perspective on monetary policy and hence on economics that could be called Islamic economics or Islamic monetary policy.

It was mainly in the 1950s, when Muslim countries got independence from colonial rule, that they had to develop their economic policy. However, these Muslim countries inherited interest-based commercial banking and hence a colonial macroeconomic framework and monetary policy. This made economists in Muslim countries follow Keynesian economists to primarily focus on the growth and stability of their economy. Keynesian economists, though, generally believed the market economy to be predominantly determined by private sector but required it to be managed by active government intervention through fiscal and monetary policy. Keynesian economics had generally become a standard economic model in the developed countries on account of the interest-based commercial banking and central banks' role in regulating their credit creation.

It was initially a slow realization in late 1960s and then more forcefully in the 1970s that the Muslim world recognized that they can have their own economic perspective instead of following the perspective of interest-based economies of developed countries. The increased financial resource created by the oil price hike made countries in the Middle East to think of making their economies Islamic. But monetary aspects of the economy created a strong bottleneck to achieve this objective.

The question of monetary policy arises when managers of the economy find that demand for money exists in the economy and is affecting their economy at a macro level, with varying consequences. Demand for money in Muslim economies has never been an issue in Islamic history. But in the contemporary world, no economy can afford to ignore demand for money due to speculative behaviour created by the interest rate banking system. Every economy, whether Muslim or otherwise, now has a monetary system regulated by the central bank of the country to supervise growth and stability in the economy. With a growing interest in contemporary Muslim economies to conform to the economic principles of Islam in all dimensions of the economy, the question arises how monetary sector and monetary policy will be managed in such an economy, where interest is eliminated from the economy.

It is believed by some Islamic economists (Naqvi, 1982; Khan, 1984, 1986 and others) that the rate of return on capital in the market can replace the monetary system in the country, which is a sensible proposition in theory when certainty is assumed in economic behaviour, particularly in investment behaviour. Rate of return on investment in the economy therefore logically becomes an effective tool for the monetary policy of an economy. To fix this in advance would require an expected rate of return based on the past return and expectations of returns in the future. But the practical situations in the economy and the pricing formulae of finance theory do not base the monetary policy rate through rate of return on investments in an economy. Instead, the monetary policy rate is determined by the government in order to meet their targets rather than the market (Jabeen and Khan, 2008). Therefore, this cannot be a viable option for monetary policy in a modern Muslim economy. In addition, in the theory of finance, the capital market rates, too, are linked to the rates of interest on debt instruments, using the proxy of a debt instrument, namely T-bills, for determining returns of assets in capital market (ibid.). Despite the theoretical recommendations, none of the contemporary Muslim economies has been able to implement monetary policy without interest because monetary policy in practice means control of flow of money and liquidity alone, delineated from the real economy and not based on real economic growth, including Iran and Sudan—where the financial system is considered to be fully Shari'ah compliant. These countries also face the challenge of designing practical instruments that allow them to conduct efficient monetary policy while remaining Shariah compliant. With the banking sector being in the public sector and under strict control of the government, there has been some progress made in innovative proposals for instruments that are comparable with conventional monetary policies. However, there is direct and tight control of the government on the banking sector, with limits on borrowing and lending rates as well as the setting of reserve rates and credit ceilings. These countries also face the same problem of identifying a proper proxy rate of return to serve as the return on government and central bank securities (di Mauro et al., 2013; Hussain et al., 2015).

According to Article 44 of the Constitution of the Islamic Republic of Iran, the economy shall have three components, which are the state, cooperative and private sector. The state sector is to include all large-scale and main industries, major minerals, banking, insurance, power generation, dams and large-scale irrigation networks, radio, and television, as well as foreign trade and other main sectors. The state is responsible for providing the basic necessities of life to all, such as housing, food, clothing, medical treatment, hygiene, education, and necessary facilities for the setting up a family.

The current application of an Islamic banking system and hence an Islamic economy with its own macroeconomic framework and monetary policy based on Islamic teaching on principles of economic activities faced a lot of questions. The political ramifications were that Western economic power and its influence on oil-producing economies could not allow rich Muslim countries to get rid of the entire interest-based financial and monetary system governing their economies. A gradual approach, therefore, was taken to transform their interest-based financial and monetary system to an Islamic system by partially introducing Islamic banking in their economies. This quickly made Islamic banking be introduced by other Muslim countries in Near East and Far East. But despite the efforts of the last half a century, no Muslim country has completely transformed its interest-based financial and monetary system. All those Muslim countries that introduced Islamic banking and financial systems in their economies have been able to reach 10–25 percent of their banking system, except Iran and Sudan, but their monetary systems are not well understood. Some Muslim countries have even less than 10 percent Islamic banking in their entire banking system. It is therefore too early to comprehend the monetary economics and monetary policy in an Islamic economy.

This historical narration of Muslim economies and hence Islamic economics suggests that monetary economics and monetary policy from an Islamic perspective be studied by understanding the following three questions with respect to monetary policies and monetary economic.

a What will be the economic model of the Muslim countries when Muslim economies can become or can be assumed to become an Islamic economy free of an interest-based financial and monetary system?
b Where Muslim economies have currently introduced partially Islamic banking and financial system, how can the Islamic banking and financial system be considered really Islamic, not merely fulfilling shariah in letter rather than embodying the Islamic spirit in Islamic economic principles?
c What will an Islamic banking and financial system look like that would fulfil the real spirit of an Islamic economic system, and what will be its monetary policy? In respect to that, what will be a macroeconomic framework and monetary economics in such a financial system in a Muslim economy?

The current state of Muslim economies is far from describing monetary policy and monetary economics in a meaningful way under the assumption of (a) and (b). This would require economies to be actually operating in situations described in (a) and (c). A meaningful discussion of monetary economics and monetary policy from an Islamic perspective can be made for contemporary Muslim economies described in (b). Even for the very meagre appearance of an Islamic and financial system, having a strong debate on several theoretical and practical aspects of this system, the discussion on monetary economics and monetary policy will not be very meaningful. Notwithstanding all ramifications about state of economies in contemporary Muslim countries, it is important that this study has been devoted to the subject of monetary issues in Islamic economics.

The stagflation in the world economy in 1970s resulting from oil entering the world financial system and, later on, the unprecedented financial crises in 2007–08 made world economists rethink their approach towards monetary economics and monetary policy. But despite their rethinking monetary economics and monetary policy, the world for 50 years in general and the past more than a decade continues to remain unable to find a solution for monetary economics and monetary policy. The world economists still could not get rid of the curse of Keynesian thought, could not even give a new thought in the textbooks for undergraduate or graduate students. It continues to be followed in different versions of Keynesian economics. This study is expected not only to help Muslim countries make their economy Islamic but also to give new ideas to world economists to get out from under the curse of Keynesian economics. This chapter therefore may give an ab initio perspective on monetary economics and monetary policy.

Structure of the chapter

The rest of the chapter is organized as follows: The next section gives a model for a Muslim economy from an Islamic perspective, with the first subsection a model of Islamic economics based on the Quran and Sunnah; the second subsection is titled "Islamic Economy's Two Segments, and another discusses monetary economics in an Islamic economy. The third section comprises an Islamic perspective on monetary policy for present-day Muslim economies, with subsections titled "Credit

Creation in a Muslim Economy in the Contemporary World" and "Cost of Holding Money from an Islamic Perspective". It is further subdivided in the following subsections: "Money Demand in Present-day Muslim Economies", "Money Supply in Present-day Muslim Economies" and "Equilibrium in the Money Market". The final two sections are "Need for Monetary Policy in Present-day Muslim Economies" and "Monetary Policy from an Islamic Perspective for Contemporary Muslim Economies". It has three subsections. Lastly, the conclusion is given, with a number of subsections.

Model for a Muslim economy in an Islamic perspective

Economics being a subject developed in the eighteenth century, when Muslim economies were mostly colonialized and had lost the Islamic perspective in their economies, Muslim economies therefore did not have much choice to think of an appropriate model for their economy and formulate economic policies, such as monetary policy, in true Islamic perspective after independence. Since the classical model of economics was conceptually more relevant to describe a Muslim economy from an Islamic perspective, let me therefore explain how we can see a Muslim economy through the glasses of classical theory before we discuss the monetary policy from an Islamic perspective. We can afterwards discourse on the possible monetary policies in the macroeconomic framework currently being used by contemporary Muslim economies.

Economics, from Adam Smith till now, is only an economics of market. Adam Smith, Alfred Marshall and other followers all based their theory of economics on the assumption that economic activity is only what exists in the market. Hence, conventionally, all economies are called market economies. Market takes place in the best way when private property is permitted in a society and the sanctity of private property and exchange of property rights is freely ensured in the economy. From an Islamic point of view, this concept of a market and its significance in the economy is not a new concept. The sanctity of private property rights and rules of free exchange and hence significance of market has been a prominent part of the Islamic system of life, as laid down in the Quran and Sunnah more than 1,000 years before Adam Smith recognized it. Unlike Adam Smith's economy, the Islamic economy cannot merely be a market economy in order to describe an Islamic model of the economy. Let us see the prominent features of the economic aspects of the Islamic system of life that would distinguish an Islamic economy from the economy assumed under the classical theory of economics or the Keynesian theory of economics.

1. The market will play predominant role if an economy decides to be an Islamic economy, but this will neither make the economy a market economy nor a capitalist economy because of its other features.
2. The market will be governed by strict laws to ensure the sanctity of property rights and the exchange of property rights. These laws are elaborately explained in *Fiqh al-Maal* and *Fiqh al-Buyu'*, based on teachings of the

Quran and Sunnah. It will be easy to see that these laws make the market free and perfectly competitive, which are meant to make the market self-clearing. This feature makes the market aspect of the economy almost similar to the economy under the classical theory of economics.

3 Interest does not exist in an economy as a time value of money. The money, therefore, will lose the opportunity to make speculative gains by holding it. Hence there will be no money demand and hence no money market. To this extent, it will be similar to the classical theory of economics, in the sense that the economy can have only a real market and therefore no money market affecting the real market.
4 Money will not receive a fixed return, neither in lending nor in so-called investment. If money holders want to use it for productive return, then this has to be used as investment and trade to earn profit or face loss afterward, whatever it produces. Otherwise it will only be a loan with no return. Money when invested as capital will lose the preferred status of getting a fixed return from investment. This identifies a clear denial of the Keynesian theory of economics.
5 Unlike in conventional economics, whether classical or Keynesian, capital will not get a fixed return irrespective of whether entrepreneurs and human resources gain or lose. Capital, too, in the form of money invested, cannot have a preferred reward. Interest does not exist in the economy or as a determinant of investment or a basis for the reward for the productivity of capital. The price of capital will be determined in the real sector as a price of other factors of production are determined. This feature suggests that an Islamic economy cannot be called even a capitalist economy because capital does not have that privileged status that it has in conventional market economies or in so-called capitalist economies.
6 A money market might not exist at all because money demand for speculative purposes is not likely to exist, but if it exists despite the absence of interest on savings or loans, it cannot affect the real market, as is assumed in classical economics.
7 Economic activities in an Islamic economy exist beyond market economy (which is not based on demand and supply forces but is based on philanthropy such as waqf and charity for giving to the have-nots). This is a significant aspect of the economy that exists side by side with market-based economic activities. This is a unique feature not found in any conventional theory, starting from Adam Smith till now. This basis of this activity is what we may call *Infaq fi sabeelillah* which will include *Zakah, Ushr*, helping the neighbours, relatives, or just charities to any one or for any reason only for the sake of divine pleasure and rewards to be received in the life hereafter. A minimum of such spending or donation is obligatory and is called *Zakah* and *Ushr*. But this spending or donation occurs much beyond the minimum required every year. This is because of the teachings in the Quran and Sunnah. In Surah al-Baqarah, more than 20 *ayaat* emphasize *Infaq fi sabeelillah* (Let us call it IFS) before giving one categorical *ayet* to prohibit *Riba* (Interest). IFS did not lose its significance even during the period of

colonial rule. A concept of waqf is used to formalize such spending with a defined social cause. IFS is not merely a charity and needs to be considered as a transfer of resources. Islamic history has proved that this IFS has been used as an economic activity as it aims at improving the economic status of the poor and making them contribute value added to the economy. The methods with which IFS has been used is to create educational institutions, hospitals, water canals, and various other productive activities simply to raise the status of the poor and enable them to earn income rather than to permanently receive charity. The significance of this activity in Islamic history has shown it to be a positive activity at a national level.

Monetary economics and macroeconomics emerged only during and after the so-called Great Depression when John Maynard Keynes' 1936 book *The General Theory of Employment, Interest and Money* appeared, which described macroeconomic concepts in explaining the unemployment as result of the failure of the (real sector) market to self-clear itself. This was attributed to the money market, which required monetary policy to increase income and employment. Monetary policy required the role of a central bank in regulating the credit creation of banks' interest-based borrowing and lending. Monetary policy was needed in managing growth and the stability of the economy at a macro level. This was the period when almost the entire Muslim world was under colonial rule and its economy could not create any development from an Islamic perspective to introduce Islamic economics and Islamic monetary policy.

In the present-day world, interest has become inevitable and indispensable for any economy in the modern world. This is what every student is taught in the initial courses of the undergraduate programs in economics in any university of repute. This leads the economy towards a Keynesian approach to adopt macroeconomic policies in general and to make monetary policy be based on an interest-based monetary system in particular. This is because, according to Keynesian theory, the interest rate affects so-called demand for money, which in turn affects the real sector of the economy as well. Classical theory where money does not matter and the real sector of the economy can be understood without a monetary sector went to the background of economics.

Model of Islamic economics based on the Quran and Sunnah

In the absence of an Islamic model formally recognized for the economy either in contemporary Muslim world or in the early history of Islam, we can only describe a model to have the following features based on the economic teachings of the Quran and Sunnah. These features will then describe a macroeconomic framework and hence a monetary policy for an Islamic economy.

1 Markets are perfectly competitive and thereby "self-clearing". For classical economic theory, this is just an assumption, but for the Islamic community it is the result of the application of Islamic laws on market operations.

2 Islamic history does not provide any significance evidence to justify that there was, in any point of time, either a money illusion or people found holding money for speculative purposes.[2] A money market, therefore, will not exist because of the absence of money demand for speculative purposes or to gain risk-free return on the short-term lending of money. There may be a possibility that people even in such a society may still like to hold some money for some transaction purposes or having some money in hand to meet some urgency needs of cash, but such demand for money cannot create a money market in the economy, and hence, other things remaining the same, the market economy will always remain as a "real market economy" irrespective of what the role of money is in the market. Even if money demand exists, it is very unlikely that economy under Islamic principles, with the absence of an interest rate on loans and rules of market transactions, will allow money demand to earn a fixed rate of return, hence making a money market that will substantially affect the real market as well.

3 Economic activity does not exist merely as a market, but it exists beyond the market as well as an integral part of economic activities in the market. The Qur'anic injunctions say that there is a right for have-nots in the wealth of haves.[3] Wealth is created in the market, and have-nots are those who are unable to create wealth for themselves in the market.

4 Savings will be equal to investments, and there will be no leakage in the economy to create inequality to save investments.

5 Economic activities in the market primarily make the economy grow by maximizing economic gains in the activities. The laws relating to property rights and exchange forces the economy in that direction. On the other hand, economic activities beyond the market primarily make the economy share the prosperity achieved by the market with that part of the economy that was unable to carry out economic activities in the market.

6 The market aspect of an economy created by Islamic laws on market operations imply following main features in the market, if the laws are properly implemented.

   a Perfect information about products. In Islamic law, a seller is required to provide all information that he knows about the product, so information asymmetry and moral hazard are minimized. Information cost, transaction cost created by contractual activities for exchange and other costs that can create market failure can also be minimized by creating an appropriate institutional framework in the economy.

   b There is freedom of entry in and exit from the market. It is not permitted to meet the supplier outside the market, depriving the sellers an opportunity to face the entire set of potential buyers.

   c There is a prohibition on economic activities in the market to acquire market power. Hence monopoly, monopolistic competition, hoarding, etc., are prohibited, preventing the buyers from negotiating the variety of sellers or suppliers.

d Transaction cost is minimized by proper documentation and enforcement of all provisions of market operations.

These features make the market efficient in increasing national wealth. Activities beyond the market become not only a source of economic and social justice, but they also contribute to raising the economic status of even those who could not increase their market status.

An Islamic economy, therefore, creates a segment in the economy where institutions are developed with the basic objective of growth in national wealth. This segment refers to the market aspect of the economy. An Islamic economy creates another segment in the economy where institutions are developed to improve the economic status of the deprived from activities in the market. This segment is created by Islamic law stating, "And those within whose wealth is a known right" (70:24). And also, "And from their properties, (there) is the right of the [needy] petitioner and the deprived".[4] This aspect is basically aiming at economic justice in national wealth. These features of Islamic economy mean the markets will always be in equilibrium and self-clearing if any shock moves them away from equilibrium. This segment will create national wealth in the economy, which will always be at its equilibrium level. Neither the market aspect nor beyond-market assets will be affected by a money market. The economy is real. Therefore, equilibrium is determined by real variables. Interest and hence a money market will not exist in the economy.

Islamic economy's two segments

Islamic economy, in theory, is a two-segment economy, one segment being a market economy and the second segment a "beyond market" economy. This will initially result in a slower growth in the short run, but in the long run the growth rate in the economy will accelerate. The unique feature of this model, however, is that efficiency and equity exist simultaneously in the growth of the economy. Since a money market will not exist in isolation from the real economy, the real economic growth of goods and services will matter and the demand and supply of money as an end in itself will not matter.

The Muslim countries in the modern world do not carry the previously mentioned features to describe the economy of an Islamic country. Due to the presence of interest-based banking in the market segment of economy, the real goods and services market exists side by side with fiat money and the banks' credit market in the economy. Discussion about monetary policy from an Islamic perspective, therefore, will make sense if it is discussed for those Muslim countries that are presently trying to eliminate interest from their economy in a gradual move towards making their economy a completely Islamic economy. This chapter, therefore, has to discuss monetary economics and monetary policy in two scenarios. In the first scenario, discussion of monetary economics can be in the framework of a truly Islamic economy and draw lessons for monetary economics and monetary policy only in theory. In the second scenario, discussion of monetary economics and monetary policy can be for present-day Muslim economies where Islamic banking exists. It will be a futile exercise to develop monetary economics and monetary policy from an Islamic perspective for present-day Muslim economies, while considering a model of a truly Islamic economy.

Monetary economics in an Islamic economy

The monetary sector in a truly Islamic economy will have money supply (MS) and money demand (MD), both determined exogenously. There is no money market. MS is determined by monetary authority (in consultation with a board of economists and shariah scholars). MD will be determined by households on the basis of several exogenous factors. There will be no question of determining equilibrium or equilibrium conditions for the monetary sector. The monetary sector will require a net balance. Households need to maintain a balance in holding money for meeting pure timely needs and money held for investment purposes. Exchange rate movements may be commensurate with economic growth and trade. This may require curbing the holding and trading of money for sheer speculative purposes regarding movements in exchange rates. Monetary authorities need to maintain a balance in growth and inflation in the economy to decide money supply.

Demand for money in an Islamic economy

The demand for money for the love of it is a matter of mindset. The mindset that Islamic rules and norms create is not in line with the mindset implicit in the Keynesian approach. We therefore assume that from an Islamic perspective, money is demanded only as medium of exchange and it has no value of itself. There is no money illusion in the mindset of a Muslim. On the contrary, the admonition in the Quran, "And those who hoard gold and silver and spend it not in the way of Allah—give them tidings of a painful punishment" (9:34), serves as discouragement to hold and accumulate money in hand for its own sake. On the other hand, the economic teachings of Islam motivate one to spend, invest or give money away rather than hold it. We therefore define demand as the set of (so-called liquid) assets that are readily available with the households to buy goods and services or to avail oneself of an investment opportunity or to give away to seek divine pleasure.

Money demand affects aggregate demand, and hence it becomes relevant to give it a role in monetary policy. We need to argue that there will be demand for money in an Islamic economy, and this demand will be a stable function of such variables as income, price level, and rate of return on investment. If this is established, then this will make the case for developing monetary economics from an Islamic perspective.

Money in the hands of a Muslim has two components:

a For pure time preference. You just want to have some money in hand to meet needs for various daily transactions, for meeting some precautionary needs or to meet the demand for help from friends and relatives (a particular consideration in an Islamic framework). This demand may depend on several factors, all exogenous.

b For investing it to make more money from it. But this has to be very short-term investment in the way that it can be liquidated to meet the expected needs.

Money demand thus will be

$$M_d = M_0 + M_i \qquad \text{(Equation 1)}$$

where
M_0 is money demand for pure time preference
M_i is money available for short-term investment

This is in fact one side of a coin. The other side of the coin is household savings, which also has two components:

$$S = S_0 + S_i \qquad \text{(Equation 2)}$$

S_0 is household savings that they want to keep liquid. This will be savings kept in hand for normal transaction and unforeseen needs

S_i is savings meant to be invested for long term

Note: In this discussion, we will avoid discussing specific macroeconomic variables and equations for an Islamic economy. We just keep in mind that the macroeconomic variables will be aggregate values of income (Y), consumption C, savings (S), and investment (I), and there will be no interest but market will not be short of some benchmark rate of return (i) on capital. The saving function in the economy would be:

$$S = S(Y, i) \text{ or } S = S_0 + a \cdot Y + b \cdot i \qquad \text{(Equation 3)}$$

where Y is national income and i is rate of return on investment

And investment function would be:

$$\mathrm{I} = \mathrm{I}(\mathrm{Y}, \mathrm{i}) \text{ or } \mathrm{I} = \mathrm{I}_0 + \mathrm{c} \cdot \mathrm{Y} - \mathrm{d} \cdot \mathrm{i} \qquad \text{(Equation 4)}$$

We cannot go into the discussion of savings function, investment function and equilibrium conditions in the real sector. This will require a whole macro model to be specified and discussed. In economics with an Islamic perspective, we do not like to talk of equilibrium and equilibrium conditions because equilibrium refers to only economics in the market. But in an Islamic economy, there is a lot of economics beyond the market where equilibrium makes no sense, and we can only try to ensure economic balance in the country. For more discussion on this, see Khan (2017).

In an Islamic economy, money demand, therefore, will be a part of the real sector of the economy. This will be determined endogenously. For the time being, to keep analysis simple, an Islamic economy is assumed theoretically to have no opportunity at present for such investment whether in the short or long run, which

a can keep the principal amount intact,
b can be liquidated immediately on demand and
c can still yield some return.

The existence of interest-based lending and borrowing makes this possible, but currently we cannot envisage that there can be any such possibility in an Islamic economy where Islamic laws relating to property rights and exchange are enforced in letter and spirit. There will thus be no money demand for the sake of keeping liquidity in the form of investment in a money market. The households will only hold an exogenously determined amount in hand to meet the household's own contingencies and contingencies of others (neighbours, relatives and friends) *fi sabeelillah*. This will be M_0, as explained earlier, and will not be a part of a money market. The other part of money demand will be only for the purpose of availing oneself of available investment opportunities. This money demand will be part of the real sector and not of a money market.

It is here that an Islamic macro model will differ from a classical model. A classical model assumes savings equal investment. They have to assume this because the savings decisions taken by households may not all go to meet investment demands from firms. The theory has to assume that nothing is leaked out of savings and all goes to investment. In an Islamic macro model, we will assume part of the savings will be held in hand in liquid or in quasi liquid form called S_0, and S_i will be part of the real sector and will be equal to investment. Thus, the assumption 4 mentioned in the beginning of this chapter will be $M_i = S_i =$ investment. M_i is investment demand and not money demand. S_0 is money demand.

This is in theory. The actual proposition of demand for money in an Islamic economy, however, will be a matter of empirical testing when an "Islamic" economy comes into existence. It is possible that empirical evidence may show money demand to be endogenously existing, and if it happens, then absolutely a new macroeconomic theory and model will need to be developed. Until this happens, we will assume that the theoretical scenario described here for discussing monetary economics and drawing lessons for monetary policy will be valid in an Islamic economy.

Monetary policy in an Islamic economy

Since money is simply a medium of exchange, it simply affects the price level, but nothing else. A change in money supply will only change the price level, but the real income, the real wage, and real rate of return on capital and level of real output in the economy will remain unchanged.

According to the classical quantity theory of money, the price level has the following relationship with the money supply:

$$MV = PT$$

where M = money supply
V = velocity of money
P = price level and
T = real total output.

In simple words, it means that a change in money supply (M) causes a proportional change in the price level (P).

Monetary policy in an Islamic framework will only be a matter of deciding an optimal level of money supply to meet desirable inflation rate and growth targets for the economy. The exercise to determine the level of money supply should therefore be a matter of a central bank decision that will be taken in consultation with an advisory board consisting of economists and shariah scholars who will advise keeping in view economic and shariah objectives for the economy. If the need arises to expand output and employment level in the economy, an expansionary monetary policy will be implemented. The increase in the money supply will increase the money in the hands of households. Liquidity rises with households who would simply spend, invest, or give away and hence increase the demand for goods and services. This will raise the price level. Real wages and real rental on capital goods will go down, hence providing incentive to employ more labour and capital to produce more goods and services. The empirical test of this theory will be possible only when an Islamic economy exists where the interest rate will be irrelevant to consider its role in money demand.

The financial system and monetary system are intertwined. The financial system provides credit to expand investment and consumption. An interest-based financial system then allows the credit to circulate in the market irrespective of the potential capacity of growth in the economy. The financial sector often lets the monetary sector grow beyond the growth of the real economy. This creates inflation and creates business cycles and hence instability in the economy and gives monetary policy a bigger role.

Can this happen in an Islamic economy? A financial system may exist in an Islamic economy allowing credit-creating financing for investment as well as consumption. Only empirical evidence can prove it. But if this would exist, can this credit create money and a money market? Shariah scholars, in principle, have yet to decide it conclusively within shariah (Islamic law). Banks can finance an economic activity on credit in an Islamic way ensuring their shariah permissible profit, but the credit created by the banks cannot be traded in the money market. Though shariah scholars advising current practice of Islamic banking and finance in contemporary Muslim economies have found ways to create a secondary market for the credit created in the process of financing investment and consumption, there are serious reservations from some shariah schools as well as from Islamic economists on the permissibility of selling credit in the secondary market.

Islamic perspective on monetary policy for present-day Muslim economies

Present Muslim countries can be considered in two categories.

a Those who have the intention to make the economy Islamic and have introduced Islamic finance partially but have not yet made their financial and monetary system completely interest-free in the economy.
b Those who have not yet taken any step in making the economy Islamic but are looking forward to doing so.

In both categories, the central bank is assumed to depend on interest rate as the linchpin of monetary regulation and policy to manage the economy. Even in the Muslim countries where Islamic finance holds a substantial share in the financial market, the monetary policy continues to be formulated by the central banks on the basis of interest. The question is what approach we should take towards monetary economics in a Muslim country which is not yet really "Islamic" in the sense explained earlier and has decided on partially going interest-free in the financial system as a starting point in the process of transforming the economy to be completely "Islamic".

It has already been discussed that it theoretically does not seem plausible to have money demand as a function of the interest rate in these economies. The economic principles in Quran and Sunnah indicate that Muslims even in the current environment would not like to have speculative demand for money. On the contrary: the empirical evidence rejects the hypothesis that the interest rate affects the money demand function. An empirical study in Pakistan (Faridi and Akhtar, 2017), where there is popular demand to make the economy Islamic, shows that "variables like real GDP, financial innovation and total population have positive effects on real demand for money while factors like deposits and exchange rates are inversely related to real demand for money". A more recent econometric study (Kemal, 2005) showed, The sign of the estimated coefficients for GDP, Demand for money for both M1 and M2 are found to be inelastic with respect to interest rate. The empirical evidence, therefore, only proves that money demand in Muslim countries is not a function of interest rate. No doubt there will still be demand for money in Muslim countries, but this demand will be for transactions, keeping money in hand for daily household needs or meeting some needs of unexpected beggars and the destitute (*saayil wal mahroom*) that one may occasionally face. However, this demand for money will not be affected by the interest rate but may understandably have a positive relationship with income. There is thus no sufficient empirical evidence to disallow a classical or neoclassical model instead of the Keynesian model for present-day Muslim economies, but there are several theoretical arguments, as discussed earlier, to assume that the monetary policy for present-day Muslim countries will be more relevant, with some adjustments to take care of some peculiarities of Islamic principles in order to formulate an appropriate suggestion for monetary policy from an Islamic perspective. Before discussing the policy, it is important to understand the cost of holding money in the Islamic perspective.

Credit creation in a Muslim economy in the contemporary world

For Muslim countries that are trying to change their financial and monetary system to change it to an Islamic system that would ultimately eliminate interest in financial and monetary transactions in the economy, the first question that arises is: If credit creation will continue to exist, then what should the monetary policy be that will allow the economy to reach the objective of ultimately eliminating interest from the economy? This is a system that allows banks to lend money that they do not have. This in principle seems to be a crime in shariah. The current global financial environment requires all banking systems in every country to commit this crime, including Muslim countries. Islamic banking is no exception. This crime creates moral hazard. For Islamic banks it creates, in addition, an information cost and transaction cost as well. This cost is more for the Islamic banks than for an interest-based bank. The scholars of shariah have not yet given any verdict against credit creation, despite the fact that Islamic economics have been discussed in academic circles—but the opinion whether Islamic banks should or should not be created is not conclusive. The discussion is mostly confined to the moral aspects of reserve requirements and hence discussing a 100 percent reserve requirement. But central bank forces allow Islamic banks to use reserve requirements and hence create credit as conventional banks do. Assuming that the creation of the current state of Islamic banks have shariah permission, Islamic banks will be creating credit as much as conventional banks of a comparable size create in order to remain competitive in the financial and monetary market. The issue, however, remains what tools in monetary policy would be needed to regulate credit creation Islamic banks when macroeconomic objectives require expansion or contraction in total credit creation in the economy.

Cost of holding money from an Islamic perspective

The cost of holding money is conventionally considered as the interest forgone by holding money. This is the price of money. The money demand is therefore a downward sloping curve with respect to the cost of holding money. Here is the main issue for present-day Muslim economies. What would be the cost of holding money in a Muslim economy other than an interest rate that households will keep in mind while holding money in hand? What alternative options will be available for the households to invest their liquidity in the short run for risk-free return when the country does not have the option of investment in interest-based products for a short period? This is basically an empirical question. The market definitely would come up with alternatives to earn a return in short-run investments on liquid assets when interest is completely eliminated in the economy. But the problem arises when a Muslim country is gradually moving towards transforming the financial system and, for some time, the economy will run a dual system, partly Islamic and partly interest-based. The maximum share of using an Islamic financial system is reported to be 30 percent in Saudi Arabia, while the rest of the financial system is interest based. In such an economy, there are households that have opportunities to earn income on their short-run investments in an interest-based money market, but there is no such opportunity for those who do not want to avail themselves of an interest-based investment opportunities. As the proportion of such households increases in the economy, the open market operations to control money demand will become less and less effective. The issue is to develop a market for short-run investment in products that can be quickly liquidated when needed. The central bank needs to allow products yielding a shariah-compatible rate of return that are easily negotiable in the secondary market. Development of these products cannot be overlooked. If an alternative to charging interest is not allowed in the money market, the population that abhors interest is forced to bear the cost of holding money. The system therefore would be inefficient. Assuming that people in these countries are moving in increasing proportions from interest-based finance towards Islamic finance and Islamic financial institutions increase in the economy, these Muslim countries will have to find a solution that would not put the population that abhors interest at a disadvantage compared to the rest of the population. Such economies need to find Islamic products for the money market that could absorb the money demand of the people who do not want to invest in interest-based products.

Free markets in the Muslim world cannot be short of opportunities for short-term investment in the real sector with almost no risk that could become a basis of Islamic money market to absorb the money demand of those who do not want to deal in the interest-based money market. It is only a matter of institutional arrangement to develop financial instrument for an Islamic money market that will offer opportunities for short-run investment, with minimum or almost no risk. Three types of financial products can be developed for this market.

a The debt-based instruments on a short-run sale of commodities carrying a fixed markup rate
b *Bai-Salam* based products
c The profit/loss sharing instruments

The short-term debt-based instruments can be generated in the commodity market. These instruments will carry a fixed markup rate. But they will not be able to be negotiated in a secondary market because of shariah restrictions on negotiating debt on discount basis. However, some institutional arrangements can allow the holder to liquidate the instruments readily, at least at face value. The short-term profit/loss sharing instruments can be generated in the commodity market as well as in the equity market. The commodity trade-based profit/loss-based sharing instruments may be more preferable than the equity market unless proper Islamic rules and laws are implemented to apply shariah rules to avoid a market that may manipulate stocks. The profit/loss sharing based instruments will be negotiable in secondary market.

A Muslim country that has a dual system of interest-based financing and Islamic financing can decide to announce an expected profit rate (instead of interest rate). Let us call it *R*. As explained earlier, expected profit will be a fixed mark up on trade-based government securities. It should be possible for the government to make all its purchases against the issuance of a fixed markup as government securities. These government securities then can serve the same purpose as the interest-based government securities (treasury bills) serve. These bills will be negotiable in a secondary market for whoever considers it permissible. Those who do not consider the debt-based securities permissible to be negotiated in a secondary market may be offered two options. The government can issue profit/loss sharing-based short-term securities. It should not be difficult for the government purchase department to issue such certificates carrying an expected profit rate with a guarantee on a narrow range variation. Government can also issue *Qard Hassan* securities and *sukuk* redeemable on demand to absorb the money demand in the Islamic money market. The government or monetary authority can announce the markup and expected rate, just as the interest rates in secular economies are announced. The central bank or monetary authority from the commodity market or equity market can determine a markup rate and expected profit rate for government securities.

Money demand in present-day Muslim economies

Liquidity preference is the demand for money. People hold money in hand to benefit from the liquidity. Liquidity is preferred for various reasons in a Keynesian framework. Under the assumption that households in present-day Muslim economies have liquidity preference and money demand is a function of interest rate even in the Muslim economies, if these economies move towards Islamic financial system in a gradual way, allowing the interest-based finance and Islamic finance to coexist in the economy, then the question arises how to estimate money demand in the economy. People who practice Islamic finance cannot use the interest-based money market to manage their money demand. The countries that are running a dual system on the way to converting the entire system, in a gradual process, face several issues with respect to their monetary system which prove to be serious hurdle in the way of transformation of the entire system.

First, for those households who do not want to manage their financial matters on interest basis, there are no formal opportunities to manage their liquidity. They keep large liquidity in informal channels. They may be using it in short-term investment, but only through informal channels, or they may keep excessive liquidity beyond their liquidity preference. The first issue, therefore, is how to bring this liquidity into the money market so that people reveal their true liquidity preference. Second, there is large majority of financial institutions in these countries that operate on the basis of interest, and there are households who do not mind investing their liquidity in the money market or keeping their savings in interest-based financial institutions, for convenience reasons or otherwise. The presence of interest and interest-based financial institutions in the economy does not allow the pricing of Islamic products in the Islamic financial market to be determined in the real market. The interest rate in the economy becomes the benchmark for pricing the products of the Islamic financial and money market. Third, the central bank has to use interest rates for managing interbank lending and borrowing because neither the central bank nor commercial banks have Islamic financial products to accommodate each other's short-term financial needs. Lending/borrowing from the banking system is an important monetary tool to regulate money supply, and this lending/borrowing can be done only on an interest basis. The interest rate therefore is a necessity for the monetary policy even for present-day Muslim economies that have a substantial component of Islamic finance in their economy. And if it remains a necessity, then money demand will continue to depend on the interest rate and a substantial part of the money demand will remain in informal channels. The dilemma of these present-day Muslim economies is that if the central bank eliminates interest from the financial and monetary system, it will lose an important tool of monetary policy, and if it keeps the interest rate, then a substantial amount of liquidity and money demand remains outside the formal money market and the entire system may never be able to convert to an Islamic system.

Money demand in present day Muslim economies is a downward sloping curve with respect to the cost of holding money, as it would be in any present-day economy. For those who do not believe in the prohibition of interest, the interest rate in the economy serves as the determinant of money demand. For those who abhor interest, an indicator of short-term return on markup on debt securities issued by the government will serve as the determinant of the money demand. A Muslim country that has a dual system of interest-based financing and Islamic financing can decide to announce a profit rate (instead of calling it interest rate). The central bank or monetary authority from the commodity market or equity market can determine a markup rate for the issuance of government securities. It should be possible for the government to make all its purchases against the issuance of a fixed markup on government securities. These government securities then can serve where they are of interest.

Money supply in present-day Muslim economies

Money supply is generated by the two sources. Central banks print currency, and the banking system creates credit. The banking system has the ability to create credit because banks can issue loans several times higher than the deposits they hold. Islamic scholars have raised no specific objection on this process of credit creation. No practical suggestion has yet come from the scholars with respect to any restriction on a banking system's ability to create credit from an Islamic perspective. Credit creation puts the money supply in the economy at the discretion of the banking system. The decisions of banks to increase or not to increase credit creation has an impact on the real economy, leading to short-run fluctuations in economic growth, hence creating instability in the economy. The credit creation ability of a banking system that the economy creates does not affect the real economy in a classical model. The classical model does not explain the financial crises. But the present-day Muslim economies may not necessarily be money neutral. A monetary policy is, therefore, needed to regulate money supply. The central banks can curtail the creating powers of banking system through reserve requirements. If a central bank requires a 100 percent reserve requirement, the banking system will not be able to create any credit or increase money supply at its discretion. The money supply will be totally at the discretion of central banks. But present-day Muslim economies do not want to do this. Currently, Muslim economies follow global patterns of keeping a low reserve requirement. The banks create credit almost as much as they want if the economy can sustain the profitability of the banking system through credit creation and it does not land the banking system in trouble by causing a run on the bank.

The first issue for the present-day Muslim economies is why the economy should be left at the mercy of the banking system by allowing banks to benefit from marginal reserve requirements. This issue was discussed in the late 1970s and early '80s by Islamic economists, but the policy makers did not pay attention to them. After the repeated crash of financial systems on a global level, and the last one (2008) that shook the entire world, it should make Islamic economic scholars raise this issue again in the context of transforming the present-day Muslim economies to conform to Islamic law.

The conventional economic thinking is sold on the idea that promoting debt in the economy is an easy way of accelerating investment and hence growth in the economy despite its adverse consequences on efficiency, equity, and stability in the economy. The economies have now become so accustomed to having easy access to a debt-creating banking system and the banks have gained so much market power that it is now impossible to think of a 100 percent reserve requirement. The economists understand this problem and have raised their voices. The policy makers, however, believe that since the monetary system is totally based on the interest rate, the governments' monetary authorities can use the interest rate as an effective tool to control and regulate money supply. The interest-based government securities and central banks' discount rates are considered sufficient to have full control of debt expansion to go beyond the limit where it will become damaging for the economy. But there is now sufficient evidence that these assumptions are wrong. Despite the central banks' power to determine the interest rates and discount rates, the banking system has sufficient leeway to expand credit in the economy beyond limits and hence become a source of financial crisis.

Islamic economic principles do not favour debt-creating investment in the economy. The absolute prohibition of charging an interest rate is a sufficient indicator of this economic principle, and if present-day Muslim economies intend to transform their financial systems to conform to Islamic financial laws, then the first step should be to curtail the powers of the banking systems to create credit at their discretion in a gradual process. The money supply needs of the economy should gradually be taken over by the central bank through printing currency. This will be the first issue that should be the concern of monetary policy.

The second issue for the monetary policy of present-day Muslim economies is what would replace the interest rate as a policy tool to control the credit-creating powers of the banking system until this power has completely been erased. The presence of interest in the economy serves two purposes for monetary policy. One, it allows the issue of interest-bearing government securities which carry no risk and can be liquidated easily on demand. The central bank can sell and purchase these securities in the money market to expand or contract money circulating in the economy. Two, it allows the central bank to fix a discount rate for interbank borrowing and lending. What policy tool will a Muslim economy have that would play the same purpose that interest helps play?

Equilibrium in the money market

Since money demand is negatively related to the cost of holding money (some rate of return investment), money demand becomes a downward-sloping function with respect to some cost of holding money in hand. With the supply of money fixed by government, there will be a money market that will determine an equilibrium amount of money held by the household and r, which is the cost that households are willing to bear for holding this amount of money.

The r will increase whenever the money demand from households shifts up or money supply is reduced by the central bank. When r goes down, investment goes up, as discussed earlier. The increase in r will increase investment, which will increase aggregate demand and hence increase output.

The higher the rate of return r on investment, the lower the demand for money, and vice versa. This negative relationship between the demand for money and the rate of return on investment provides a link between changes in the monetary system with the real sector.

Need for monetary policy in present-day Muslim economies

In Keynesian analysis, the rate of interest is determined by the demand for and supply of money. If either the demand for money or the supply of money changes, the equilibrium rate of return on capital (r) would change.

Changing the supply of money can effectively change real variables like employment, output, and income by influencing aggregate demand. The effect on output will depend on the elasticity of the supply of aggregate output. As long as there is excess capacity in the economy, the increase in the supply of money will increase investment by raising the return on capital, which will raise effective demand through the multiplier effect, thereby increasing income, output, and employment.

Unless the rate of return is too low in a Muslim economy, the money demand curve will remain on a downward slope if the Keynesian hypothesis of liquidity preference is valid for present-day Muslim economies, and there will remain the need for monetary policy. None of the Muslim countries, particularly those who are introducing Islamic finance, have a rate of return on investment too low to imply an infinitely inelastic demand for money, so that monetary policy will become redundant. As long as the Keynesian hypothesis remains true in present-day Muslim economies—that households do have liquidity preference, even without any love for money for its own sake—monetary policy will continue to be needed. Though the Keynesian original view, that money supply can affect output, went through several transformations, the Keynesians no longer believe that monetary policy can affect employment and output, but still the New Keynesians advocate using monetary policy for other macroeconomic objectives such as stability, if not for employment or output. The need for monetary policy is now also being emphasized to offset the effects of unexpected external shocks to the economy.

Current economic management in present-day Muslim countries is apparently sold on the Keynesian approach, and the Keynesian approach advocates that the discount rate rather than the money supply is the preferred monetary policy tool.

In the prevailing process to transform their entire financial system to conform to shariah, Muslim countries are faced with a question about what monetary policy tools they need for the interim period until the transformation is completed. Continuing with the interest rate as a policy tool will be counterproductive in any effort to move towards bringing an Islamic financial and monetary system into the economy.

Monetary policy from an Islamic perspective for contemporary Muslim economies

In the background of this discussion, if we are sold on the idea that present-day Muslim economies need monetary policy to increase output employment and for the purpose of stability and therefore the central bank needs adequate monetary tools to regulate money supply and the interest rate or its equivalent is needed in the economy, then let us see what options present-day Muslim economies have to move towards transforming their financial and monetary systems to conform to shariah without losing policy tools to intervene in the money market for growth and stability in the economy.

Three policy directions are suggested:

a Rationalizing the reserve requirement and the utilization of credit created through it
b Replacing the secondary market of debt-based instruments with a profit/loss sharing-based secondary market
c Introducing an Islamic alternative to the discount rate right away

Rationalizing the reserve requirement and utilization of the credit created through it

Economists thinking from an Islamic perspective have always questioned the shariah justification in two respects:

a Why should the credit creation from the banking system continue to be the source of creating money supply when government has the sole authority to change money supply by its power to print money?
b Why can credit created not be used productively without letting it become inflationary?

Economists provide no economic rationale for letting the banking system do it despite its negative implications for efficiency, stability, and equity in economic growth. On the contrary, world economists have recognized that world is in a mess and the crises the world is facing has no solution because of the economic policy makers' permission to banking systems to continue to create credit.

Loans through credit creation by the banking system allow money to be given to the rich as much as they want even after living luxurious life; it makes the rich turn to high-risk economic activities, hence making economy inefficient. The current economic scenario overwhelmingly has shown that loans and credits are not only being acquired unfairly but are also being used in economically inefficient activities such as in gambling, investing in junk bonds, etc. At the occasion of the last Davos meeting, an economist, while commenting on an article published in *The Economist* in London, concluded "Saving is sin and spending is virtue". It implies, according to the economist,

> Get some fools to save so that you can borrow from and spend more they can do from their own resources and hence become rich, leaving the fools poor. This irrational economic situation is occurring due to two undesirable elements taking place in world economic phenomena. First, aggregate consumption is being raised through loans and credits all around the world, and this is creating a propensity to consume to reach towards unity. But the loans have to be generated and credit has to be created on the basis of savings deposited in banking and other financial institutions. If savings have to be enough to make investment and hence the economy grow, then to achieve desired economic progress the poor must save enough to make the financial and monetary system create credit and generate loans to do nothing but make the economy bankrupt. This craze of the world, therefore, is causing economists to believe that a nation cannot grow unless the people spend (in personal consumption), not just spend but borrow and spend

And this cannot happen unless borrowing keeps growing through money and credit creation. The world therefore has to remain an economic mess, and there is no way out for this. Muslim countries will continue to have growing involvement in this mess because their banking system is following the credit creation irrationally adopted by developed world. It is the credit creation from the savings of the poor that is allowing rich people to increase their luxurious and wasteful consumption to create the mess. Even current Islamic banking system and prevailing monetary policies is doing the same and making the economy in Muslim countries a mess. A monetary policy from an Islamic perspective can get Muslim economies to exist apart from this mess, and this will require making the banking system truly Islamic.

The starting point for making monetary policy with respect to credit creation in a banking system should be:

- a Not to allow credit created to go to highly risky (gambling-type) consumption or investment
- b To increase aggregate consumption for economic growth by making credit creation to go to the poor for fulfilling their needs for consumption as well for increasing their productive capacity

In addition, monetary policy should directly or indirectly aim at:

- a Increased *Infaq fi sabeelillah*, as the teachings of Quran and Ahadith require to help poor and needy through formally organized channels. A properly developed system of *Awqaf* can create more economic efficiency, stability, and social harmony along with economic growth that the credit creation of a banking system can aim at.
- b Replacing *Riba* with Islamic alternatives so that Muslim economies will not be indulging in creating unnecessary credit and loans in their countries.
- c Prohibiting gambling-type investments from banking loans. In other words, taking a high risk of losing one's resources with a clear zero-sum game or negative-sum game would not be allowed.

Strategy for gradually reducing trading of debt-based financial instruments in a secondary market

Thanks should be given for the efforts of shariah scholars in the contemporary Muslim world, who have engineered a variety of financial instruments to suit every need of every person that cannot be called *Riba*-based financial instruments. Currently these instruments in the form of debt-creating instruments and profit/loss sharing instruments can meet the risk-return profile of every person in the economy and are shariah compatible. These instruments are asset based and are not merely monetary instruments, and the rate of return on these instruments relates to the real market and not the money market. The following need to be taken care of with respect to formulating monetary policy from an Islamic perspective.

The first step that Muslim countries that are introducing an Islamic financial system may like to consider is to replace the terminology of interest rate with markup or profit rate. This may initially be a change in name only, but it will mentally prepare people at home and abroad to accept the modalities when the markup or profit rate will refer to the rate determined from the real market, not from the money market. This will also make people conscious to look into the details of their financial contracts and deals when making a markup-based or profit rate-based financial deal.

Second, irrespective of whether the term "markup" or "rate of profit" is used instead of "interest rate", it should be same rate that the central bank will announce as a bank rate, benchmark rate, interbank rate, or discount rate. This rate will be determined on the basis of data from the real commodity market or equity market. Actual profits and markup determined from the real market will be applicable in the interest-based financial and monetary market running parallel to the Islamic financial and monetary market. The central bank will declare the markup or profit rate determined from the real market instead of announcing the interest rate for interbank transactions or to become the benchmark for the interest-based financial institutions to determine their own markup on their lending transactions.

Shariah supervision of monetary policy

From an Islamic perspective, the central bank and government may not have absolute powers to intervene in the economy on the pretext of regulating the monetary sector by taking arbitrary decisions of what objective to pursue through monetary policy and what policy tools to be used for economic policy. Monetary policy intervenes in the market and in the economy. Several questions may arise from a shariah point of view. These questions will arise about government intervention in the market. Several scholars deny that government can intervene in the market and economy. But there are some scholars that give government substantial authority to intervene in the economy in public interest or in the interest of society. Some say that government intervention would be subject to certain conditions and certain limits.

The first question about the supervision of monetary policy would be the shariah objective for monetary policy in an Islamic economy. Growth and stability are valid shariah objectives for an economy. Stability, however, loses its significance when macroeconomic models assume money neutrality. The shariah question arises, "Why is monetary policy needed for an Islamic economy?" The monetary authority and shariah authorities together should analyze costs and benefits of monetary policy objectives and tools to be used to achieve economic and monetary objectives.

The second question about shariah provision can be about the extent of discretion to be given to government for the use of monetary policies. What is the safeguard against the abuse of any discretion used by the government? Monetary authorities need to be given shariah guidelines to ensure judicious use of monetary policy and its tools. Monetary policy can generate inflation. How much inflation would be feasible is not only an economics issue but also a shariah issue. Some shariah rules will have to be laid down along with economic rules for the monetary authority with respect to monetary policy.

Conclusion

Islamic economics could be taken as a real alternative to current economics if it had been introduced in a distinct way. The 2008 crisis became the last nail on the coffin of the current economic paradigm. Current economics for all academic and application purposes became conceptually dead. The world has desperately been looking for an alternative economic paradigm since then, and Islamic economics has not yet been able to create any impact on current economic thought. The current economic paradigm based on "creation of wealth" has to be practically proved to be replaceable by the Islamic economic paradigm that, although it will "create wealth", will do so with humane and moral considerations so that it can create peace and harmony along with economic growth and stability in the society.

Monetary policy issues would have been discussed meaningfully if we had seen an Islamic economic paradigm implemented in the practice of current Islamic banking and financial institutions. But the current form of Islamic banking and finance has failed to create any impact in the name of Islamic economics. The practice has only been reflecting the same Adam Smith paradigm of "creating wealth" *from a market perspective* without any morality and humanity put in it. If we had been able to show economic principles of Islam (particularly *Infaq fi sabeelillah* through such institutions as *Awqaf*) for conducting *economic activities beyond the market* as well as reflecting humane and moral considerations in economics while "creating wealth" from the institution of the market, we would have been in a better position to have productive discussions on monetary policy issues.

Having said this, we are therefore not presenting "Monetary Issues in Islamic Economics" but instead presenting "monetary economics and monetary policy issues in Islamic perspective for those contemporary Muslim economies that are trying to make their economies Islamic". Ideally speaking, even this presentation is premature. If a present-day Muslim country wants to make its economy truly Islamic, then the question of what monetary economics will be and what issues will arise in formulating monetary policy could be very easy and straightforward. But the fact is that none of the present-day Muslim economies can be claimed to be truly Islamic economies.

The first issue to be settled therefore, is

What macroeconomic model should be assumed for an economy in order to identify monetary issues?

A discussion on this will then make us understand monetary economics issues in the economy and what issues will then arise for monetary policy and how to solve them from an Islamic perspective.

If we make a simple assumption that implementing an Islamic system of property rights (*Fiqh al-Mall*) and Islamic laws of exchange of property rights in the market (*Fiqh al-Buyu'*) can make the economy of a present-day Muslim country Islamic, then understanding monetary economics and hence identifying monetary issues and discussing their solutions will be simple without posing any big challenge for such a Muslim country. The chapter has described from the outset how a Muslim country would make its economy Islamic and how we will describe the economic model of this economy under which we can discuss monetary economics and monetary issues. Under this assumption, the discussion would have been similar to what has been discussed in economics literature under the classical theory of economics. Under this theory, the monetary sector does not affect the real sector, and there will therefore be no significant monetary issues. But we cannot assume this for any contemporary Muslim country. Present-day Muslim economies are far from the scenario of a properly and correctly defined macroeconomic model for the discussion of monetary economics for the model. We cannot even define a classical macroeconomic model for a Muslim country. Influenced by Keynesian thought, all economies have assigned interest a central role in economic management.

However, since almost all major Muslim economies are in the process of introducing an Islamic finance and monetary system, probably as a part of a policy to gradually convert the entire financial system to confirm to shariah, we can therefore discuss, for such Muslim economies, the issues about how to manage their monetary sector so that they can gradually eliminate the role of interest in the monetary policy while effectively managing the monetary sector for growth, equity, social harmony, and stability in the economy.

In this perspective and in the theoretical background discussed in this chapter, we propose that the following may be considered for discussion:

a Reduce the private sector's dependence on debt creating investment and let the economy grow not on debt but on profit/loss sharing-based financing.
b The secondary market of debt-based financial instruments should be eliminated, whether the debt is interest based or is Islamic debt based on markup. A secondary market should exist only for profit and loss sharing-based instruments.

Reduction of the private sector's dependence on debt-creating investment

Presently, all Islamic banking activities mostly use the concept of what is called markup for financial accommodation in giving or receiving financing, fulfilling shariah rules only in letter rather than spirit or in form rather than in substance. And this is under the instructions of a central bank approved by shariah scholars. The concept of markup, directly or indirectly, is based on the interest rate that is to be used by the rest of the banking and financial institutions in the economy. If, in the process of making economy Islamic, central banking continues making the system on markup-based financing and markup determined on global interest-based banking system, then monetary policy will, therefore, remain the same as in the interest-based system, making no impact on the economy to achieve desired objectives of growth and stability with equity and peace in society.

The issue is how to get rid of this situation. One issue relates to central bank functions and the other relates to security markets.

Central bank functions

We have two suggestions to be discussed in this respect:

- i The central bank can determine markup rate or profit rate whatever they like to distinguish the rate from the interest rate on the basis of actual market transactions in trading or on selling and buying over short-term future payments. The market of goods and services should determine these rates to be used in monetary policy. It is said (though we do not have reference) that in *Khilafat Usmanya*, Khalifa used to announce mark-up in financial transactions on the basis of actual trade transactions.
- ii A strategy to rationalize the reserve requirement should have the objective of determining such a reserve requirement that is essential for creating credit sufficient to achieve shariah-approved macroeconomic objectives in the economy. The credit creation resulting from such a reserve should be in a planned way to help in funding the poor sections of the system to improve their economic status. It should not be used in spending the loans so obtained in luxurious consumption and wasteful economic activities.

Rationalizing a secondary market to reflect the Islamic spirit

The secondary market currently even in those Muslim countries who are aiming at making their financial system Islamic are based on financial instruments, whether the debt in these instruments is interest based or is Islamic debt based on markup. Monetary policy should consciously eliminate market of debt-based securities, and the secondary market should exist only for PLS-based instruments.

Monetary policy aims at slowly reducing the debt content in the investments in the economy in order to design monetary policies to make monetary and financial systems to fully conform to shariah.

Notes

1 This chapter is a substantially modified version of a chapter from M. Fahim Khan published in the Book published recently by IRTI. Though a few portions of this chapter may be a verbatim reflection of the previous chapter, it should not be confused with the substance of the previous paper. This chapter changes the substance by changing the assumption of model of an Islamic economy underlying the explanation of monetary economics and monetary policy in this chapter.

2 "And those who hoard gold and silver and spend it not in the way of Allah—give them tidings of a painful punishment". The Quran (9:34)

3 The Quran (51:19 and 70:24)

4 The Quran (70:24), (51:19)

References

di Mauro, Filippo, Pierluigi Caristi, Stéphane Couderc, Angela Di Maria, Lauren Ho, Baljeet Kaur Grewal, Sergio Masciantonio, Steven R. G. Ongena and Sajjad Zaheer. (2013). Islamic Finance in Europe. ECB Occasional Paper No. 146, Available at SSRN: https://ssrn.com/abstract=2251204

Faridi, Muhammad Zahir and Muhammad Hanif Akhtar. (2017). *An Estimation of Money Demand Function in Pakistan: Bound Testing Approach to Cointegration*. Multan: Bahauddin Zakaria University.

Hussain, M.M., A. Shahmoradi and R. Turk. (2015). *An Overview of Islamic Finance* (No. 15–120). International Monetary Fund, Washington D.C.

Jabeen, Z. and M.R. Khan. (2008). An Inquiry into the Usage of Real Assets in Islamic Transactions and Their Benchmarking: The Implications for Islamic Capital Markets. *Islamic Capital Markets*, Vol. 69.

Kemal, A.R. (2005). Macroeconomic Management: Breaking Out of the Debt Trap. *Lahore Journal of Economics*, Vol. 10(Special Edition), 45–62.

Khan, M. F. (1984) Macro Consumption Function in an Islamic Framework, *Journal of Research Islamic Economics*, 71–73.

Khan, M. Fahim. (2017). Economics of Philanthropy, *Journal of Philanthropy*, Vol. 1, No. 1, Islamabad.

Khan, Mohsin S. (1986). Islamic Interest-Free Banking: A Theoretical Analysis, Staff Papers, *International Monetary Fund*, Vol. 33, No. 1 (March), 1–27. Published by Palgrave Macmillan Journals on behalf of the International Monetary Fund Stable. www.jstor.org/stable/3866920

Naqvi, Syed Nawab Haider. (1982). On Replacing the Institution of Interest in a Dynamic Islamic Economy, in *Essays in Islamic Economic Philosophy* 3, Islamabad: Pakistan Institute of Development Economics.

3 Economic analysis of Islamic monetary framework and instruments

Salman Ahmed Shaikh and M. Kabir Hassan

Introduction

It is well established in the literature that financial development complements economic growth. North (1990) and Neal (1990) conclude that regions that developed more sophisticated and well-functioning financial systems were the subsequent leaders in the economic development of their times. Odedokun (1998) also concludes that the growth of financial aggregates in real terms has positive impacts on the economic growth of developing countries, irrespective of the level of economic development attained. Levine (2002), using cross-country data, argues that financial development is robustly linked with economic growth. Furthermore, Hassan et al. (2011) find a positive relationship between financial development and economic growth in Organization of Islamic Cooperation (OIC) developing countries.

Figure 3.1A plots data of 48 OIC member countries for broad money (as a percent of GDP) and annual real GDP in 2016. It can be seen that increase in the monetary assets is positively linked with GDP. Figure 3.1B plots data of 50 OIC

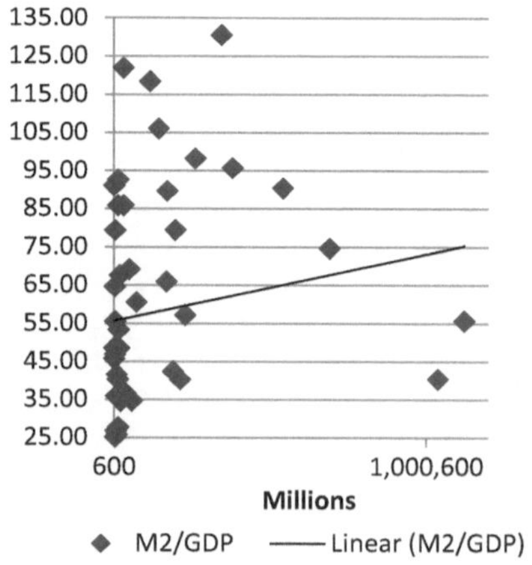

Figure 3.1 M2 (% of GDP) on GDP (in millions)

Source: World Development Indicators 2016

member countries for private sector bank credit to GDP and annual GDP in 2016. The graph reveals that increased private sector credit penetration is positively associated with higher levels of GDP.

However, in interest-based financial intermediation, the access to finance is only available primarily to rich capitalists who can reveal financial capacity in the form of endowments that are acceptable as collateral. This enables the rich capitalists to smooth the path of consumption by borrowing as well as engage in productive enterprise to enhance their incomes. On the other hand, the majority of people who do not have ownership of assets that are acceptable as collateral remain excluded, especially from financial credit services. Hence, increased penetration and deepening of such a financial architecture brings about growth but also exacerbates income inequality, as shown in Figures 3.2A and 3.2B.

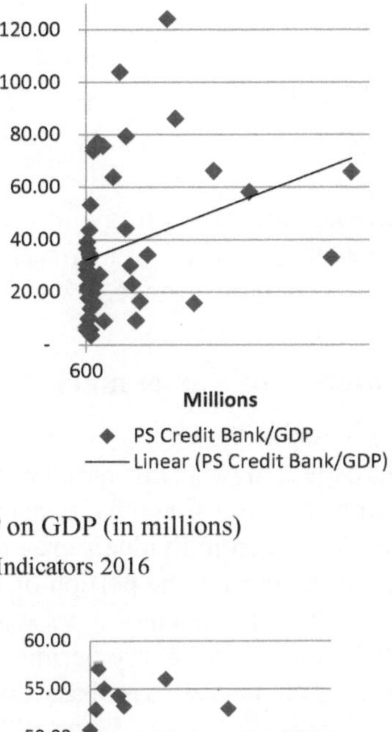

Figure 3.2 PS credit/GDP on GDP (in millions)
Source: World Development Indicators 2016

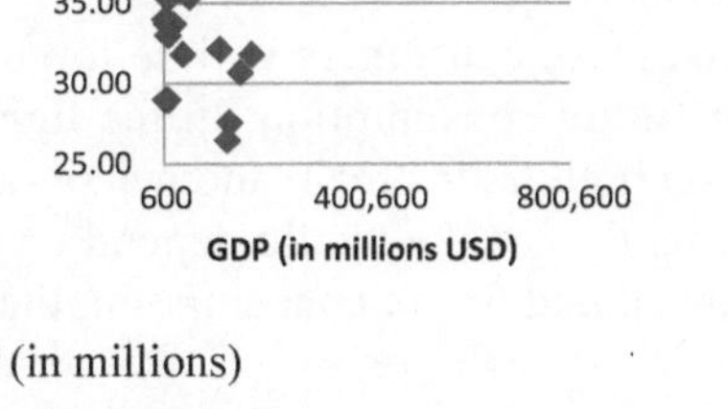

Figure 3.3 GINI on GDP (in millions)
Source: World Development Indicators 2016

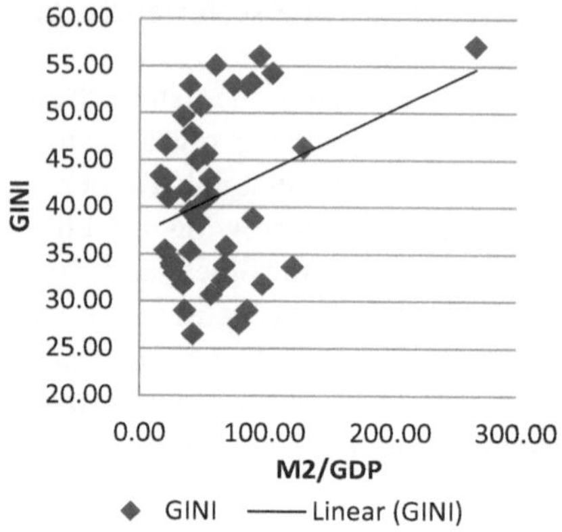

Figure 3.4 GINI on M2/GDP
Source: World Development Indicators 2016

An alternate financial architecture needs to avoid these negative effects on income inequality; at the same time, it has to ensure financial inclusion and accessibility, which is a precursor to economic growth.

Asset allocation in the interest-free asset market

In the Islamic monetary framework, the capital market avoids the elements of interest and instead allocates capital investments based on the profit-sharing ratio. In an economy, there are some consumers who have income which is more than their consumption for the period. Such individuals are known as saving surplus units, where the savings in a period (S_t) is the portion of income that is not consumed in the same period ($Y_t - C_t$). These consumers would be required to pay *Zakāt* on their surplus wealth endowment every period if their wealth is above the value of *Nisāb*. In contrast to the interest-based asset market, there is no fixed return that they can earn at the prevailing rate of interest by simply lending their surplus savings to a financial institution or debt issuer in the interest-based capital markets. Thus, in order to avoid reduction in wealth and to earn any legitimate return on their surplus savings, these saving surplus units will have to undertake investment in the real economy.

In making investments, these consumers will be forgoing present consumption for possibly higher future consumption. In the light of economic theory and empirical evidence on both mainstream and behavioural finance literature, the amount of investments they make would depend on their marginal rate of substitution between current and future consumption, the reward-to-variability ratio of the investment undertaking, and the degree of loss aversion in their preferences. They will reveal their preferences by responding in terms of making different levels of capital investments at different levels of profit-sharing ratio. Steep indifferences curves, that is, a higher marginal rate of substitution for intertemporal consumption and loss aversion, would make them demand a higher profit-sharing ratio for themselves. On the other hand, a higher Sharpe ratio (i.e., higher reward to variability) of a potential investment undertaking would enable them to reap the target level of return even with a lower profit-sharing ratio.

In addition to that, in an economy there will be individuals or groups of individuals who would be looking to pursue productive investments but remain short of funds. Such individuals would require capital investments. In return, they would offer profit-sharing in the investment undertaking. As is the practice, the ex-ante profit-sharing ratio is offered by saving deficient units looking to source finance. The factors that determine this offered profit-sharing ratio include the amount of capital needed, the duration of investment, and the reward-to-variability ratio of the investment undertaking. The greater the capital requirement and the duration of investment undertaking, the higher will be the offered profit-sharing ratio. However, the higher the reward-to-variability ratio, the lower will be the offered profit-sharing ratio. Thus, unlike the debt-based financing where the savers and investors have opposite reactions to the rate of return since the return for savers is the cost to investors, the interest-free equity financing-based capital markets do not have an inherent tension between savings and investments. Both

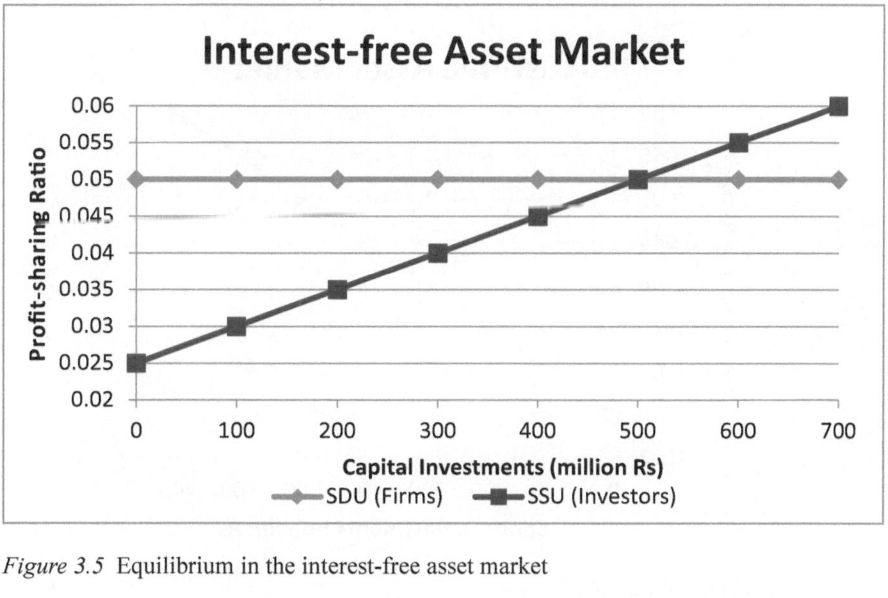

Figure 3.5 Equilibrium in the interest-free asset market

react uniformly to the internal strength of the investment undertaking, that is, the reward-to-variability ratio.

Since there is no fixed return to money capital alone in the loanable funds market, all savings must necessarily be invested in the real economy to earn any return. If no return is required, then surplus savings can either be paid to charity or given as an interest-free loan. Any return on investments will have to be earned in the real economy. The equilibrium is shown in Figure 3.3, where the horizontal line represents the saving deficient units demand for capital investments, whereas the upward sloping line illustrates the saving surplus units supply of investable funds at the different levels of profit-sharing ratios. Equilibrium occurs at the equilibrium profit-sharing ratio; the amount of capital invested by the investors equals the capital investment required by the firm.

Higher capital requirement, longer duration of investment, and lower Sharpe ratio will compel the firms to offer a higher profit-sharing ratio and vice versa. Figure 3.4A and Figure 3.4B show both the upward and downward shift in SDU investment demand curves.

An increase in the Sharpe ratio of investment indicating greater strength of the project will shift the SDU curve down as well as shift the SSU curve to the right and make it flatter as it shifts, with the intercept remaining the same. The intercept for SSU curve is the rate of *Zakāt*, since it is assumed that *Zakāt* is not paid on surplus wealth that is not available for either use or consumption in that period. Another argument giving way for this assumption is that capital investment becomes a means of earning income. Hence, as with income from produce on rain-fed lands, the investment income in this case would be subject to *Ushr*

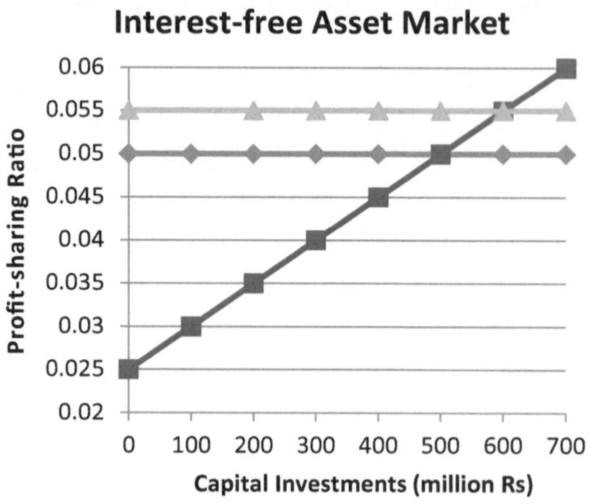

Figure 3.6 Upward shift in SDU curve

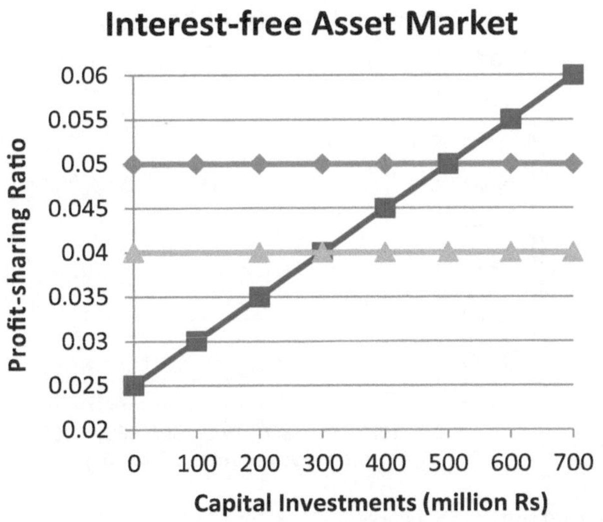

Figure 3.7 Downward shift in SDU curve

since the means of production would be exempt from wealth *Zakāt*. Thus, firms sourcing funds can access greater investible funds even if they do not increase their investments, they can source the required funds at a lower profit-sharing ratio as the SSU curve becomes flatter and shifts to right following an increase in the Sharpe ratio.

On the other hand, greater impatience in the consumers would make their indifference curves steeper and hence shift the SSU curve on the left and make it steeper as well. Furthermore, higher loss aversion would also result in the SSU curve becoming steeper. As a result, firms will have to respond by increasing the profit-sharing ratio for inducing patient and loss-averse consumers to engage in capital investments. Figure 3.5A and Figure 3.5B show both the upward and downward shift in SSU investment supply curves.

Thus, the preceding analysis shows that movement in the profit-sharing ratio can perform the asset allocation function in the interest-free capital market. Furthermore, investment acceleration can be achieved through institutionalizing *Zakāt*, which levies a charge on idle wealth. In an economy where there is prohibition of interest, the surplus and idle wealth would accelerate conversion of saving into investment. Thus, it can enhance the scale of decent employment opportunities and contribute to economic growth.

In addition to that, since there is no return on money balances and direct participation possibilities in the investment projects through asset markets, there will be lower risk for the economy to fall in the liquidity trap. Circulation of wealth is

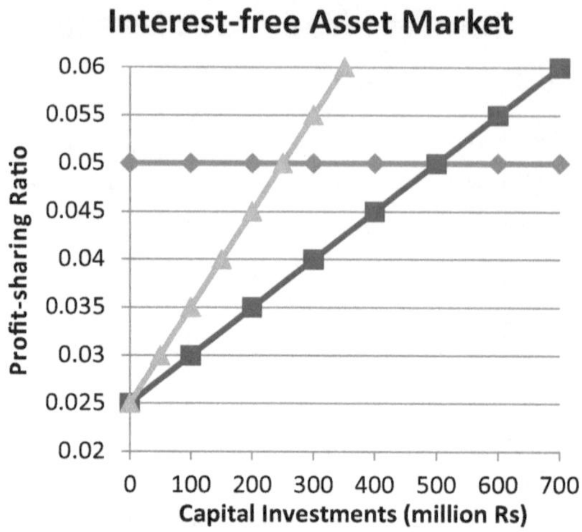

Figure 3.8 Upward shift in SSU curve

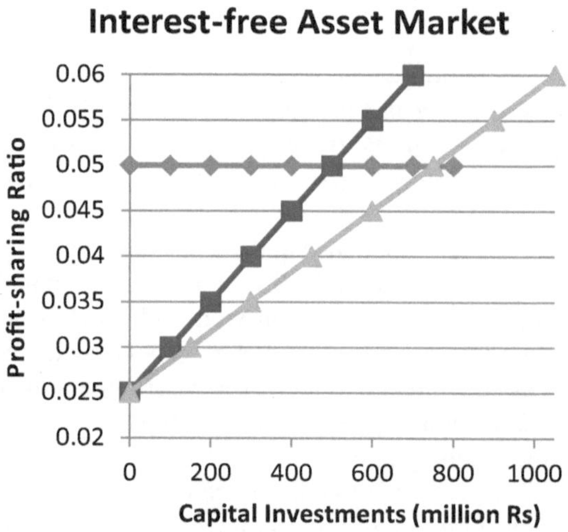

Figure 3.9 Downward shift in SSU curve

also bolstered by *Zakāt*. If the investments are made exempt from *Zakāt* until they are at least redeemed, consumers will be further incentivized to invest.

The effects of Islamic capital market operations on the macro economy are also positive. There is less pressure on current account balance if there is no or a limited gap between savings and investments. In an open market economy, the gap between savings and investments is filled by the current account balance. Thus, a stable current account can have a stabilizing effect on the exchange rate and on domestic currency as a store of value in the interest-free economy.

Interest free banking for short-term financing and investments

Islamic banking enables short-term intertemporal finance between risk-averse investors and individual and corporate clients who require short-term finance. Risk-averse investors want to minimize risk and delegate the responsibility of credit portfolio monitoring to the Islamic banks. There are certain short-term finance needs which might be difficult to finance through long-term equity finance or which can be more efficiently funded through employing trade and lease-based modes of financing. Interest-free Islamic banking primarily caters to short-term finance needs involving an asset, and the investor client base of Islamic banks are investors who want to smooth the path of consumption through regular incomes with limited chances of risk. Thus, Islamic banking investments are suitable for impatient, risk-averse, and loss-averse investors who invest in a limited way by sharing in the financing of real assets where the returns are linked to the assets' sale or use rather than their long-term productivity.

The basic structure of Islamic banking can be explained mathematically as follows. First, an Islamic bank creates an asset pool (AP) which consists of the bank's equity ($E = \Sigma\, p{\cdot}n$) and deposits. Deposits include two further classifications, that is, remunerative deposits ($RD = \sum_{j=1}^{n} RD_j$) and non-remunerative deposits ($NRD = \sum_{i=1}^{m} NRD_i$). Remunerative deposits are mobilized using partnership mode *Mudarabah*, with a bank's shareholders and depositors as partners. The profit-sharing ratio is agreed at the start of this partnership. Non-remunerative deposits are mobilized using *Qard* (non-compensatory loan) or *Wadiah* (safekeeping deposits). Mathematically, the asset pool is funded by a bank's equity and deposits, including both remunerative and non-remunerative deposits:

$$AP = \sum p{\cdot}n + \sum_{i=1}^{m} NRD_i + \sum_{j=1}^{n} RD_j \qquad \text{(Equation 1)}$$

Where p is par value of the bank's share price, n is the number of outstanding shares, NRD_i is the non-remunerative deposit of the ith depositor and RD_j is the remunerative deposit of the jth depositor. This pool of assets is used to provide asset-backed financing (ABF). In accounting terminology, the asset pool is the liability side of the Islamic bank's balance sheet, whereas the asset-backed financing assets and receivables make up the asset side of the Islamic bank's balance sheet. In economic terms, both should be equal, that is,

$$AP = ABF \qquad \text{(Equation 2)}$$

ABF consists of various financing assets based on different underlying financing contracts, that is, *Ijarah*, Diminishing *Musharakah*, *Murabaha*, *Salam*, and *Istisna*. An Islamic bank does not lend money. It provides asset-backed financing in which the asset is owned by the bank. These financing modes can be categorized as lease-based financing ($LBF = \sum_{k=1}^{0} LBF_o$) or credit sale-based financing ($CSBF = \sum_{l=1}^{p} CSBF_p$).

Hence, equation 2 can also be written as:

$$AP = ABF = \sum_{k=1}^{0} LBF_o + \sum_{l=1}^{p} CSBF_p \qquad \text{(Equation 3)}$$

Where LBF_0 is the lease-based financing provided to the *o*th client and $CSBF_p$ is the credit sale-based financing provided to the *p*th client. Income stream is generated either through profit on credit sale or rent for the use of asset. Thus, income (I) comes in the form of rent ($R = \sum_{k=1}^{0} R_o$) or profit on sale ($P = \sum_{l=1}^{p} P_p$).

$$I = \sum_{k=1}^{0} R_o + \sum_{l=1}^{p} P_p \qquad \text{(Equation 4)}$$

If rental income is some stable proportion of *LBF* and profit income from the deferred sale is some stable proportion of *CSBF*, then equation 4 can also be written as:

$$I = \alpha\, LBF + \beta\, CSBF \qquad \text{(Equation 5)}$$

We can assume the average rental rate or profit rate to be the same, except for term premia and counterparty risk premia in customized financing assets. If *r* is average rental and profit rate, then equation 5 can also be written as:

$$I = r \times (LBF + CSBF) \qquad \text{(Equation 6)}$$

Using equation 3 in equation 4, we can see that income is distributed among the contributors in the pool, including the bank's shareholders and depositors. To achieve spreads for financial intermediation function, profit-sharing is done between the bank and the depositors as per the pre-agreed profit-sharing ratio and pre-assigned weights to different types of depositors. Thus, the Islamic bank is able to achieve competitive matching returns, and where a significant deviation occurs, the Islamic banks can use profit equalization reserves (PER) to smooth returns.

An illustration of capital to assets ratio against the Gini coefficient does reveal that there is an inverse relationship between the capital-to-assets ratio in banks and income inequality, as shown in Figure 3.6. The OIC member countries where the banks have higher capital adequacy ratios usually have lower inequality of income.

Thus, in the full reserve banking system or the system where there is only asset-backed financing or a greater capital buffer, the distribution effects are expected to be more egalitarian. Since remunerative investment accounts in Islamic banking are operated through *Mudarabah*, the capital buffer would be greater in Islamic banking, leading to greater solvency, resilience, and lesser volatility in net banking

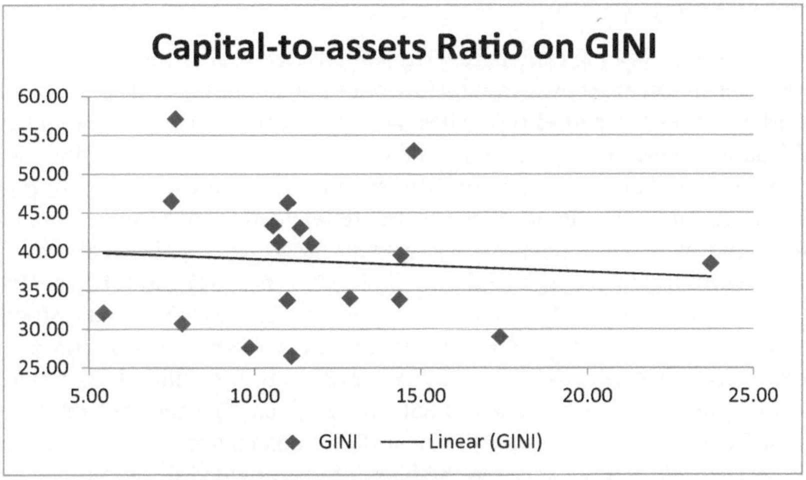

Figure 3.10 Capital-to-assets ratio on GINI coefficient
Source: World Development Indicators 2016

Table 3.1 Islamic banking indicators globally

Country/ Indicators	*CAR*	*Gross NPF*	*ROA*	*ROE*	*Net Profit Margin*	*Cost to Income*	*Liquid Assets to Total Assets*
Bahrain	19.00%	12.07%	1.33%	9.84%	26.46%	82.28%	17.57%
Brunei	21.22%	5.74%	1.73%	12.31%	52.39%	40.54%	49.93%
Egypt	13.54%	7.60%	2.70%	47.86%	59.21%	31.45%	68.36%
Indonesia	15.74%	4.69%	0.91%	9.39%	8.96%	91.09%	12.93%
Jordan	22.26%	2.96%	1.70%	17.90%	48.32%	51.67%	36.65%
Kuwait	17.97%	2.95%	1.21%	10.34%	21.41%	36.73%	32.01%
Malaysia	15.69%	1.30%	1.05%	15.23%	39.43%	41.62%	11.23%
Nigeria	38.31%	1.67%	0.06%	0.74%	4.93%	89.90%	21.06%
Oman	40.74%	0.06%	−2.02%	−3.42%	−71.01%	158.24%	20.38%
Pakistan	14.11%	5.98%	1.04%	15.88%	24.57%	74.76%	30.72%
Saudi Arabia	20.30%	1.18%	2.14%	14.37%	47.73%	51.98%	26.29%
Sudan	18.69%	5.96%	2.62%	25.70%	52.93%	43.81%	37.11%
Turkey	15.48%	4.31%	1.08%	12.35%	18.66%	49.28%	48.65%
UAE	16.46%	7.91%	1.52%	12.63%	33.85%	66.15%	15.01%

Source: Author's calculations from IFSB data

spreads due to pass-through of returns in the risk-sharing model. Indeed, Islamic banks in different jurisdictions seem to have enough capital adequacy to guard against exacerbating income inequality, which is a tendency in interest=based fractional reserve banking. Table 3.1 gives the average capital adequacy ratios in Islamic banks in different jurisdictions.

Pricing benchmark, money market instruments, and monetary policy

In the literature on pricing capital, few studies have focused on the price of capital in an interest-free context by using shadow price in place of the regular accounting price (Mannan, 1982), and some studies have shown concern over the applicability of Islamic finance principles beyond the commercial banking into the pricing of loans between countries and IFIs (Reddy, 2001) and monetizing public debt (Darrat & Bashir, 2000). In academic literature relevant to the role and functions of the central bank and monetary management based on Islamic ideals, we find concepts such as refinance ratio (Siddiqi, 1982), *Qard-e-Hasan* ratio (Khan, 1982), *Mudarabah*-based lending between commercial and central banks and restricting high-powered money by way of required reserve ratio (RRR) than relying on open market operations (OMO) (Chapra, 1983), Time Multiple Counter Loan (Shaikh, 1990), composite stock (Zangeneh & Salam, 1993), and the central bank having equity stake in commercial banks (Uzair, 1982), to name a few. In this section, a brief overview of pricing capital in the literature is provided followed by practicable alternatives suggested by Islamic economists.

In proposing the financing arrangement between the central bank and the government, Kurrihara (1951) explained that since a central bank is the government's bank, if the government sells securities to the central bank, interest paid by the government will eventually come back to the government without economic or payoff difference.

In another proposal to price capital in an intertemporal transfer of funds, Mannan (1982) proposed the use of the accounting price of capital, which will neither add to the cost of production nor form part of the profits but instead will be used to appraise projects.

Pricing capital in an interest-free economy has been a problematic issue to deal with. Responding to Kurrihara's viewpoint, we argue that interest is prohibited in an absolute sense, and it cannot be accommodated even if the same transaction is reversed over a period of time, thereby nullifying the economic impact. Responding to Mannan's viewpoint, we think that if interest is criticized on the presumption that it is not a rightful mechanism to allocate resources, then this accounting price will be no different. Capital rationing is useful to avoid the free-rider problem so long as an artificial and rigid scarcity of capital can be avoided.

But the vacuum still exists as to how to effectively price capital in a holistic way to encompass both private and public finance. Reddy (2001) highlighted an important problem in an interest-free economy as to how it will deal with external debt management which is primarily interest based. Similar concern was shown by Darrat and Bashir (2000) as to how deficit financing can be monetized in an interest-free economy and how expectations about the rate of return can be formulated.

Now we come to the various suggested alternatives to price capital holistically and look for ways in which a central bank in an interest-free economy can carry out its functions. Chapra (1983) realized that the two important instruments of monetary policy in the capitalist economy, that is, discount rate and open market operations (OMO) in interest-bearing government securities, will not be available in an Islamic economy. Based on this, he recommended the following important measures.

i *Managing monetary base, deposit mobilization and fund utilization*

The central bank should make the total money supply created by it available partly to the government and partly to the commercial banks and the specialized financial institutions. The government would pay an actual service charge to the commercial banks for their deposit mobilization services.

ii *Public share of demand deposits*

In addition to the amount diverted to the government by the central bank for expanding the monetary base (*Mo*), a proportion of commercial bank's demand deposits, for example, 25 percent, should be diverted to the government to enable it to finance socially beneficial projects in which profit-sharing is not feasible.

iii *Statutory reserve requirement*

Commercial banks should be required to hold a certain proportion, say, 10 percent or 20 percent, of their deposit liabilities with the central bank as statutory reserves. The central bank should pay the commercial banks the cost of mobilizing these deposits just as the government would pay the cost of mobilizing, that is, 25 percent of demand deposits diverted to the government.

Coming to other proposals, Siddiqi (1982) supported the use of a "refinance ratio", that is, the central bank refinancing a part of the interest-free loans provided by the commercial banks to influence the volume of short-term credit extended by the commercial banks. Khan (1982) advocated the use of *Qard-e-Hasanah* ratio, that is, the percentage of demand deposits that commercial banks are obliged to lend as an interest-free loan to influence the availability of credit.

Uzair (1982) proposed that a central bank can acquire equity stake in commercial banking by holding 25 percent of the capital stocks of the commercial banks to get a permanent source of income and play its role as a lender of last resort. However, his proposal can bring conflict of interest between the regulator and the private banking institutions.

Shaikh (1990) introduced the Time Multiple Counter Loan (TMCL) model, which is based on the basic idea that in a loan arrangement, both the amount of loan and time to maturity are important. Thus, if the amount of any loan is multiplied by the period of lending, the result would be a unit, that is, loan value (LV). Thus, Rs.1,000 lent for one year has the same loan value as Rs.125 lent for eight years, that is, both sum up to the same loan value of Rs.1,000. Therefore, any combination of giving bilateral loans whereby the loan value remains the same is in conformity with Islamic principles, as it will fall in the realm of *Qard-e-Hasanah*. Therefore, if a borrower needs a loan of Rs.1,000 for one year, he can give away a loan of Rs.125 for eight years and get a loan of Rs.1,000 for one year. According to the author, the TMCL concept could be used in interbank lending and borrowing and between central banks and commercial banks. Zaheer (1996) criticized the TMCL concept, arguing that TMCL is based on the premise that money ought to have time value and the Islamic prohibition of *Riba* requires no time value of money in loan transactions.

Zangeneh and Salam (1993) presented two alternatives for money management, the discount rate and OMO. They recommended that the central bank could charge the borrowing bank a weighted average rate of return in different sectors of the economy plus or minus a discretionary premium to discourage borrowing if the economy is facing inflation.

They also recommended that the central bank could perform its OMO in terms of a "composite stock" representing the central bank's ownership of all of the government and government agencies' owned enterprises. By trading a "composite stock" rather than individual private or public company's stocks, the potential problem of exerting undue influences on the price of a company's stocks is avoided.

Some scholars have proposed in the past to index financial loans in the inflationary periods with some inflation index. Here, we analyze the potential problems with this proposal. If this proposal is suggested at the macroeconomic level in financial intermediation (such as in banking; as banks become an intermediary between those who have surplus funds and those who need funds, and banks profit by the difference in interest rates on the deposit and financing side), then it is not practicable in the financial system. Indexing loans with inflation will not yield any return for the intermediary (the bank) in two-tier loan-based banking.

Furthermore, inflation is measured by an index which has an urban bias, because the consumer price index (CPI) inflation is calculated looking at only the prices in urban areas. It has a period bias, as in indexing; the choice of base year makes the calculations very different. It also has a representative bias, because inflation in urban areas is not a true representative of inflation in all areas if rural areas make up two-thirds of the population in some developing countries. Plus, inflation is just an estimated measure, and there are at least four varieties of inflation measure used by the Pakistan Bureau of Statistics—Consumer Price Index, Wholesale Price Index, Sensitive Price Index, and Producer Price Index. The results depend on the methodology, the particular commodities in the index which change from time to time, and not everyone has the same basket of goods relevant for them.

Finally, cost-push inflation is driven by supply shocks, such as an increase in oil prices and a decrease in supply and hence increases in prices of electricity, gas, etc. Therefore, deterioration in real purchasing power is caused by factors not in the control of the borrower. He cannot be held liable to compensate in a matter in which he was not responsible.

To sum up, it can be seen that efforts have been made in the past to delineate a mechanism for managing money supply, for instruments to be used in an Islamic money market, and for managing liquidity in the financial sector and on the determination and delineation of functions of the central bank in the Islamic economy.

But much of that academic research has not translated into practice, and limited attention has been paid to the issue of establishing the benchmark for an Islamic monetary system. This non-existence of a distinct and standardized benchmark has created obstacles in the creation and wide acceptance of more preferable Islamic alternatives like *Mudarabah* and *Musharakah*.

An alternate pricing benchmark and money market instrument

Time value of money is the basis of interest. As per Islamic principles, time value of money is the problem for the investor to avoid keeping his money idle and to avoid forgoing the use of money that may bring positive value to his investment. However, it does not mean that the investor can demand an arbitrary increase as the cost of using money without taking the market and price risk of a productive enterprise. As per Islamic principles, the person who owns money has to undertake the risk of productive enterprise by becoming a self-entrepreneur or an investing entrepreneur as an equity partner in others' businesses to have any justifiable compensation out of the production process.

In contemporary monetary system, interest-based T-bills are not Islamic, since they involve *Riba*, which is prohibited in Islam. As a substitute for T-bills, the governments can issue Treasury *Sukuk Ijarah* Bills to source funds. This instrument can also be used in open market operations. In place of reverse repo and repo, ready buy deferred sale can be used to inject and mop up funds. If the commercial banks want to deposit funds with the central bank, they will buy Treasury *Sukuk Ijarah* Bills at a lower price on the spot and sell at a higher price in future. Likewise, if they want to access funds from the central bank, they will sell Treasury *Sukuk* Bills at a lower price on the spot and buy at a higher price in future. The difference in price will be the financial cost to the party that is obtaining funds and return to the counterparty that is providing funds. The imputed rate of return will be higher on reverse repo than on repo. A unilateral undertaking will separate the two legs of the transaction. To ensure that it is not an outright buyback transaction, it is important to ensure proper identification of the *Ijarah* asset, transfer of ownership, constructive possession, and prior valid offer and acceptance to execute the sale of *Ijarah* assets.

In outright open market operations where the objective is to buy and hold the treasury securities till maturity, *Murabaha Sukuk* can also be used where there is no need for a secondary market and for multiple sales between counterparties during the life of the security.

The question arises as to what the profit rate benchmark should be. To solve this issue, the government can set up a trading corporation that trades in commodities like food crops and petroleum products. In some countries, such a trading corporation already exists, and the governments procure goods through these trading corporations to achieve the objective of smooth supply, exports of surplus and imports of shortage, protecting the small growers, and regulating prices. In these trading operations, the government can set prices to reflect its target profit rate. This target profit rate can become a benchmark for issuing Treasury *Sukuk Ijarah* Bills and affect the other rates of returns in Islamic short-term debt financing instruments.

Open market operations would involve injecting and mopping up funds. This will be achieved through purchasing and selling Treasury *Sukuk Ijarah* Bills. Credit controls can utilize a *Qard e Hasan* ratio (for cash reserve ratio) and sovereign investment ratio (for statutory liquidity ratio) where investments are made in Treasury *Sukuk Ijarah* Bills or composite equity certificates.

In corporate finance, the weighted average profit rate in commodity trade operations of the government could be used in valuation models to provide a quantitative mechanism to rank investment alternatives. In project valuation, this benchmark rate could be used to find the "estimated intrinsic value" of cash flows.

From the perspective of rules governing Islamic finance, this proposal would be appropriate because we are using a real sector-oriented profit rate benchmark rather than an interest-based benchmark. *Mudarib* or a capital deficient partner will not be obliged to provide the returns based on these valuations. But the investor can use this indicative valuation to rank investment alternatives.

It will provide a quantitative mechanism to rank investment alternatives. In actual distribution of income between investors and firms using equity modes of financing, a profit-sharing ratio (PSR) would be used and agreed upon at time (t) and applied to the actual gross profit earned in time period ($t + 1$).

In ranking projects, a project with the highest net present value would be most preferable for investment, so the *Rabb-ul-Maal* (investor) could prefer to enter that contract with even a slightly lower PSR. A project with the lowest NPV is least preferable for investment, so the *Rabb-ul-Maal* could prefer to enter that contract only with a slightly higher PSR. Ranking would be facilitated by using the profit rate as a benchmark in financial valuation models. This process of bargaining will lead to equilibrium in an Islamic investible funds market. With *Zakāt* on idle capital, the investible funds supply in an Islamic economy will be more than in a conventional economy. Plus, with no excessive taxation, the distortions and idleness will be lower, and that will enhance the set of feasible investments between capital surplus and deficient units.

Conclusion

This chapter showed how an asset market would operate in the interest-free economy. The model included the factors that will affect the investment supply and demand. It showed how that profit-sharing ratio could perform the capital investment allocation. *Zakāt* on idle wealth and prohibition of interest would necessitate conversion of saving into investment. Since the returns on capital are shared, it also limits the risk of a liquidity trap. Furthermore, there is less pressure on the current account balance if there is no or a limited gap between savings and investments. This has a stabilizing effect on the exchange rate and on domestic currency as a store of value in the interest-free economy. In addition to that, asset-backed monetization checks unbridled multiplication of money, which causes inflationary effects in the economy. For sourcing funds, the government can issue Treasury *Sukuk Ijarah* Bills and a composite equity certificate representing a stake in state-owned enterprises which are having positive profits. In monetary instruments, credit controls can utilize the *Qard e Hasan* ratio (for the cash reserve ratio) and the sovereign investment ratio (for the statutory liquidity ratio), where investments are made in sovereign *sukuk* or composite equity certificates. Finally, the empirical evidence presented in this study shows that countries where the banks have higher capital adequacy ratios usually have lower inequality of income. Thus, in the full reserve banking system or the system where there is only asset-backed financing or a greater capital buffer, the distribution effects are expected to be more egalitarian. Since remunerative investment accounts in Islamic banking are operated through *Mudarabah*, the capital buffer would be greater in Islamic banking, leading to greater solvency, resilience, and lesser volatility in net banking spreads due to pass-through of returns in the risk-sharing model.

References

Chapra, M. U. (1983). Monetary Policy in an Islamic Economy. *Money and Banking in Islam*. International Centre for Research in Islamic Economics. Jeddah: King Abdul Aziz University.

Darrat, A. F., & Bashir, A. H. M. (2000). Modeling Monetary Control in an Interest-Free Economy. *JKAU: Islamic Economics*, *12*(1), 3–19.

Hassan, M. K., Sanchez, B., & Yu, J. S. (2011). Financial Development & Economic Growth in the Organization of Islamic Conference Countries. *Journal of King Abdul Aziz University: Islamic Economics*, *24*(1), 145–72.

Khan, M. A. (1982). Inflation and the Islamic Economy: A Closed Economy Model. International Centre for Research in Islamic Economics. Jeddah: Kind Abdul Aziz University Press.

Kurrihara, K. K. (1951). *Monetary Theory and Public Policy*. London: Allen and Elwin.

Levine, R. (2002). Bank-Based versus Market-Based Financial Systems: Which Is Better? *Journal of Financial Intermediation*, *11*(4), 398–428.

Mannan, A. M. (1982). *Interest Free Islamic Economy: A Comparative Policy Approach*. International Centre for Research in Islamic Economics. Jeddah: Kind Abdul Aziz University Press.

Neal, L. D. (1990). *The Rise of Financial Capitalism: International Capital Markets in the Age of Reason*. Cambridge, UK: Cambridge University Press.

North, D. (1990). *Institutions, Institutional Change, and Economic Performance*. Cambridge, UK: Cambridge University Press.

Odedokun, M. O. (1998). Financial Intermediation & Economic Growth in Developing Countries. *Journal of Economic Studies*, *25*(3), 203–24.

Reddy, B. M. (2001). Of Religion and Economics. *Frontline*, *18*(11).

Siddiqi, M. N. (1982). *Monetary Policy: A Review*. *International Centre for Research in Islamic Economics*. Jeddah: Kind Abdul Aziz University Press.

Shaikh, M. A. (1990). *Towards Interest Free Banking*. Lahore: Institute of Islamic Culture.

Uzair, M. (1982). Central Banking in an Interest-Free Banking System, in Mohammad Ariff (Ed.), *Monetary and Fiscal Economics of Islam*, pp. 211–235. Jeddah: International Centre for Research in Islamic Economics.
Zaheer, K. (1996). A Critical Look at the Alternatives to the Popular Models of Interest Free (IF) Banking. *Renaissance*, *6*(6).
Zangeneh, H., & Salam, A. (1993). Central Banking in an Interest Free Banking System. *JKAU: Islamic Economics*, *5*, 25–36.

4 Re-examining monetary and financial stability in a modern economy

Evidence from Turkey and Malaysia

Adam Abdullah

Introduction

According to the IMF, there have been 425 instances of monetary, debt, and financial crises since 1970 (Lietaer, 2017, p. 48), and despite this financial instability, regulatory requirements, which assume that banks are financial intermediaries, have failed to stop a single financial crisis. Money is the common denominator for all economic transactions. In Islam, money is defined as an instrument of transfer (Al-Ghazali, 1994), whilst mainstream economics defines money as a commodity that comes at a price in order to justify a theory of interest and a theory of banking. The store of value function of money is a litmus test as to the validity of a medium of exchange (monetary economics) in terms of the objectives of the *Shari'ah* (*maqasid al-Shari'ah*) and the protection of wealth (*hafiz al-mal*). In terms of evaluating monetary stability in Turkey over 540 years (1469–2009), 1.1 gold *lira* coins exchanged for GBP 1.00 gold sovereign coins in 1844, but then 1.5 million paper *lira* exchanged for USD 1.00 in 2005. After redenomination, 1.5 *lira* equalled USD 1.00, but with the onset of another crisis, at one point the USD exchanged for 7.00 *lira* in 2018, before falling back to about 5.15 *lira* in early 2019. Similarly, in Malaysia over 48 years (1970–2018), in terms of gold, the price of gold (PG) was RM 110/oz in 1970 and is now worth RM 5,138 in December 2018; hence the value of RM 1.00 in 1970 is now worth only 2 cents (RM 110/5,138). This massive loss in monetary value has occurred during the fiat standard, causing an exponential decay in the purchasing power of money (PPM) and an exponential increase in prices (Abdullah, 2013, Dec., 2015). This monetary and price instability implies a problem with banks and the alchemy associated with money creation and related interest, and also monetary authorities who have outsourced the production of money, such that private commercial banks typically issue about 97 percent of a nation's money supply (McLeay et al., 2014, p. 15).

In a modern economy, money and banking are supposed to provide monetary and financial stability. However, financial instability has been a recurrent phenomenon in contemporary economic history, affecting countries with varying intensity. The most enduring crisis was the Great Depression of the 1930s. Eminent economists who lived through the Great Depression endeavoured to articulate a banking system capable of preserving long-term financial stability. Their proposals became known as the Chicago Reform Plan, as elaborated by economic professors at the University of Chicago. Indeed, Irving Fisher wrote *100% Money* (1935) in support of a 100 percent reserve banking system. After World War II, from 1945 to 1970, the Bretton Woods gold exchange system witnessed monetary stability as the denominator for economic savings and investment that saw no financial crises. Under the fiat standard, the monetary and financial system changed, such that money was no longer backed by gold but rather by debt at interest, such that price and financial instability has rapidly deteriorated.

In banking, financial instability is associated with notions of default or insolvency. It manifests itself through a deficient treasury position, whereby the sources of funds fall short of the application of funds with respect to payment obligations. When financial instability persists, access to borrowing results in illiquidity. In this case the bank may have to recapitalize, liquidate assets, restructure liabilities, require a public bailout, or require a bail-in by depositors (as a solvency restructure with a hair-cut in deposits in exchange for bank equity), or may be subjected to merger or even liquidation. On the other hand, stability inherently implies that asset and liability maturities are matched, where assets preserve their values and do not depreciate and IOUs are fully backed by deposits. Any over-issuance of credit may cause instability that results in a run by domestic or international depositors. At the time of the global financial crisis, a run on a commercial bank such as the UK's Northern Rock involved queues of depositors physically withdrawing their deposits over a number of days. Such a bank run would likely occur much more quickly, ten years later, given today's information technology infrastructure and the ability of customers to transfer sums instantaneously to other (even non-bank) accounts.

Mirakhor (1988) showed that Islamic banking could be modelled as a non-speculative equity ownership model that is directly linked to the real sector and where demand for new equity is determined by real savings in the economy. All causes of financial instability, in particular credit or money creation out of thin air, speculation, or interest-based financial assets at the time value of money (TVM), should be absent in Islamic finance. Banks should directly own real assets and operate like an equity holding system. Savings are thus redeployed into productive investment with no money creation. Mirakhor demonstrated that the rate of return on equities is determined in a growth model by the marginal efficiency of capital and time preference and is significantly positive in a growing economy, implying that Islamic banking is always profitable provided that real economic growth is positive. Mirakhor's findings established a basic difference that ought to be exist between Islamic banking, where profitability is fully secured by real economic growth, and conventional banking, where profitability is not driven primarily by the real sector. In this case, the Islamic bank would be a genuine 100 percent reserve institution, as an investment intermediary performing the function of an Islamic wealth manager for the demanders and suppliers of capital and related Islamic financial services. This would also eliminate the overall reliance on debt in an economy. Indeed, the intent of the Islamic Financial Services Act 2013 (Bank Negara Malaysia [BNM]) in Malaysia was to encourage Islamic banks

Table 4.1 100% reserve system—a society free from debt

Liabilities		*Assets*	
equity	1,000	state money	10,000
demand deposits	9,000	loans	0
	10,000		10,000

Source: Adapted from El Diwany (2003)

to increase their role in Islamic investments. However, the reverse has happened, with risk-free debt products at the TVM appearing on both sides of the bank's balance sheet. Some Islamic economists and writers have wondered if the fractional reserve-banking model is the correct monetary and financial vehicle for an Islamic economic system (El Diwany, 2003), since it inherently requires an economy to get into debt.

On the other hand, one of the important hallmarks of a 100 percent reserve system is that society is free from debt (Table 4.1). Credit (money) creation in form of demand deposits is not feasible, since all equity and demand deposits can only reflect the supply of money that the state has issued. There is a separation of the public issuance of state money and the private issuance of equity finance and investment. Since there is no debt, there is no incentive for an institution to extend debt finance at interest, and since a debt is greater than cash received, there would be no incentive to create money. Equity and profit sharing are endogenous to profits generated in the real economy and society is free of debt, which is structured on the basis of investment.

However, modern commercial banks provide a unique role in extending credit, a process that involves the creation of money in the money supply process. William Patterson, the first governor of the Bank of England, on obtaining the charter of the Bank of England in 1694, stated: "the Bank has benefit of interest on all money which it creates out of nothing" (Quigley, 1966, p. 49). Apparently only licensed commercial banks are permitted to do this.

> If the two parties, instead of being a bank and an individual, were an individual and an individual, they could not inflate the circulating medium by a loan transaction, for the simple reason that the lender could not lend what he didn't have, as banks can do. . . . But if [an individual] incorporates himself into a commercial bank . . . he can do this very thing. . . . Only commercial banks . . . can lend money, which they manufacture by lending it . . . by the same token two individuals cannot deflate the circulating medium.
>
> (Fisher, 1935, p. 38)

There is also a time mismatch over a bank's liabilities, comprising bank deposits, being a promise to pay upon demand, against its assets, comprising loans, being a promise to pay a debt at some point in the future. The associated mismatch in income streams explains the entire nature of a bank's liquidity dilemma, because the bank's deposits liabilities are "short" and its loan assets are "long". The bank requires exponential growth of deposits and debt for it to remain solvent. However, in terms of money supply, the rate of growth in deposits (and thus money supply) is being determined by the combination of the aggregate deposit as well as the lending rates of interest (Abdullah, 2015). These aggregate rates of interest are the primary determinant in increasing money supply, since a debt at interest is greater than cash received, which inevitably leads to more bank credit (money) being created into circulation. In order to find future money to pay for future interest obligations, the banking system must create money into existence involving the money creation process.

This chapter is organized into the following sections: in the second section, we begin with a literature review on the three theories of banking, as well as incorporate related views and analysis on credit creation, including views on its regulatory and economic impact. The third section presents a methodology to evaluate monetary performance over the long term. The fourth presents the empirical findings from Turkey and the fifth analyzes the mechanics of banking and its role in monetary devaluation under the fiat standard, whilst the sixth section presents the evidence from Malaysia. The last section concludes by developing an Islamic monetary theory of value and equation of exchange, as well as recommending a solution for monetary reform.

Literature review

Werner (2014) highlighted the importance of a stable monetary and financial system in developing sustainable economic growth, free of banking crises. He also noticed that the historical literature has recognized three theories of banking.

i The *credit creation theory of banking* (Macleod, 1883, 1894) maintains that each individual bank creates money out of nothing and does so when it extends credit.

i The *fractional reserve theory of banking* (Marshall, 1890) supposes that banks are merely intermediaries, like other non-bank financial institutions, collecting deposits that are then lent out, as often described in modern textbooks.

ii The *financial intermediation theory of banking* (Keynes, 1936) suggests that individual banks are mere financial intermediaries that cannot create money, but collectively they create money through systematic interaction when money is created (multiplied) through the textbook explanation of the money-multiplier.

With regard to the *credit creation theory of banking*, Macleod stated that

> deposits are not deposits at all: they are nothing but credit and are merely so many bank notes in disguise. They are nothing bit an enormous superstructure of credit, reared up on a comparatively small basis of bullion. . . . [The

> financial statements of banks] . . . do not show the quantity of cash the banks have at their command to trade with, but they show the quantity of business *they have done* [assets] and the *liabilities they have created.*
>
> (Macleod, 1883, 1, p. 329; emphasis in original)

Indeed, "a bank is, therefore, not an office for 'borrowing' and 'lending' money, but it is a Manufactory of Credit" (Macleod, 1894, II/1, p. 594).

Werner empirically established that individual banks create money out of nothing, thereby affirming the credit creation theory of banking and also disproving both the fractional reserve and financial intermediation theories of banking (Werner, 2014). The findings of Werner's empirical research were confirmed by the Bank of England (BoE) as the pioneer model for all fractional reserve banks in two papers in 2014 titled "Money Creation in a Modern Economy" (McLeay et al., 2014) and "Banks Are Not Intermediaries of Loanable Funds—and Why This Matters" (Jakab and Kumhof, 2015). It was also confirmed by both the German central bank, the Bundesbank, in an article in its monthly report, "How Money Is Created" (2017, Apr), and in a speech by Thomas Jordan, the Chairman of the Swiss National Bank, titled "How Money Is Created by the Central Bank and the Banking System" (Jordan, 2018, Jan.);

- Money creation in practice differs from some popular misconceptions—banks do not act simply as intermediaries, lending out deposits that savers place with them, and nor do they "multiply up" central bank money to create new loans and deposits. . . . In the modern economy, most money takes the form of bank deposits. But how those bank deposits are created is often misunderstood: the principal way is through commercial banks making loans. Whenever a bank makes a loan, it simultaneously creates a matching deposit in the borrower's bank account, thereby creating new money. The reality of how money is created today differs from the description found in some economics textbooks. Rather than banks receiving deposits when households save and then lending them out, bank lending creates deposits. In normal times, the central bank does not fix the amount of money in circulation, nor is central bank money "multiplied up" into more loans and deposits.

  (McLeay et al., 2014, p. 14)

- In the intermediation of loanable funds model of banking, banks accept deposits of pre-existing real resources from savers and then lend them to borrowers. In the real world, banks provide financing through money creation. That is, they create deposits of new money through lending, and in doing so are mainly constrained by profitability and solvency considerations. . . . [As compared to financial] intermediation models, financing [through money creation] models predict changes in bank lending that are far larger, happen much faster, and have much greater effects on the real economy.

  (Jakab and Kumhof, 2015, pp. i–ii)

- The majority of the money supply is made up of book money, which is created through transactions between banks and domestic customers. Sight deposits are an example of book money: sight deposits are created when a bank settles transactions with a customer, i.e. it grants a credit, say, or purchases an asset and credits the corresponding amount to the customer's bank account in return. This means that banks can create book money just by making an accounting entry: . . . this refutes a popular misconception that banks act simply as intermediaries at the time of lending—i.e. that banks can only grant credit using funds placed with them previously as deposits by other customers.

  (Bundesbank, 2017)

- When a bank provides a loan, it credits the amount in question to the borrower in the form of a deposit.

  (Jordan, 2018, p. 4).

However, the accounting nature of credit creation also reveals credit destruction. Ryan-Collins et al. (2012) observed that

> just as banks create new money when they make loans, this money is extinguished when customers repay their loans as the process is reversed. Consequently, banks must continually create new credit in the economy to counteract the repayment of existing credit.
>
> (Ryan-Collins et al., 2012, p. 71)

Since deposits are continuously extinguishing loans, and notwithstanding that new loans create new credit, ultimately, the amount of credit issued equals the principal borrowed; what remains is the difference, that is, aggregate interest. Hence, as empirically established by Abdullah (2015), broad money supply must increase at aggregate interest, since a debt is greater than cash received, and new money must be created to fund future interest obligations.

The three theories of banking are based on a different description of how money and banking function, and they differ in their policy implications. It is fundamentally important to determine which of the three theories is true, not only in analyzing the function and role of banks correctly within an economy but also for the design of appropriate bank regulation that aims at sustainable economic growth without crises. The modern approach to bank regulation, as reflected in Basel I (1988), is predicated on the understanding that the *financial intermediation theory* is correct. The capital-adequacy based approach to bank regulation as reflected in Basel I and II has so far not been successful in preventing major banking crises. If the *financial intermediation theory* is not an accurate description of reality, as has been empirically established by Werner (2014) and confirmed by the BoE (McLeay et al., 2014; Jakab and Kumhof, 2015), the Bundesbank (2017), and the Swiss National Bank (Jordan, 2018), it would also cast serious doubt on the suitability of Basel III and similar national approaches to bank regulation (Werner, 2014, p. 2).

This would also include related stability measures, as reflected in capital adequacy, assets, management capability, earnings, liquidity (asset-liability management), and sensitivity to interest rate risk (CAMELS, initially introduced in the United States in 1979), which is designed to classify the overall condition of a conventional bank. Also, ECB bank stability measures (2013), IMF macro-prudential indicators of financial soundness (2000), and bank stability measures (2009), IFSB measures of Prudential and Structural Islamic Financial Indicators (PSIFIs), are all designed to facilitate macro-prudential analysis and assess the structure and state of development of IFIs. IFSB data is separately compiled for prudential and structural indicators for stand-alone Islamic banks and Islamic windows of conventional banks that are especially pertinent in a dual banking system. None of these regulations have stopped any of the 425 instances of monetary and financial crises since 1970. Therefore, Werner's findings and central bank admissions highlight the inability of the current regulatory framework to diagnose and prevent monetary and financial instability under the fiat standard and bring into sharp focus the problems associated with Islamic banks, which have similarly adopted the underlying English fractional reserve-banking model (El Diwany, 2003).

Werner initially developed his empirical research whilst at the Bank of Japan and the Japanese Finance Ministry. He subsequently published a *New Paradigm in Macroeconomics* (Werner, 2005) and further went on to co-author *Where Does Money Come From?* (Ryan-Collins et al., 2012). In these works, Werner discusses the credit theory of money and why capital adequacy requirements (including leverage ratios as a variant of capital adequacy rules) do not protect against insolvency and do not limit credit creation, since these rules neglect the crucial fact that banks are the creators of money supply. Requiring banks to raise more capital in a boom will not stop asset bubbles, since the boom is caused by increased bank credit and also the expansion in the money supply can be tapped by banks to fund higher capital ratios. Werner identified a quantity theory of credit, or disaggregated credit, in terms of productive and speculative credit that recognizes banks ration and allocate credit and create new money in the process. Thus, the supply and not the demand of credit by the banks ensures that they have a decisive influence over the allocation of money in an economy. Regulation would require understanding and monitoring of these processes involving a credit guidance regime, and economies could achieve non-inflationary growth by creating credit in a domestic banking system and guiding it towards productive use—that is, productive credit affecting economic growth and GDP (Ryan-Collins et al., 2012; Werner, 2016). This is supposed to be what Islamic banking does, but in reality, the direction of Islamic bank financing by economic activity (IFSB, 2017, AD06) often involves speculative non-GDP financing and real estate transactions.

Whilst Werner's (2014) empirical analysis on the money creation theory of banking is decisive, Abdullah (2015) rejected Keynesian and quantity theory approaches and detailed an Islamic monetary theory of value. Since a debt is greater than cash received, it requires new money to be created to pay for future interest (TVM) obligations; hence, interest is driving the growth in money supply.

> The exponential decline in the value of fiat currencies, as a result of an excessive increase in the supply of money (due to aggregate deposit and loan interest), in relation to demand, the result of which is an exponential increase in prices—the cause is the decline in the value of money, the effect is an increase in prices.
>
> (Abdullah, 2015)

Genuine monetary and financial stability should thus target the public provision of a high value currency, separated from the private provision of equity finance and profit-sharing, within a 100 percent reserve framework. Since fiat money is debt organized into money, economies inevitably experience higher debt:GDP ratios, as a function of aggregate interest, credit creation, debt-backed currencies, and the fractional reserve banking system (Abdullah, 2015). In fact, absent of interest, investment and in turn employment are expected to be higher in an Islamic economy. Even Keynes stated that interest sets "a limit to the level of employment . . . [and] . . . holds back investment in production" (Keynes, 1936, pp. 222, 235).

Duncan (2012), in discussing a quantity theory of credit, analyzed the margin efficiency of credit (MEC) or the ratio of GDP to total credit market debt (the return on credit). In the United States, for example, the return on credit has declined from 65 percent in 1970, to less than 30 percent at the time of the global financial crisis (GFC) (Duncan, 2012, p. 49). The US economy has therefore steadily generated less output for every dollar borrowed and reflects the extraordinary mal-investment that has accumulated under the fiat standard. Nonetheless, this reinforces Werner's assessment that all banking crises are a function of speculative credit crises (Werner, 2012), as reflected in Table 4.2. Mervyn King, the former governor of the Bank of England (2003–2013), subsequently published *The End of Alchemy* in 2016 and admitted that "For centuries, alchemy has been the basis of our system

Table 4.2 The cause of previous banking crises

Crisis	*Cause*
US, 1920s—margin loans	Speculative credit creation
Scandinavia, 1980s	Speculative credit creation
Japan, 1980s	Speculative credit creation
Asian Financial Crisis, 1990s	Speculative credit creation
UK property bubble until 2007	Speculative credit creation
US property bubble until 2006	Speculative credit creation
Irish property bubble until 2007	Speculative credit creation
Spanish property bubble until 2007	Speculative credit creation

Source: Werner (2012, p. 29)

of money and banking. . . . For society to base its financial system on alchemy is a poor advertisement for its rationality" (King, 2016, pp. 250–1).

Adnair Turner worked alongside King during the GFC, as the former Chairman of the United Kingdom's Financial Services Authority (FSA). Turner published *Between Debt and the Devil* in 2016 and stated,

> Textbook descriptions of banks usually assume that they lend money to business to finance new capital investment . . . but in most banking systems most credit does not finance new capital investment. Instead, it funds the purchase of assets that already exist and, above all, existing real estate . . . banks left to themselves will produce too much of the wrong sort of debt.
>
> (Turner, 2016, pp. 61–2)

In the United Kingdom about 80 percent of lending was allocated to real estate by the banks (Table 4.3). Indeed, real estate is the cause of much financial instability, "credit and real estate prices . . . have been not just part of the story of financial instability in advanced economies, they are close to the whole story" (Turner, 2016, p. 175). Thus, banks fuel the real estate market as a function of the credit cycle through increases in speculative financial transactions and credit creation that cause property asset bubbles. Accordingly, speculative real estate non-GDP credit creation typically results in a financial crisis, whereas productive GDP investment and financing would result in real economic stability.

Furthermore, whilst productive credit transactions are captured in GDP, speculative financial transactions as well as the majority of real estate transactions are non-GDP items (Werner 2005, 2012, 2014, 2016; Ryan-Collins et al., 2012). Thus, the causality of bank lending, credit creation, and credit allocation significantly impacts the economy and not the other way round. "We need to build economies that do not rely on rapid credit growth to achieve adequate demand. We need to manage the quantity and influence the allocation of credit that banks create" (Turner, 2016, p. 174). However, is a credit guidance regime realistic if credit creation is outsourced almost entirely by the central banks to commercial banks? It would seem that, rather than developing productive financing to small to medium-size enterprises (SMEs) by small community banks, such as in Germany, in reality the general trend is towards bank mergers and acquisitions, resulting

Table 4.3 The components of UK bank lending (2012)

By Economic Sector	*Per Cent of GBP 1.6 Trillion*
Business Non-Real Estate	14%
Commercial Real Estate	14%
Residential Mortgages	65%
Consumer Credit	7%
Total	**100%**

Source:Turner (2016, p. 63)

in larger financial institutions, requiring larger customers and larger loans. The United Kingdom has only five large banks, who are clearly not catering to SMEs, which adversely affects the general level of employment, since SMEs are the largest employers in an economy. Therefore, what is the overall impact of money creation and interest in terms of the monetary side of the balance sheet under the fiat standard, and how does it compare with previous monetary systems in terms of performance? We can test monetary performance in terms of evaluating prices in nominal and real terms over the long term, in order to ascertain which medium of exchange retains its store of value and also to determine the effect on price stability.

Methodology

In relation to meeting the objectives of the *Shari'ah* (*maqasid al-Shari'ah*) and the protection of wealth (*hafiz al-mal*), the test for any valid medium of exchange is to hold its store of value function of money. A number of empirical investigations have been conducted by Abdullah (2016), including Ottoman-Turkish data from 1469–2009 (Abdullah, 2013, Dec.) and Malaysian data from 1971–2014 (Abdullah, 2015).[1] This study combines Abdullah's approach at a macro level with library and content analysis of Werner (2014, 2016) at a micro level and his empirical analysis of the accounting view of money to analyze the mechanics of banking, in order to explain devaluation under the fiat standard.

Given Abdullah's historical analysis on high value coinage in the form gold and silver currency (Abdullah, 2016), this study provides an overall impact assessment by measuring the performance of a monetary system in terms of the store of value function of money in determining any debasement in coinage or any devaluation in fiat money from money creation and interest and the impact on nominal and real prices over the long term. Accordingly, the debasement of Ottoman silver coinage, or the devaluation of Turkish paper *lira*, involves a reduction in the value of money—as reflected in the rate of exchange with a fixed amount of silver (a higher price of silver)—as a result of an excessive increase in supply of money in relation to demand, the effect of which is higher nominal prices—and similarly with the paper *ringgit* in terms of gold. The decrease in value of money is the cause, and the increase in prices is the effect. As reflected in Abdullah (2013, Dec., 2015), the value of money involves the construction of indices for the price of gold (*PG*) or silver price (*PS*), the inverse of which reflects the gold (*GC*) or silver content (*SC*) of money, reflecting the intrinsic value of money. The statistical definition of a change in general prices over the long term involved the construction of a geometric mean (Fisher, 1922) and wholesale (*WPI*) or commodity price index (*CP*) (Abdullah, 2013, Dec., 2015).

When the value of money is corrected, real gold or real silver—that is, the purchasing power of gold ($PPG = PG/CP$) or silver ($PPS = PS/CP$)—and real prices expressed in terms of pure gold (*CPgc*) or silver (*CPsc*) are constant and low over the long term (Abdullah, 2013, Dec., p. 202). Real prices in terms of gold or silver are nominal prices adjusted for any loss in the intrinsic value of money, so *CPgc*

$= CP \times GC$. As with the purchasing power of money (*PPM*), which equals the inverse of prices ($PPM = 1/CP$), so with the purchasing power of gold (*PPG*) or silver (PPS); since gold and silver are money, then real gold or real silver is also the reciprocal of real prices, where $PPG = 1/CPgc$ and $PPS = 1/CPsc$.

Findings and discussion: evidence from Ottoman-Turkey

The monometallic monetary standard under Ottoman Empire was the silver *akche*, which was first minted in 1326, and comprised a coin that was ¼ of the Tabriz *mithqal*, weighing 1.152 g of pure silver. Whilst there was debasement of the silver *akche* under the Ottoman Empire, there was also devaluation that occurred when Turkey became a republic, especially under the fiat standard. In 1469 the silver content of the *akche* was 0.86 g, but by 1844, when the Empire became a bimetallic standard with the introduction of the gold *lira* coin, the silver content of the *akche* had shrunk to a mere 0.0083 g. The gold *lira* coin comprised 6.615 g of pure gold and exchanged with the GBP (gold *sovereign* coin) at 1.1 *lira*:£1. By 2005 the *lira*:USD exchange rate was 1.5 million *lira*:USD1. The paper *lira* had become the world's most devalued currency and was subsequently redenominated by simply cutting six zeros from the old *lira* to obtain 1 new *lira*, so that in 2009 the exchange rate was 1.5 *lira*:USD1 (more recently, the USD exchange rate would further deteriorate to 7:1 in 2018, although it has marginally recovered since). This represents a profound loss in the value of money, such that the paper *lira* experienced an exponential decay in the purchasing power of money, especially under the fiat standard (Figure 4.1).

The purchasing power of money is the inverse of prices ($PPM = 1/P$), so that a decline in the *PPM* reveals increased inflation. What caused the decline the *PPM*

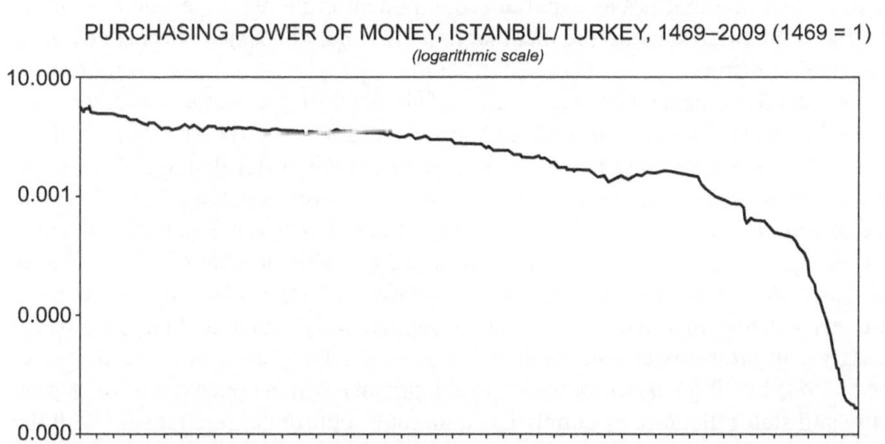

Figure 4.1 The purchasing power of money in Turkey (1469–2009)
Source: Abdullah (2013, Dec.)

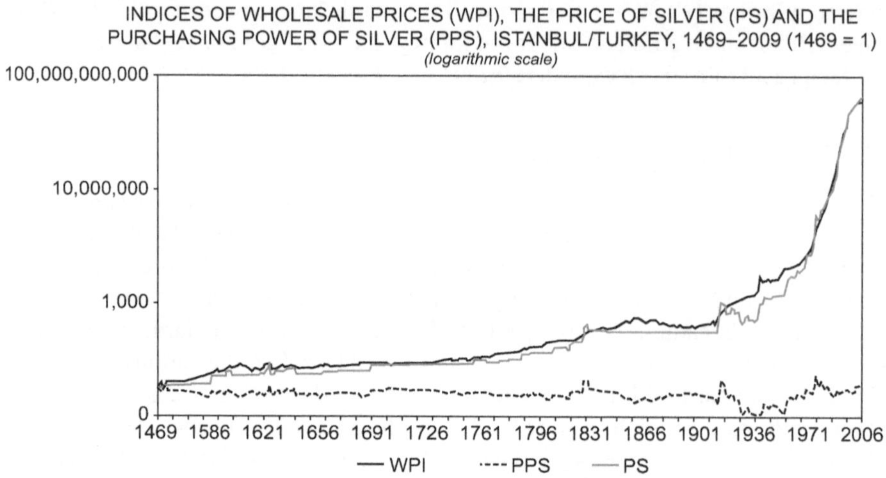

Figure 4.2 Commodity, silver prices, and the purchasing power of silver, Turkey (1469–2009)

Source*:* Abdullah (2013, Dec.)

was the fact that the intrinsic value of circulating coins and paper *lira* decreased due to debasement and devaluation, as reflected in a higher price of silver, which is strongly correlated with higher wholesale prices (Figure 4.2), as reflected in a whole price index (*WPI*). The purchasing power of silver is constant over the long term, whilst nominal prices experienced exponential increase, particularly under the fiat standard, reflecting the fact that *lira* ultimately became the most devalued currency in history.

Figure 4.3 presents real prices in terms of silver (*WPIs*) when the loss of intrinsic value has been corrected in order to show what prices would have been had the value of money been maintained, without debasement or devaluation. Real prices are low and stable over the long term, and since silver is money, the *PPS* is the reciprocal of real prices (*PPS* = *1* / *WPIs*) expressed in silver. Therefore, precious metals and not paper money hold their store of value and satisfy the *maqasid al-Shari'ah* and *maslahah*, whereas fiat money is harmful (*darar*). An Islamic monetary theory of value involves value, supply, and demand and targets a stable currency in order to achieve stable prices over the long term. This should not to be confused with the quantity theory (monetarism), which concentrates on supply only and states that money supply has a direct, proportional relationship with the price level, or even the purchasing power theory (mercantilism, Keynesian economics), and involves altering the value and PPM in order to target stable prices by managing money through interest rates (Keynes, 1936) or the supply of money (Friedman, 1956) through central bank monetary policy (Abdullah, 2013, Dec.).

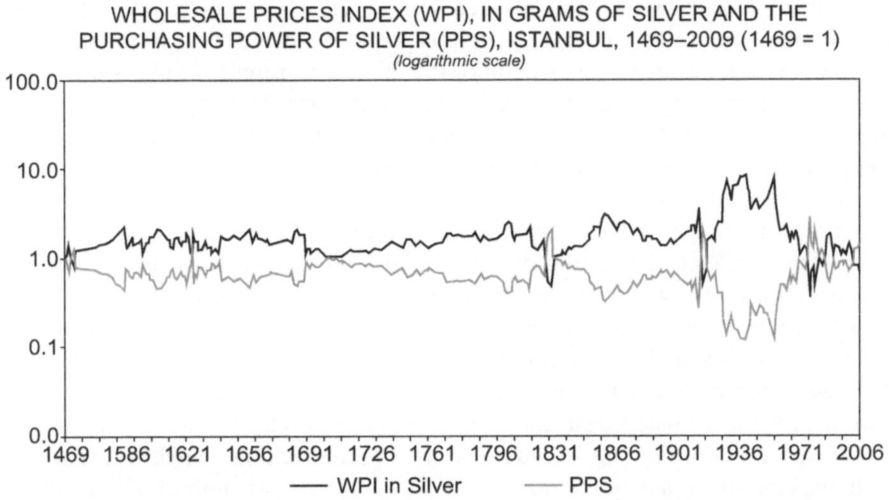

Figure 4.3 The purchasing power of silver, real prices in silver, Turkey (1469–2009)
Source: Abdullah (2013, Dec.)

The mechanics of banking: empirical evidence

Having already observed the exponential decline in the PPM with the Turkish data, and before proceeding to analyze Malaysian fiat data, it is necessary to analyze the mechanics of banking under the fiat standard. As mentioned earlier, only recently was the first empirical study conducted on the mechanics of banking, by Professor Werner from the University of Southampton. Werner (2014) investigated the accounting nature of credit creation involving a live empirical test by tracking the documentation and processing of a live loan through the accounts of a commercial bank, then interpreting the accounting treatments according to each theory of banking before confirming what actually occurred, thereby serving as a test in order to support the correct theory. Werner empirically established that individual banks create money out of nothing, thereby affirming the credit creation theory of banking and also dis-proving both the fractional reserve and financial intermediation theories of banking (Werner, 2014).

Essentially, in analyzing Werner's test and understanding the mechanics of banking, we could ask the question: "Where does the conventional or 'Islamic' bank obtain the money to lend?" (for example, to finance the purchase of a house). A typical answer might be "from depositors' money", but in response we could ask, "What are the accounting entries when they disbursed the loan?" Some bankers, but certainly the accountants, may answer: "Debit" for the borrower's account (i.e., borrower's loan/financing account—the buyer) and "Credit" for the seller's account (i.e., the seller of the house or the developer if they have a savings or deposit account at the bank, or the bank will pay via a banker's cheque). In this case, banks do not use existing deposits or reserves to fund lending, since the transaction involves debit and credit book-keeping entries, where new "credit" (money, in the form of unfunded non-cash deposits) is created out of nothing from lending. Hence, lending creates deposits and not the other way round, which is contrary to most contemporary economics and finance textbooks. The impact will not just be on education but should be upon the provision of finance and regulation, since counterfeiting money into existing from a debt transaction is simply fraud, and should be treated as such.

Indeed, in analyzing the *financial intermediation theory of banking*, as with a non-bank financial institution or a merchant (Table 4.4), we would expect a decline in cash reserves of the same amount that customer loans increase. If the bank borrowed from another financial institution in order to fund the loan (implying a decrease in shareholder's equity), we would not expect an increase in deposits or an increase in the balance sheet. Indeed, as with any trader, a merchant can only lend what is owned from the capital of the firm, that is, equity capital. To create capital out of nothing would be deemed counterfeiting, which is fraud.

In the case of the *fractional reserve theory of banking*, an individual bank cannot start lending without first having money deposited at the bank, so it cannot create money and is still a financial intermediary, except that there is a regulatory

Table 4.4 Accounting entries and balance sheet for financial intermediation

Accounting entries for disbursement of a loan by a merchant

Account	*Amount ('000s)*	*Notes*
Dr Cash A/C	200	Cash A/C
Cr Debtor's A/C	200	Debtor's A/C

Balance Sheet of Merchant (before lending)

Liabilities		*Assets*	
equity capital	250	cash	250
	250		250

Balance Sheet of Merchant (after lending)

Liabilities		*Assets*	
equity capital	250	cash	50
		debtor	200
	250		250

No change in liabilities

No increase in assets, only a change in asset class

Source: Adapted from Werner (2014)

requirement that reserves must be held with the central bank. A bank cannot at any moment lend more money than its excess reserves, and it will have to draw down the reserve balance in order to lend. With this theory, balance sheet expansion is driven by a prior increase of a deposit to boost excess reserves, not by the granting of a loan. However, an increase in the balance sheet cannot be reconciled with the fractional reserve theory of banking, if reserves (involving cash or claims with other financial institutions, including the central bank) are unchanged (Table 4.5), in which case the fractional reserve theory of banking is not applicable.

In reality, with the *credit creation theory of banking*, whether with a conventional bank (Werner, 2014) or with an Islamic bank (Abd. Wahab, 2016), such as in Table 4.6, a borrower first arranges financing to purchase an asset (house/car) and the seller (or developer) opens a deposit account. Whilst accounting entries are shown for shareholder's equity, in fact, a bank branch needs no prior deposit or capital and can just begin the business of banking by lending credit into existence, and lending will not be constrained by reserve requirements.

The asset account is offset by the contra asset account, which therefore leaves *Dr* borrower's account and *Cr* seller's account on the completion of the transaction, as the borrower must agree to the financing (loan) first before a matching amount is created in the seller's deposit account. The title of the asset has simply

Table 4.5 Accounting entries and balance sheet for fractional reserve theory

Accounting entries for disbursement of a loan by a bank

Account	*Amount ('000s)*	*Notes*
Dr Reserves A/C	200	Reserves A/C
Cr Borrower's A/C	200	Financing A/C

Balance Sheet of Bank (before lending)

Liabilities		*Assets*	
equity capital	250	cash reserves	250
	250		250

Balance Sheet of Bank (after lending)

Liabilities		*Assets*	
equity capital	250	cash reserves	50
		financing	200
	250		250

No change in liabilities

No increase in assets, only a change in asset class

Source: Adapted from Werner (2014)

Table 4.6 Accounting entries and balance sheet for credit creation theory

Accounting entries for disbursement of a loan by an Islamic bank

Account	*Amount ('000s)*	*Notes*
Dr Asset A/C	200	Asset A/C
Cr Seller's A/C	200	Seller's Deposit A/C
Dr Borrower's A/C	200	Financing A/C
Cr Asset A/C	200	Contra Asset A/C

Balance Sheet of a Bank (before lending)

Liabilities		*Assets*	
equity capital	250	cash reserves	250
	250		250

Balance Sheet of a Bank (after lending)

Liabilities		*Assets*	
equity capital	250	cash reserves	250
seller's deposit	200	financing	200
	450		450

Bank lending creates money

No change in cash, but bank assets increases by the loan amount

Source: Adapted from Werner (2014), Abd. Wahab (2016)

changed from the seller to the buyer but is charged to the bank as collateral until the deferred "marked-up" credit price has been repaid by instalments. Thus, a debt made by the bank on the asset side of the balance sheet, with the borrower as a debtor to the bank, is matched by an unfunded bookkeeping entry on the liability side of the balance sheet. Bank lending creates non-cash credit ("money") in the form of a deposit, with the depositor as an unsecured creditor to the bank. Islamic banks are able to increase their assets and balance sheet by the financing (loan) amount, such that they create money out of nothing (i.e., they create fictitious purchasing power). A similar example can be found with the "Islamic" "credit" card. The accounting entries when the cardholder conducts a transaction are *Dr* cardholder's account and *Cr* merchant's account. No cash is involved, just debits and credits, so that "credit" (money) is created and the bank's balance sheet expands accordingly. By counterfeiting credit into existence from risk-free debt contracts at the TVM, the *Majallah* (no. 52), points out that, "if something is void (*batil*) then all that flows from it is also void (*batil*)". This manifests itself in Islamic banking financing products, since Islamic banks are not traders, as they have no stock or inventory. They structure risk-bearing sales contracts and arrange them, as a stratagem, into risk-free debt contracts at the TVM (Abdullah, 2016, Oct.). Ibn Qayyim condemned this practice by citing a *hadith* from the Prophet (s.a.w.s.), "A time is certainty coming to mankind when they legalize (*yastahillun*) *riba* under the name of *bay*"' (Rosly and Sanusi, 1999, p. 9). This is emphasizing substance over form (*Majallah*, no.2), we can block the legal means to an unlawful outcome (*sadd al-dhara'i*) in order to protect the public interest (*maslalah*) and avoid harm (*al-darar*).

Evidence from Malaysia

If debasement and devaluation was the cause of a decline in the value of money under the Ottomans, then devaluation also occurred in Malaysia. To be a credible medium of exchange, a measure of value and a standard of deferred payment, a currency has to retain its store of value function of money and preserve its purchasing power. All fiat currencies are backed by debt, and the *ringgit* (MYR) is also backed 99.7 percent (= 1,548.6/1,553.8) by debt, which are IOUs owed to banks (Table 4.7). Additionally, BNM currency in the form of notes and coins represents only 4 percent (= 68.2 / 1,553.8) of total *M3* money supply, with the balance of 96 percent of money creation being outsourced to private commercial banks. Furthermore, interest accrues on both sides of the monetary balance sheet, on loans and on deposits, thus implying that money supply must grow to accommodate future interest obligations. Meanwhile, BNM data affirms that Islamic banking assets comprise 40 percent of total banking assets in 2018, in which case Islamic banks must accept an equivalent level of responsibility with regard to any economic impact.

Since deposit money is created from lending, the amount of a loan creates an unfunded bookkeeping entry, which is being recorded as a debt and at the same time as a deposit on both sides of a bank's balance sheet. Thus, money creation provides cover for the total aggregate deposit and lending rates of interest, to inevitably grow money supply at the combined rate of interest, since debt is greater than cash received.

An alternative money supply (*M3e*) can be constructed by growing the money supply (less currency in circulation) at aggregate interest and then comparing it to the actual growth in the *M3* monetary aggregate (Figure 4.4); indeed, the correlation between *M3e* and *M3* is almost unity, at 0.996 (Abdullah, 2015). In fact, between 1970 and 2014 the monetary aggregates equally grew at the aggregate

Table 4.7 The monetary balance sheet of the MYR as of 31 December 2014

Assets (Billions)		*Liabilities (Billions)*	
Gold	5.2	BNM Currency	68.2
IOUs Owed to Banks	1,548.6	Bank Deposits	1,485.6
	1,553.8	**M3**	**1,553.8**

Source: BNM Statistics (Abdullah, 2015)

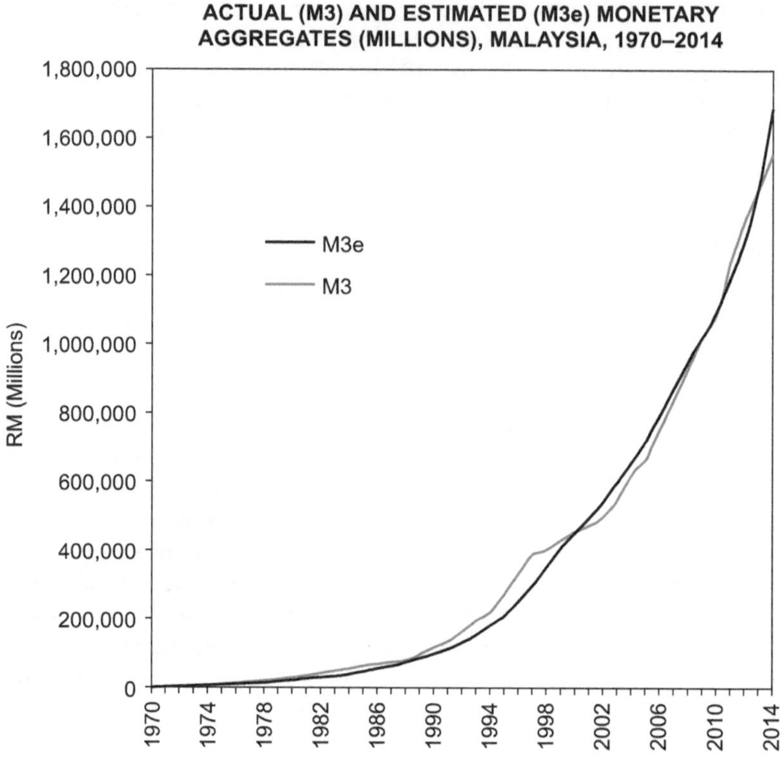

Figure 4.4 Actual and estimated *M3*, 1970–2014
Source: Abdullah (2015)

deposit and lending rates of interest at about 14 percent (Abdullah, 2015), so aggregate rates of interest are the primary determinants of the increase in money supply (*M*).

In assessing the growth in Malaysian monetary aggregates since 1970 (Figure 4.5), we may observe the significant rise in Malaysian monetary aggregates, which has been exponential since the demise of the Bretton Woods gold exchange standard in 1971. How does growth in the monetary sector compare with growth in the real economy? We may observe a similar pattern of growth in the market value of final goods and services produced over the same period, as measured by nominal GDP at current prices (Figure 4.6). Indeed, the correlation between *M3* and GDP is 0.997 (Abdullah, 2015).

Accordingly, aggregate interest drives *M3*, which in turn drives nominal GDP at current prices. Essentially, a predictable relationship exists between *M* and aggregate interest but a similar such relationship also exists between *M* and nominal GDP. In the quantity theory, if velocity is stable, then a direct, predictable relationship must exist between money supply (*M*) and nominal GDP (Friedman and

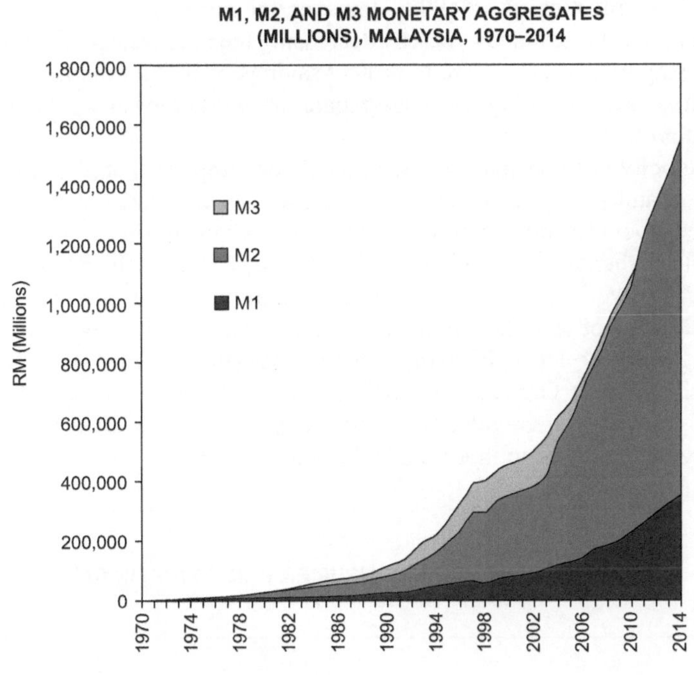

Figure 4.5 Malaysian money supply, 1970–2014
Source: Abdullah (2015)

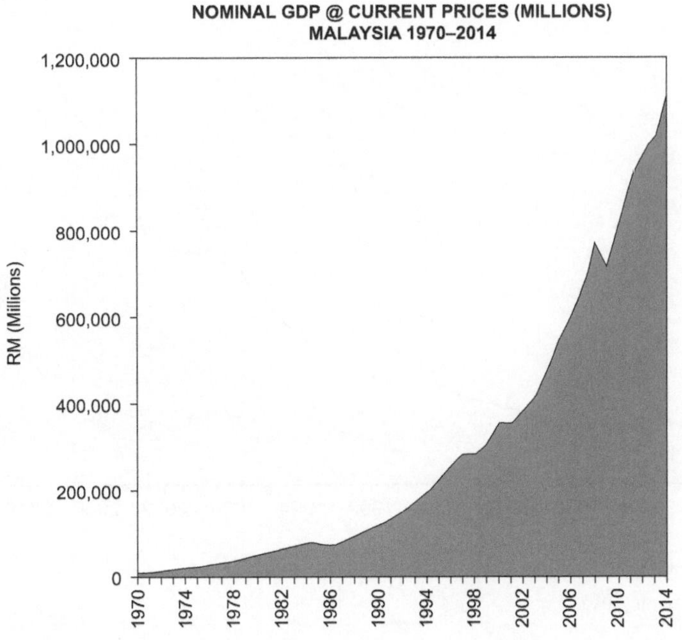

Figure 4.6 Malaysian GDP, 1970–2014
Source: Abdullah (2015)

Schwartz, 1963). Indeed, the correlation coefficient between *M3* and GDP from 1970–2015 is almost unity, at 0.997. However, the quantity theory hides the role of interest in devaluing money, thereby decreasing the purchasing power of money and increasing prices. The desire to protect savings from inflation from a deposit interest rate is self-defeating, since aggregate interest is the cause of devaluation and not its protector.

With velocity (*V*) constant, the quantity theory implies that $P = M/Y$. Given published *M* and *Y* macroeconomic variables, we can calculate the annual change in the price level (*P*) and construct a price index where 1970 = 1. Since *P* represents inflation, then the purchasing power of money (*PPM*) is the inverse of prices ($PPM = 1/P$). We can then adjust the purchasing power of one *ringgit* (MYR 1.00) in 1970 and observe how monetary inflation has steadily devalued domestic purchasing power to levels in 2014 far below that which existed 45 years earlier (Figures 4.7 and 4.8). Our consumer prices index (*CP*) revealed that as a function of the *M2* monetary aggregate, prices rose exponentially to 24.6 by 2014, and conversely the *PPM*, as an inverse of *CP*, sank to 0.04.

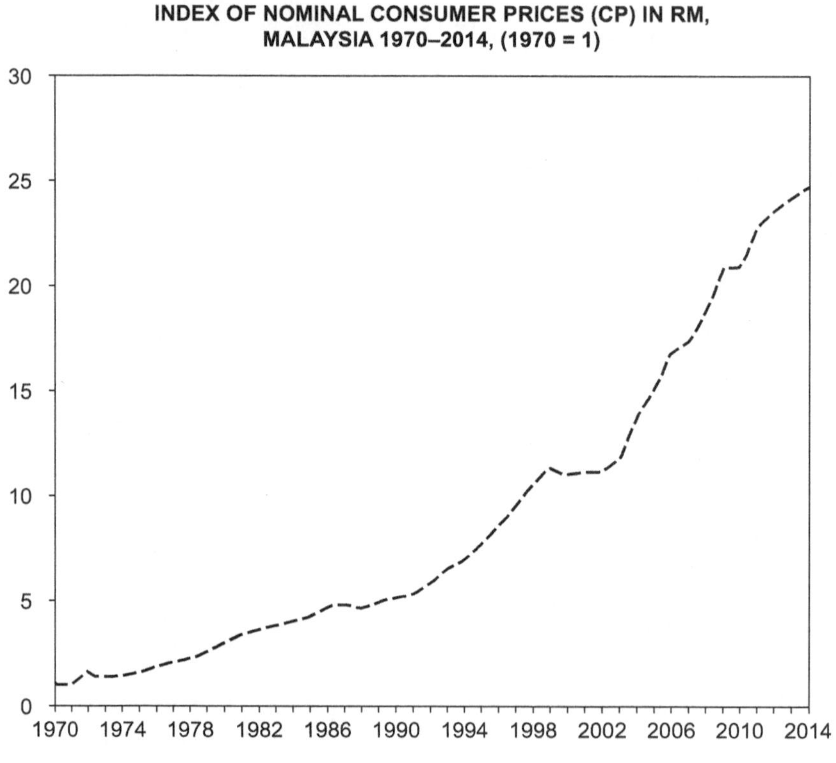

Figure 4.7 CP, 1970–2014

Source: Abdullah (2015)

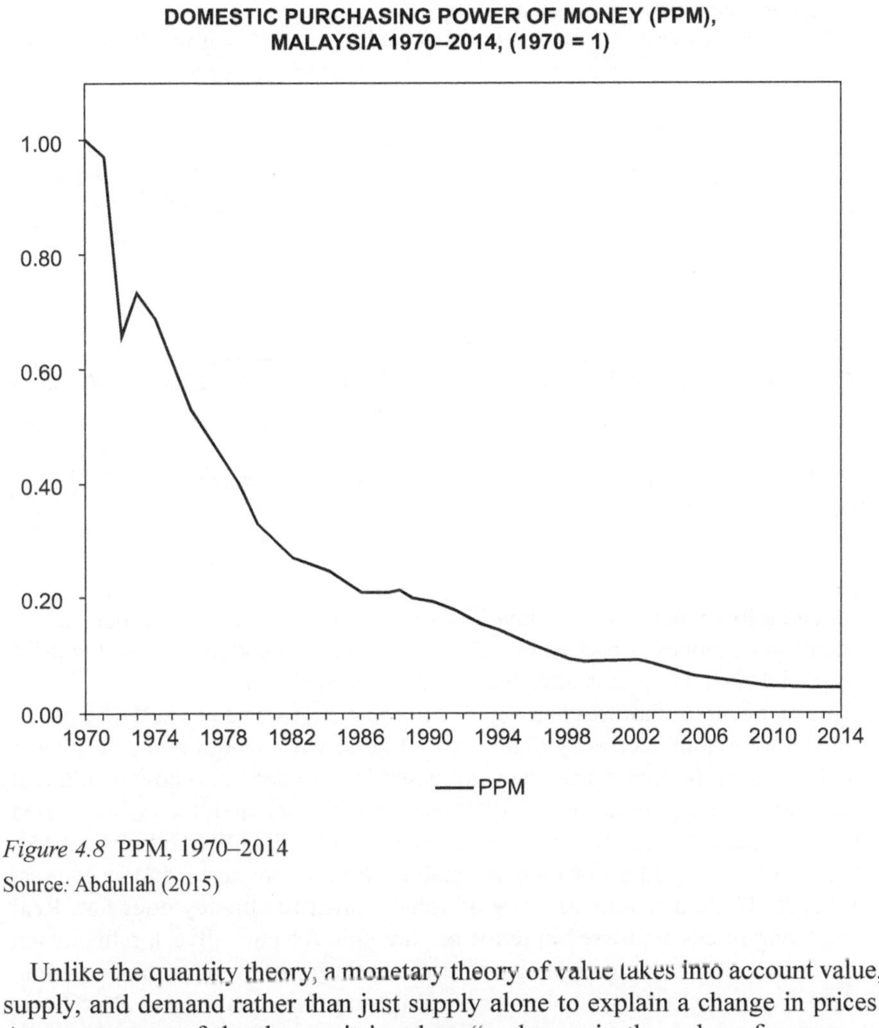

Figure 4.8 PPM, 1970–2014
Source: Abdullah (2015)

Unlike the quantity theory, a monetary theory of value takes into account value, supply, and demand rather than just supply alone to explain a change in prices. As a statement of the theory, it involves "a change in the value of money, as reflected in its rate of exchange with gold (or silver), as a result of a change in the supply of money in relation to demand, the effect of which is an increase in the price level" (Abdullah, 2015). Thus, a decline in the value of money is the cause and an increase in prices is the effect. An inflationary monetary policy is thus to weaken the value of money (*VM*), reflected in a higher gold price (being the currency value of a fixed amount of gold, in terms of its rate of exchange with gold), as a result of an increase in the supply of money, in relation to demand, the effect of which would be to increase prices. Equally, a deflationary monetary policy involves increasing the value of money—reflected in a lower gold price as a result of a decrease in the supply of money—in relation to demand, the effect of which would be to lower prices. In summary, the effect of a high value currency is low

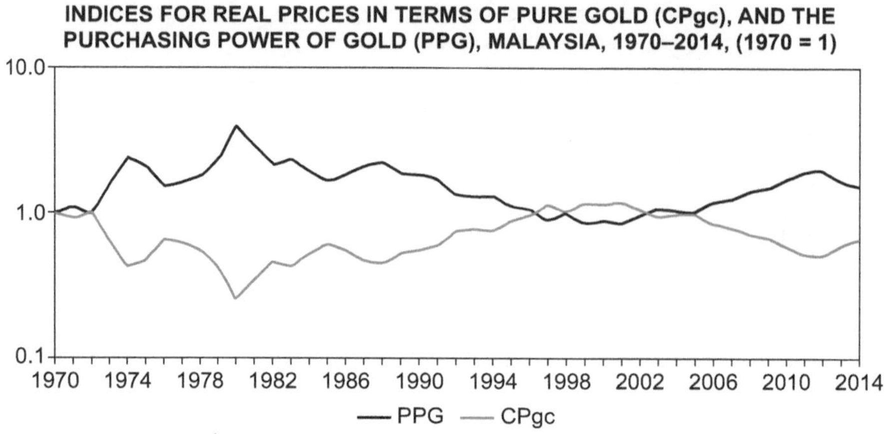

Figure 4.9 Indices of real gold (*PPG*) and real prices expressed in gold, 1970–2014

Source*:* Abdullah (2015)

prices and a low value currency involves high prices. In Malaysia, under the fiat standard, since money is backed by debt growing at cumulative interest, the PPM has decayed such that prices have increased exponentially.

If the monetary authorities had decided not to compromise on the *VM* and had targeted a high value currency that involved gold, what would real prices have looked like over the long term when expressed in pure gold, and how would real prices relate to real gold (or the *PPG*)? Real gold is a function of the *PG* expressed in MYR and adjusted for prices (*CP*), such that *PPG* = *PG*/*CP* (Abdullah, 2015). In Figure 4.9, real gold is constant and stable over the long term, and in contrast with the *PPM*, gold retains its store of value, whilst fiat money does not. Real prices, being prices expressed in terms of pure gold (or pure silver), reflect what the price level would have been absent any monetary distortion or manipulation. Real prices remain low and stable over the long term. The reciprocal of *PG* reflects the intrinsic value of the gold content (*GC*). Real prices (*CPgc*) are nominal prices adjusted for any loss in intrinsic value, so $CPgc = CP \times GC$; but of course, as with the purchasing power of money, so with the purchasing power of gold; since gold is money, then real gold (*PPG*) is also the reciprocal of *CPgc* ($PPG = 1/CPgc$). In summary, if monetary authorities had targeted a high value currency that was fully redeemable and 100 percent backed by allocated gold, then prices would have been low and stable over the long term since 1970.

It follows that we must re-examine the quantity theory to reflect changes in the value of money. We should begin with *PY* and the real economy rather than *MV* and monetary sector and reconfigure Fisher's equation of exchange to $PY = MV$ (Fisher, 1911), where *V* no longer means the velocity of money in circulation but the value of money (*VM*). In fact, we ought to emphasize *VM* rather than *MV*, since both the quality and quantity of money will have to be taken into account. Indeed, money does not circulate; it is exchanged against goods and services and must equally apply to *M* as well as *Y*. Furthermore, velocity cannot be independently measured, since it is a residual calculation of the other variables. Therefore, our restated equation of exchange is no longer an identity; it is a monetary theory of value, for it takes into account the quality and quantity of money that is being exchanged against goods and services in the real economy.

$$PY = VM \quad \text{(Equation 1)}$$

Where *P* reflects real prices (*CPgc*) and *Y* output or the quantity of goods and services (*Q*), so that *PY* is real output or real GDP. *V* is the value of money reflected in its rate of exchange with gold (or silver), and *M* is the money stock exchanged against *Y*. *VM* is the real value of the quantity of money, expressed in terms of gold (*Mgc*) rather than adjusted for prices *M/P*. Moreover, nominal GDP or the market value of output may be expressed in terms of gold (*GDPgc*), and therefore, real output (*GDPgc*) must equal the amount of real money (*Mgc*) exchanged against it (Figure 4.10). As we have already observed, real gold (*PPG*) and real prices (*CPgc*) revolve around a constant of 1 over the long term; indeed, $PPG \times CPgc = 1$.

Where changes in real prices or output occur, the market value of final goods and services (GDP) does not change because there has been a change in the value of real money (*Mgc*), since we have corrected the loss in value in the stock of nominal money, but because the quantity of real cash transactions must equal the quantity of goods exchanged and so changes occur in real prices in relation to output, being a function of supply and demand of goods and services. When real prices reach equilibrium at a constant 1, the curves for the *PPG* and *CPgc* coincide. In fact, with the loss in the value of money corrected during the Asian financial crisis and later

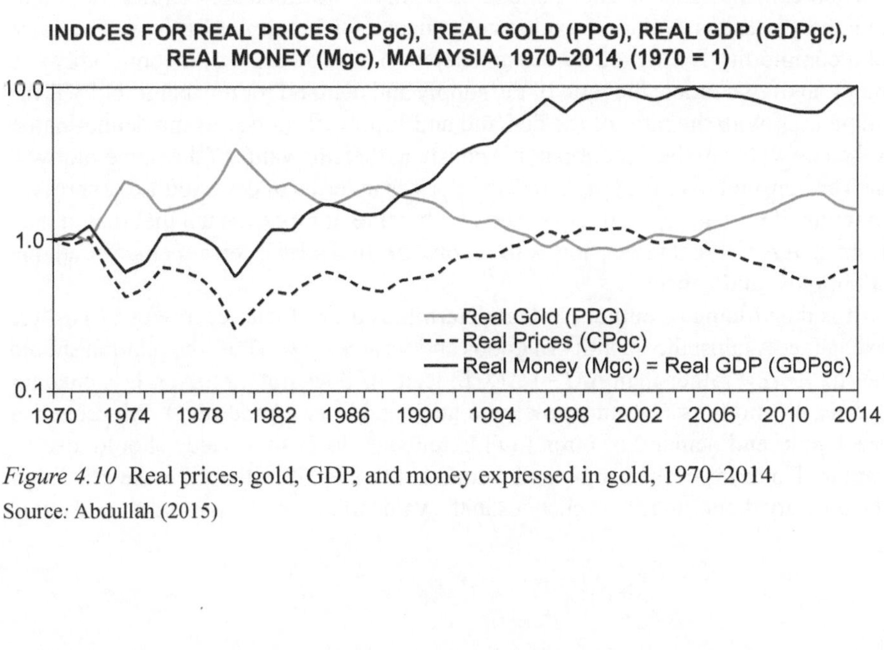

Figure 4.10 Real prices, gold, GDP, and money expressed in gold, 1970–2014

Source: Abdullah (2015)

with the global financial crisis, we may observe that instead of being a period of instability, it would have been a period of monetary and price stability supporting sustainable economic growth. Thus, the Asian financial crisis was not a financial crisis, it was a monetary crisis.

Conclusion: an Islamic monetary theory of value and equation of exchange

Given the empirical evidence from Turkey and Malaysia, we have established that conventional monetary theories and policies combined with the mechanics of credit creation have served only to disguise the effects of aggregate rates of interest on deposits and loans in devaluing money, inflating the supply of money and causing monetary inflation. The solution is to apply an Islamic monetary theory of value, which may be derived as follows:

> The value of money, as reflected in its rate of exchange with a fixed amount of precious metal, depreciates (or appreciates) due to an excessive increase (or decrease) in the supply of money in relation to demand, the effect of which is to increase (or decrease) the price level.

This takes into account value as a function of supply and demand and should not be confused with the quantity theory, or the relationship between the quantity of money and the price level, which altered the meaning of inflation: it does not mean a fall in the value of money as a result of an excessive supply of money relative to demand but instead means any increase at all in the supply of money, so that inflation is now interpreted as a process of steadily rising prices resulting in diminishing the purchasing power of a given nominal sum of money, and it has become the cause rather than the effect. Inflation and deflation are purely monetary phenomena, and price changes due to monetary distortions are distinct from non-monetary reasons. Value in exchange is measured in terms of prices. The price of a commodity is affected by the underlying *VM*. The price of a commodity is a function of two ratios: the ratio of the supply and demand for that commodity is the numerator, with the ratio of the demand and supply of money as the denominator. When the value of the denominator is constant, then the value of the numerator will also be constant over the long term. Real prices in terms of commodities expressed in terms of pure gold or silver reflect a high value of money, such that real money is the inverse of real prices and both revolve around a long-term secular trend that is both low and constant.

It is the volume of output (Y) that determines the velocity of money (V) as it is exchanged against the quantity of goods and services (Q). Thus, the relation should be $\Delta Q \rightarrow \Delta M$ rather than $\Delta M \rightarrow \Delta Q$. Indeed, M does not circulate, it exchanges against Y, and thus V cannot solely be attributable to M and not Y. Moreover, if the supply and demand of output (Y) is reflected in P, then value should also be captured in terms of the supply and demand of money. It follows that we must alter the quantity theory to reflect changes in the value of money (VM), and should begin with PY and the real economy rather than MV and the monetary sector. Thus, we can restate the equation of exchange and emphasize VM rather than MV, since both the quality and quantity of money will have to be taken into account. As reflected in Abdullah (2015, p. 240), our re-stated equation of exchange, is no longer an identity, it is a theory involving an Islamic equation of exchange, which includes an Islamic monetary theory of value:

$$PY = VM \qquad \text{(Equation 2)}$$

Where P reflects an index of real commodity prices (CPg or CPs expressed in pure gold or silver) for currently produced output and Y reflects current output or quantity of goods and services (Q) expressed in terms of gold ($GDPgc$) or silver. V should represent the value of money reflected in its rate of exchange with gold (or silver), and M is the money stock exchanged against goods and services. VM is the real value of the quantity of money, expressed in terms of gold (Mgc) rather than adjusted for prices M/P. Real gold (PPG) is the reciprocal of real prices ($CPgc$), and they are constant over the long term; indeed, $PPG \times CPgc = 1$. When the PPG and $CPgc$ are in equilibrium, then nominal GDP, or the market value of output expressed in terms of gold, and real GDP coincide, such that real output ($GDPgc$) = real money (Mgc). Changes in real prices occur in relation to real output, as a function of the supply and demand of goods and services (Abdullah, 2015, p. 241). This confirms the observations of Al-Ghazali (1994) and Ibn Khaldun (1958) that gold and silver, as instruments of transfer, mirror the value of goods and services, such that only the value of real output of goods and services changes (as intended by *Allah* s.w.t.), absent of monetary devaluation and distortion (by man).

The monetarist MV or the Islamic VM represents the monetary sector, as the counterpart to the Keynesian aggregate expenditure (AE) model. However, it was Ibn Khaldun and not Keynes who observed that, "Income and expenditure balance each other in every city. If the income is large, the expenditure is large, and vice versa. And if both income and expenditure are large, the inhabitants become more favourably situated, and the city grows" (Ibn Khaldun, 1958, 2, p. 275). For Keynes to argue that effective demand for finished goods and employment occurs only when aggregate expenditure is in equilibrium with income (Y) cannot be accurate, since Y must equal AE ($= C + I$) by definition, and the aggregate supply function must be identical with the aggregate demand function, regardless of whether Y and employment are in equilibrium: the supply and demand for goods and services is not the supply and demand for labour, and this "apprehension is, perhaps, the best test of a sound economist" (Stephen, 1881, 2, p. 197). Accordingly, we have to re-assert that Ibn Khaldun anticipated the classical law of the markets, and given our findings and analysis, it refutes the mercantilist Keynesian AE model, which should be recast as the Ibn Khaldun income and expenditure model. The relationship between AD, AE, AS, AMD, and Y, $AE = Y$ and $AS = AD$ is reflected in Figure 4.11.

Monetary policy should not target stable prices but a stable currency, which involves a stable value of money and purchasing power over the long term; for

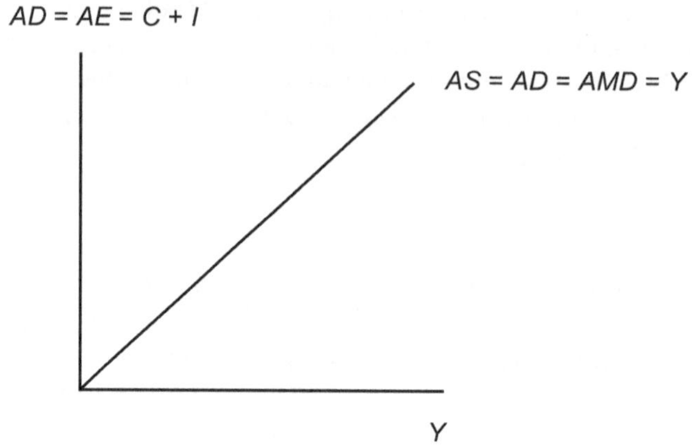

Figure 4.11 The Ibn Khaldun income and expenditure model ($AE = Y$)

"a currency, to be perfect, [it] should be absolutely invariable in value" (Ricardo, 1816, pp. 13–14). The management of the value and purchasing power of money implies an ability to provide stable prices, and yet prices are supposed to change in order to efficiently transmit information and organize an economy. An Islamic monetary policy should not target stable prices by devaluing money and its purchasing power, but we should target a stable currency, which in turn implies a stable purchasing power and thus stable prices. Moreover, wealth is transferred to the issuer as a result of the over-issuance of currency, since wealth is confiscated through inflation: "the decrease in purchasing power incurred by holders of money due to inflation imparts gains to the issuers of money" (Reubling, 1975, p. 22). Well before his appointment as chairman of the Federal Reserve, as an economist, Alan Greenspan mused over a gold standard, equating it with economic freedom, although his sentiments equally apply to a gold or silver commodity standard, in the absence of which,

> there is no way to protect savings from confiscation through inflation. There is no safe store of value . . . no way for the owners of wealth to protect themselves. . . . This is the shabby secret . . . [it] is simply a scheme for the confiscation of wealth. Gold [or silver] stands in the way of this insidious process. It stands as a protector of property rights.
>
> (Greenspan, 1966)

Indeed, the Islamic monetary theory of value exposes the true nature of the fiat standard, which is subject to the exponential decay in the *VM* due to an exponential increase in the supply of money (increasing at aggregate interest) in relation to demand, the effect of which is an increase in prices. We have to lower our standard of living to accommodate higher prices as a result of aggregate interest, such that our wealth is confiscated and transferred to the profit and loss statement of the banking system. Conventional monetary policy manages money supply through monetarism (Friedman, 1956) or via interest rates (Keynes, 1936) with the objective of price stability, but under the fiat standard, prices have increased exponentially and the financial system has become unstable. Indeed, the liquidity preference theory, and as Von Mises also observed, the quantity theory, "fails to explain the mechanism of variations in the value of money" (Mises, 1912) and does not touch upon this question at all, because these theories are disguising the effects of interest. In reality, interest does not protect wealth, as Fisher and Keynes would have us believe. On the contrary, it transfers wealth: the modern fractional reserve banking system is a wealth transfer mechanism. The TVM and the theory of interest is a circular argument, for it is the cause of the monetary devaluation and cannot exist when the value of money is constant over the long term. The intrinsic value of precious metals does not change—what changes is the value of paper money in relation to a precious metal.

Recommendation: monetary reform

On an international level, the United States should not imagine it has a trade problem but should consider that it has a monetary problem. The same decline in the value of money this study presented on Turkey and Malaysia was also found in America from 1792–2009 (Abdullah, 2013, Oct.). A modern monetary system based on a USD (fiat) international reserve currency is unsustainable and inevitably requires reform. Any increase in foreign official dollar reserves equals the net exports of the rest of the world, which means it must also equal U.S. international payments deficits. This unsustainable situation is not solved by trade policy in the form of protectionism and tariffs but by monetary reform. Under an international gold standard, combined net exports are equal to the total increase in world gold reserves (which in turn approximated gold exports). Thus, if real prices expressed in gold decreased, real gold would increase, thereby increasing the profitability of gold mining to meet the demand for gold exports as a function of reserves.

A gold standard has historically implied monetary stability. A nation is said to be on a gold standard if its unit of money is defined as so many grains of gold (Chown, 2001, p. 72). A fractional reserve gold standard implies that the ratio of gold to notes and deposits is not 1:1 as a result of credit creation occurring over the monetary base consisting of gold held in reserve. In fact, in analyzing the combined monetary data of the United Kingdom, the United States and France from 1815 to 1913 under the classical gold standard, total money supply as a multiple of gold (66%), including notes and deposits (34%), was already 1.5 in 1815. However, total money supply as a multiple of gold (10%), including notes and deposits (90%), expanded to 10 by 1913 (Chown, 2001, p. 72). Hence, in times of economic shocks, such as war (e.g., the Napoleonic War in 1815 and World War I in 1914), central banks broke their promise and were simply unable to redeem paper bank notes or deposits for gold coins held on reserve.

Thus, the UK gold standard "did not ensure short-run stability nor did it prevent trade cycles and financial crises. Those arose from the fluctuations in the size of the credit superstructure built on the gold base" (Chown, 2001, p. 72). On the other hand, a 100 percent pure gold standard involves the issuance of a unit of account that is 100 percent backed by gold and held on reserve. Interestingly, following the global financial crisis, the President of the World Bank, Robert Zoellick, called for a new gold standard:

> A new system should consider employing gold as an international reference point of market expectations about inflation, deflation and future currency values. Although textbooks may view gold as old money, markets are using gold as an alternative monetary asset today.
>
> (Zoellick, 2010)

A 100 percent pure gold standard or a 100 percent reserve system implies monetary and financial stability.

Hence, one solution is a return to a bimetallic standard involving the physical settlement in payments with precious metals by redeeming fiat for gold and silver. Given the stability of gold and silver over the long term, might there be a future role for gold and silver, and indeed, is there enough gold or silver to restore stability to our monetary system in terms of monetary reform? After all, *Rasulullah* (s.a.w.s.) has said, "A time is certainly coming over mankind in which there will be nothing (left) which will be of use save a *dinar* and a *dirham*" (Imam Ahmad ibn Hanbal, *Musnad*).

At of the end of 2017, the total above-ground stock of gold was 190,040 MTs (WGC), and the total above-ground stock of silver was 1.65 million MTs (USGS, 2005, Silver Institute).[2] According to updated gold market data (based on Abdullah, 2016, p. 226), an astonishing 181,000 MTs[3] of gold was cleared in cash in 2017 (LBMA, 2017). However, total physical gold supply was 4,440 MTs (WGC). So, the ratio of gold traded to physical gold = 41 (181,000/4,440). Thus, for every 41 oz of gold currently being traded globally, 40 oz are unallocated and 1 oz is allocated, which represents a fractional reserve ratio for gold of 2.5 percent (1/40). Therefore, in the presence of unallocated gold derivatives and paper trades, the *PG* is currently USD 1,250/oz. Absent of these paper trades, the true *PG* is USD 50,000 (1,250/0.025). Accordingly, the *PG* is being manipulated, involving a huge synthetic supply of unallocated gold, to give a false impression of the value of the USD (Abdullah, 2016, p. 226, 2018, p. 27).

With this in mind, Abdullah (2016, p. 133) also established that the above-ground stocks of gold and silver are more than enough to redeem global money supply, at the true *PG* and true price of silver. With updated data, official gold stocks of 32,575 MTs, combined with private investment gold stocks of 40,035 MTs, equals 72,610 MTs in 2017 (WGC), which at the true *PG* would equate to USD 116.7 trillion.[4] This would easily exceed the redemption of global *M2* money supply at the end of 2017, of USD 96.1 trillion (CIA, 2018), and we have not factored in the contribution of the global stocks of silver. When gold and silver are physically settled internationally, the unallocated paper trades would be eliminated, ensuring that the intrinsic value and true *PG* and *PS* would emerge.

For policymakers to redeem fiat money for gold and/or silver as part of any monetary reform, then an Islamic monetary theory of value derived from historical data is a prerequisite to understanding the fundamental importance of the store of value function of money as part of a value-based Islamic economic system. This necessarily involves the protection of wealth (*hafiz al-mal*) in adhering to the objectives of the *Shari'ah* (*maqasid al-Shari'ah*). We can therefore successfully link this to new developments involving fintech by providing historical lessons from the past, in order to support new solutions for the future, involving perhaps a return to a 100 percent international gold and/or silver standard coupled with block-chain technology involving the public issuance of a gold and/or silver backed medium of exchange, coupled with the private issuance of Islamic partnerships (Abdullah and Mohd Nor, 2018) that contains justice (*'adl*), so important in fulfilling the true objectives of Islamic economics and finance. It is imperative to restore value and stability to the monetary system, since money is the common denominator of all economic transactions, whilst at the same time providing financial stability with Islamic equity-based investment based on profit-sharing, which eliminates both the alchemy of money creation and usury associated with banking in a modern economy.

Notes

1 For Turkey, a full population of secondary silver and commodity prices data was compiled from the Central Bank of Turkey (CBRT), the Office of Turkish Statistics (TurkStats), and Silver Fixing (London Bullion Market Assoc.—LBMA) (Abdullah 2013, Dec., 2016). For Malaysia, a full population of secondary gold price, deposit and loan rates of interest, GDP, money supply, and price data was derived from Bank Negara Malaysia (BNM), Malaysian Dept. of Statistics (DoS), International Monetary Fund (IMF) and the LBMA (Abdullah, 2015, 2016).

2 With a specific gravity (SG) of 19.32 g/cm^3 for gold, then 190,040 MTs/19.32 = 9.836 cubm, or a cube of pure gold measuring 21.4 m on each side. With a SG of 10.49 g/cm^3 for silver, then 1.65 million MTs of silver/10.49 = 157,293 cubm, or a cube of pure silver measuring 54 m on each side.

3 LBMA (2017) total monthly average daily clearing statistics = 20.7 Mn.Ozs (per day) × 253 (trading days) = 5,237.1 Mn ozs p.a. Hence, 5,237,100,000 ozs/32,150.7 (troy ozs/MT) = 162,892 MTs. LBMA controls about 90 percent of the market = 162,892 MTs/0.90 = 181,000 MTs.

4 72,610 MTs × 32,150.7 ozs/MT × USD 50,000/oz = USD 116.7 Tn

References

Abdullah, A. (2013, Oct.). "Examining the Value of Money in America over the Long Term (1792–2009)". *International Journal for Economics and Finance*, Vol.5, No.10, pp. 58–84.

Abdullah, A. (2013, Dec.). "Examining the Value of Money in Turkey over the Long Term (1469–2009)". *Asian Social Science*, Vol.9, No.17, pp. 187–208.

Abdullah, A. (2015, Dec.). "Economic Security Requires Monetary and Price Stability: Analysis of Malaysian Macroeconomic and Credit Data". *Al-Shajarah*, Special Issue on Islamic Banking & Finance, pp. 205–47.

Abdullah, A. (2016, Oct.). "Examining US Approvals of Islamic Financing Products and the Islamic Theory of Lawful Profit". *International Journal of Islamic and Middle Eastern Finance and Management*, Vol.9, No.4, pp. 532–50.

Abdullah, A. (2016). *The Islamic Currency*. Kuala Lumpur: ICIFE.

Abdullah, A. (2018). *Money and the Real Economy*. Kuala Lumpur: IIiBF.

Abdullah, A. and Mohd Nor, R. (2018, Sept.). "A Framework for the Development of a National Crypto-Currency". *International Journal of Economics and Finance*, Vol.10, No.9, pp. 14–25.

Abdul Wahab, A. M. (2016, 3 Dec.). "Dato' Abdul Manap Abdul Wahab, Former CEO of Bank Muamalat, Presentation on 'Islamic Finance: An Alternative' at the Movement of Monetary Justice seminar on Establishing a Just Monetary System". International Islamic University Malaysia, Kuala Lumper.

Al-Ghazali M. (1994). *Ihya Ulum-id-Din (The Book of Religious Learnings)*, Vols.4, revised ed. New Delhi: Islamic Book Service.

Bank Negara Malaysia [BNM] (2013). retrieved from www.bnm.gov.my/

Bundesbank. (2017, 25 Apr.). "How Money Is Created". *Monthly Report*, retrieved from www.bundesbank.de/en/tasks/topics/how-money-is-created-667392

Central Bank of the Republic of Turkey [CBRT]. retrieved from CBRT's Electronic Data Delivery System https://evds2.tcmb.gov.tr/

Chown, J. (2001). *A History of Money*. First published (1994), re-printed London: Routledge.

CIA. (2018). "World Fact Book", retrieved from www.cia.gov/library/publications/the-world-factbook/rankorder/2215rank.html

Department of Statistics [DoS], Malaysia. retrieved from www.dosm.gov.my/v1/

Duncan, R. (2012). *The New Depression: The Breakdown of the Paper Money Economy*. Singapore: John Wiley & Sons.

European Central Bank [ECB]. (2013, 9 December). "Opinion of the European Central Bank on Measures to Strengthen Bank Stability". (CON/2013/86), retrieved from www.ecb.europa.eu/ecb/legal/pdf/en_con_2013_67_f_sign.pdf

El Diwany, T. (2003). *The Problem with Interest*. 2/e. London: Kreatoc.

Fisher, I. (1911). *The Purchasing Power of Money*. New York: Macmillan.

Fisher, I. (1922). *The Making of Index Numbers: A Study of Their Varieties, Tests, and Reliability*, originally published (1922). Boston: Houghton Mifflin Company, reprinted (2008) by Whitefish, MT: Kessinger Publishing.

Fisher, I. (1935). *100% Money*. New York: Adelphi.

Friedman, M. (1956). *The Quantity Theory of Money: A Restatement*, reprinted (1969) in *The Optimum Quantity of Money*, Chicago: Aldine.

Friedman, M. and Schwartz, A. J. (1963). *A Monetary History of the United States, 1867–1960*. Princeton: Princeton University Press.

Greenspan, A. (1966). "Gold and Economic Freedom". *The Objectivist Newsletter*. Retrieved from www.321gold.com/fed/greenspan/1966.html

Ibn Khaldun. (1958). *The Muqaddimah*, trans. by Rosenthal, F. Vols.3. New York: Pantheon Books, retrieved from www.muslimphilosophy.com/ik/Muqaddimah/

Islamic Financial Services Board [IFSB]. (2017, Q1). "Prudential and Structural Islamic Financial Indicators (PSIFIs)". retrieved from http://ifsb.org/psifi_01.php?selfolder=

International Monetary Fund [IMF]. (various years). *International Financial Statistics*. Washington, DC: International Monetary Fund.

International Monetary Fund [IMF]. (2000, Apr.). "Macro-Prudential Indicators of Financial System Soundness". IMF Occasional Paper (OP) No. 192, retrieved from www.imf.org/external/pubs/ft/op/192/OP192.pdf

International Monetary Fund [IMF]. (2009, Jan.). "Bank Stability Measures". IMF Working Paper, WP/09/4, retrieved from www.imf.org/external/pubs/ft/wp/2009/wp0904.pdf

Jakab, Z. and Kumhof, M. (2015, May). "Banks Are Not Intermediaries of Loanable Funds and Why This Matters". Bank of England, Working Paper No. 529, retrieved from www.bankofengland.co.uk/research/Pages/workingpapers/2015/wp529.aspx

Jordan, T. R. (2018, 16 Jan.). Speech on "How Money Is Created by the Central Bank and the Banking System". Swiss National Bank, Zurich.

Keynes, J. M. (1936). *The General Theory of Employment, Interest and Money*, originally published (1936), re-published (2007) for the Royal Economic Society. Basingstoke: Palgrave Macmillan.

King, M. (2016). *The End of Alchemy: Money Banking and the Future of the Global Economy*. London: W. W. Norton & Co.

London Bullion Metals Association [LBMA] (2017). retrieved from www.lbma.org.uk/prices-and-data

Lietaer, B. (2017). "A Possibly *Shari'ah*-Compatible Global Currency to Stabilize the Monetary System". *JKAU Islamic Economics*, Vol.30, No.2, pp. 47–58.

MacLeod, H. D. (1883–1886). *The Theory and Practice of Banking*, 2 Vols., 4/e, Vol.1 (1883), Vol.2 (1886). London: Longmans, Green & Co.

MacLeod, H. D. (1889–1891). *The Theory of Credit*, 3 Vols., Vol.1 (1889), Vol.2 Part 1 2/e (1894), Vol.2 Part 2 (1891). London: Longmans, Green & Co.

Marshall, A. (1890). *Principles of Economics*, originally published (1890), eighth ed. published (1920), re-printed (2013). Basingstoke: Palgrave Macmillan.

McLeay, M., Radia, A. and Thomas, R. (2014, Q1). "Money Creation in a Modern Economy". *Quarterly Bulletin*, Bank of England's Monetary Analysis Directorate, retrieved from www.bankofengland.co.uk/publications/Pages/quarterlybulletin/2014/qb14q1.aspx

Mirakhor, A. (1988). "Equilibrium in a Non-Interest Open Economy". International Monetary Fund, Working Paper, WP/88/111.

Mises, L. von. (1912). *The Theory of Money and Credit*, originally published in German (1912), translated (1934) by Baston, H.E., published (1981). Indianapolis: Liberty Fund.

Quigley, C. (1966). *Tragedy & Hope*. First published (1966). New York: Macmillan, re-published (1975). San Pedro: GSG & Associates.

Ricardo, D. (1816). *Proposals for an Economical and Secure Currency: With Observations on the Profits of the Bank of England, as They Regard the Public and the Proprietors of Bank Stock*. 2/e. London: John Murray.

Rosly, S. A. and Sanusi, M. M. (1999). "Application of *Bay' al-'Inah* and *Bay' al-Dayn* in Malaysian Islamic Bonds: An Islamic Analysis". *International Journal of Islamic Financial Services*, Vol.1, No.2, p. 9, citing Ibn Qayyim (1991). *Ighathat al-Lahfan min Masayid al-Shaytan*, 2 Vols. Cairo: Dar al-Hadith, Vol.1, p. 352.

Ruebling, C.E. (1975, Feb.). "Financing Government Through Monetary Expansion and Inflation". *Federal Reserve Bank of St. Louis, Review*, pp. 15–22.

Ryan-Collins, J., Greenham, T., Werner, R. and Jackson, A. (2012). *Where Does Money Come From? A Guide to the U.K. Monetary and Banking System*. London: New Economics Foundation.

Silver Institute (2018). retrieved from www.silverinstitute.org/

Stephen, L. (1881). *History of English thought in the Eighteenth Century*, 2 Vols., originally published (1876) and 2/e published (1881). London: Smith, Elder & Co., re-printed (2007). Boston: Adamant Media Corporation.

[TurkStat]. (2000). *500 Years of Price and Wages in Istanbul and Other Cities*, prepared by Sevket Pamuk, Ankara: Turkish State Institute of Statistics.

Turner, A. (2016). *Between Debt and the Devil: Money, Credit and Fixing Global Finance*. Princeton and Oxford: Princeton University Press.

United State Geological Survey [USGS] (2005). *Mineral Commodity Profile: Silver, Open-File Report 2004–1251*, retrieved from https://pubs.usgs.gov/of/2004/1251/

Werner, R. (2005). *New Paradigm in Macroeconomics*. Basingstoke: Palgrave Macmillan.

Werner, R. (2012, 30 Oct.). "The Quantity Theory of Credit and Some of Its Applications". Centre for Banking, Finance and Sustainable Development, Southampton University, retrieved from www.postkeynesian.net/downloads/Werner/RW301012PPT.pdf

Werner, R. (2014). "Can Banks Individually Create Money Out of Nothing?: The Theories and Empirical Evidence". *International Review and Financial Analysis*, Vol.36, pp. 1–19.

Werner, R. (2016). "A Lost Century in Economics: Three Theories of Banking and the Conclusive Evidence". *International Review of Financial Analysis*, Vol.46, pp. 361–79.

World Gold Council [WGC]. retrieved from www.gold.org/

Zoellick, R. (2010, 8 Nov.). President of the World Bank, "The G20 Must Look beyond Bretton Woods II". *Financial Times*, retrieved from www.ft.com/content/5bb39488-ea99-11df-b28d-00144feab49a

5 The impact of external shocks on the dynamics of macroeconomic variables in Iran (Islamic versus conventional monetary rule)

Zahra Afshari and Maryam Soleimani Movahed

Introduction

The 2008 crisis revealed a major failure of the present financial system. In parallel to the malfunction of the financial instruments, it also revealed an important ethical failure related to the present economic system. Some scholars have even referred to the collapse of the ethical values system. Islamic banks were largely spared from the crisis, even though they had suffered a slowdown in overall economic activity (Ben Daoud, 2012). Saymeh and Orieqat (2013), in their article "The Global Financial Crisis: Is Islamic System a Potential Solution?", made a list of academicians, economists, and policymakers who argue that the Islamic system is more sustainable and efficient than conventional models. Islamic banks have been more resilient to the global financial crisis. They have been able to avoid its consequences due to their ethical policy and to the ethical principles on which they rely.

In conventional economics, interest rates play an important role in the money allocation between borrowers and lenders. Also, interest rates are core and conventional tools of monetary policy, such as discount rate and open market operations. From the theoretical view, Islamic economics is different from conventional economics because interest rate—*riba*—is prohibited in Islam, it means that banks are not allowed to offer a fixed rate of return on deposits and are to charge interest on loans. An exclusive feature of Islamic economics is its profit-and-loss sharing paradigm, which is predominantly based on the *Mudharabah* (profit sharing) and *Musyarakah* (joint venture) concepts. Under the profit-and-loss paradigm, the assets and liabilities of the Islamic financial system are integrated in the sense that borrowers share profits and losses with the financial institutions and similarly share profits and losses with depositors. The first experiments of Islamic banking in the world began in the twenty-first century. According to Ahmad et al. (2011), Islamic and conventional banking are separated due to interest rate, risk-sharing, and materialism. Iran is among the pioneering countries whose banking operations comply with the shariah rules of Islam, while many other Islamic countries have established mixed systems that combine aspects of conventional and Islamic banking practices. Islamic banking refers to a system of banking that is based on legally shariah-compliant financial instruments and transactions. In particular, conventional transactions based on an ex-ante promise of a risk-free rate of return are forbidden in Islamic economic jurisprudence. Partnership contracts in Islamic banking are innovative as well in the sense that they are neither fully equity nor a debtor-creditor relationship.

Islamic economics, as well as conventional economies, may face macroeconomic issues like economic growth and price stability. While price stability or inflation is incompatible with the goals of an Islamic economy, prolonged recession and unemployment that cause human sufferings are also unacceptable. Monetary policy has, therefore, aimed to reach a high rate of economic growth with full employment and full utilization of productive resources. However, it should not lead to excessive and overly rapid use of resources at the expense of future generations, and it should not be harmful to present or future generations. Monetary policy has to be as important an instrument of public policy in an Islamic economy as it is in its capitalist counterpart. The objectives and tools must, however, be different because of the differences in the goals and the nature of the two systems and because of the prohibition of interest in Islam, while it is a key ingredient in the capitalist system. This chapter represents an attempt to highlight the role that monetary policy should be designed to play in an Islamic economy and to show how it can be made to play its role effectively if interest is abolished and two important instruments of monetary policy in the capitalist economy, discount rate and open market operations in interest-bearing government securities, are not available. Thus, the role of monetary policy in Islamic economics is undeniable. In conventional economics, however, the interest rate is the key instrument for executing monetary policy. The Taylor (1993) rule is a simple monetary policy rule mechanically linking the level of the policy rate to deviations of inflation from its target and of output from its potential (the output gap). Other researchers have computed policy rules that are optimal, in respect to a particular macroeconomic model and loss function (Ball, 1997, 1999; Clarida et al., 1999; Jaaskela, 2005; Jensen, 2003; Jondeau & Le Bihan, 2002; Svensson, 2000). Meanwhile, other researchers have computed rules that maximize a representative agent's welfare in a typically small dynamic stochastic general equilibrium model (Adjemian et al., 2007; Jondeau & Sahuc, 2008; Sofia et al., 2008; Woodford, 2003)

Advocates of Islamic economics thus argue that the Islamic financial system is theoretically better structured than conventional financial institutions in terms of absorbing external shocks because the financial institutions' financing losses can be partially absorbed by the depositors (Khan & Mirakhor, 1989; Iqbal, 1997). Correspondingly, the profit-and-loss paradigm featured the risk-sharing function, in theory, allows Islamic banks to make a longer-term basis loan with higher risk-return profiles and, ultimately, to promote economic growth (Chapra, 1992; Mills & Presley, 1999).

The aim of this chapter is to design a simple new Keynesian dynamic stochastic general equilibrium model for the Iranian economy based on the participation of the private sector and the government on funding the investment by introducing an Islamic instrument, the *Musharakah* contracts. Then a policy rule based on *Musharakah* contracts is derived. The dynamics of macroeconomic variables in confronting technology, government expenditure, oil revenue, and monetary policy shocks under Taylor and so-called *Musharakah* rules are compared. Finally, an optimal policy based on *Musharakah* is derived. The rest of the chapter is organized as follows: The second section provides an overview of conventional and Islamic literature. The third describes the model undertaken in this study. The last two sections are devoted to the empirical findings and concluding remarks, respectively.

Literature review

The effectiveness of monetary policy in overcoming the business cycles both in the theoretical and empirical literature is controversial. In the following, we will have an overview of the empirical literature on previous issues both in conventional and Islamic research. Grohe and Uribe (2004) in their study computed welfare-maximizing monetary and fiscal policy rules in a real business cycle model augmented with sticky prices, a demand for money, taxation, and stochastic government consumption. Their main findings are first, the size of the inflation coefficient in the interest-rate rule plays a minor role in welfare. It matters only insofar as it affects the determinacy of equilibrium. Second, optimal monetary policy features a muted response to output. More importantly, interest-rate rules that feature a positive response to output can lead to significant welfare losses. Third, the welfare gains from interest-rate smoothing are negligible. Fourth, the optimal fiscal policy is passive. Finally, the optimal monetary and fiscal rule combination attains virtually the same level of welfare as the Ramsey optimal policy. Gerali et al. (2010) studied the role of credit-supply factors in business cycle fluctuations. For this purpose, they introduced an imperfectly competitive banking sector into a DSGE model with financial frictions. Banks issue collateralized loans to both households and firms, obtain funding via deposits, and accumulate capital from retained earnings. Margins charged on loans depend on bank capital-to-assets ratios and on the degree of interest rate stickiness. Bank balance-sheet constraints establish a link between the business cycle, which affects bank profits and thus capital, and the supply and cost of loans. The model is estimated with Bayesian techniques using data for the euro area. The analysis delivers the following results. First, the existence of a banking sector partially attenuates the effects of demand shocks, while it helps propagate supply shocks. Second, shocks originating in the banking sector explain the largest share of the fall of output in 2008 in the euro area, while macroeconomic shocks played a limited role. Third, unexpected destruction of bank capital has a substantial impact on the real economy, and particularly on investment. These results align with several conventional models that indicate that the effectiveness of conventional models based on the interest rate in confronting the business cycles is questionable.

Khan (1984), in his paper "Macro Consumption in an Islamic Framework," developed a macroeconomic model to examine consumer behaviour and the allocation of resources within the Islamic economy. Gan and Hue (2009) determine optimal Taylor rule from an Islamic perspective for open and emerging market economies. Using data from Malaysia and by applying the Svensson (2000) method, the empirical results indicate that the fluctuations of the output gap, inflation, and exchange rate to the macroeconomic shocks under Islamic monetary policy rule are less than the conventional one. Anvari et al. (2011), by applying an interest=rate rule consistent with the objectives of the Islamic economy, simulated the inflation and output gap in a dynamic stochastic general equilibrium framework. They concluded that the minimum interest rate will obtain when the inflation rate reaches 3 percent within six years. Faizi (2008) makes an attempt to develop a New Keynesian small open economy DSGE model for Iran in an Islamic framework. He argues that the central banks should develop innovative types of shariah-compliant financial instruments to manage the economic fluctuations. He introduced the nominal exchange rate as an alternative monetary policy instrument for the Iranian economy. Rasoulinezhad (2012) in his article integrated the concept of Islamic finance in a DSGE model. Soleimani et al. (2016) studied the impact of supply and demand shocks on macroeconomic variables in Iran in an Islamic framework. For this purpose, the share of government participation in capital funding is a substitute for the interest rate. The results reveal that in respect to the impact of both supply and demand shocks on macro variables, fluctuation with Islamic instrument is less than the conventional one. They conclude that the *Mushrekah* instrument introduced in this model is quite capable to confront economic fluctuations, and it can be used as an alternative superior instrument for implementing the stabilization policies. Dahani and Aboulaich (2018) design a Dynamic Stochastic General Equilibrium model for Morocco as an Islamic economy. This model is based on the replacement of interest rates by the rate of return on the capital. In addition, the model integrates *Zakat* into the model. The results show that the introduction of the Islamic instrument was not fully successful in overcoming the negative impact of shocks on the macroeconomic and financial conditions of Morocco.

The theoretical framework

The revolution put an end to nine decades of Western-oriented banking expansion. In June 1979, all banks, along with a number of other financial and industrial establishments, were nationalized, and banking regulations changed with the approval of the Islamic banking law (interest free). The nationalization and the subsequent consolidation of the banks paved the way for the launching of Islamic banking. In 1983, the Islamic Banking law of Iran was passed by the Islamic Parliament of Iran. According to this law, Iranian banks can only engage in interest-free Islamic banking (Global Islamic Finance Report, 2017). In the third phase, which began in 1986, the banking system was rapidly being integrated with the rest of the government. Thus, the banking system is perceived not only as the major source of financial resources to finance the government's fiscal deficits but also as an effective tool for processing economic objectives, such as shifting in the pattern of consumption, investment, and production behaviour in the economy as well as restructuring of the economy and income redistribution. Finally, a highly activist rule is defined for the central government for allocating funds and restructuring the economy. Therefore, the interventionist posture of the government in the economy was legitimized (Khan & Mirakhor, 1990).

In Iran *Musharakah* (partnership) is the most important Islamic contract. The law recognizes two different forms of partnership, namely civil and legal partnership. A civil partnership is a project-specific partnership for short and medium terms. It is defined as the mixing of capital from a bank with the capital from a partner or partners (in cash or kind) on a joint-ownership basis for the performance of a specific job (Parveen et al. 2015; Nili, 2014). In 2017, 42.3 percent of outstanding facilities extended by banks to the non-public were in the form of a civil partnership (Afshari, 2020). The legal partnership is a joint venture for a long duration. In a legal partnership contract, the bank finances part of the capital for a start-up or purchases corporate shares in order to compensate for a shortage of capital in joint-stock firms. The bank receives a dividend at the end of each fiscal term. This kind of deal aims at the long-term provision of resources for productive, commercial, and service companies (Central Bank of the Islamic Republic of Iran, 1997). In 2017, 3.6 percent of outstanding facilities extended by the banking system to the non-public sector was in the form of a legal partnership (Afshari, 2020).

The economy of Iran is a mixed and transition economy with a large public sector. It is dominated by oil and gas production. With 10 percent of the world's proven oil reserves and 15 percent of its gas reserves, Iran is considered an "energy superpower" (petroleum constitutes 56 percent of Iran's exports, OPEC, 2019). Oil and natural gas are Iran's most important exports, accounting for 82 percent of the country's export revenues. As a result, oil price shocks are an important part of business cycles in Iran.

In this chapter, an attempt was made to design a new Keynesian DSGE model compatible with the previously mentioned characteristic of the Iranian economy. The model consists of three representatives: households, firms, and government. Other assumptions of the model are as follows:

1 A small open economy.
2 Apart from the oil exports, the country has no trade with the rest of the world.
3 The country produces two kinds of goods: intermediate and final goods
4 The intermediary producers confronted with two kinds of costs: labour costs and capital costs.
5 Households are firm owners; their savings are used for partial capital financing of intermediary producers. The rest of the firms' capital needs finance through government *Musharakah*.
5 The final producer works in competitive markets and acts as an aggregator.
6 The factors of production are not internationally mobile.
7 Goods are normal.

Households: At the beginning of each period, the representative household spends a part of its income (gained from wage and profit share) for buying final goods and services. The rest of its income is spent on financing part of the next period capital needs of intermediate producers. At the end of each period, money is returned to households as wage and profit-share, which again are consumed and saved. The purpose of representative households is to choose the path of consumption, labour, and capital financing (savings) in order to maximize the present value of lifetime utility:

$$E_t \sum_{t=0}^{\infty} \beta^t u(c_t, l_t) = E_t \sum_{t=0}^{\infty} \beta^t \left[\frac{c_t^{1-\varphi}}{1-\varphi} + \frac{(1-l_t)^{1-\chi}}{1-\chi} \right] \quad \text{(Equation 1)}$$

E_t shows the conditional expectation at time t, and $1 < \beta < 0$ is a subjective discount factor of representative household. The utility function $(1/\varphi)$ represents the intertemporal elasticity of substitution, $(1 - l)/\chi l$ is Frisch elasticity of labour supply, and l is the amount of the steady-state labour. It is assumed that the household will face two kinds of constraints: First, cash in advance (CIA) constraint; the household should pay money for buying goods and services. It implies that $c_t = m_t$. Second, the budget constraint. At the beginning of each period the household has two sources of money income, labour income, $w_t l_t$, and capital income (the net profit gained through Musharakah in the previous period, $pr_t \frac{s_{t-1}}{1+\pi_t}$. The household budget constraint can be written as follows:

$$m_t + s_t = w_t l_t + pr_t \frac{s_{t-1}}{\pi_t} + (1-\delta)\frac{s_{t-1}}{\pi_t} - \tau_t \quad \text{(Equation 2)}$$

Where m_t and l_t are real balances and hours of labour, respectively, τ_t is the net tax payments to the government, and $\pi_t = P_t / P_{t-1}$ is inflation. We assume that money growth follows an AR (1) exogenous process, as follows:

$$mu_t = \rho_m mu_{t-1} + (1-\rho_m)\overline{mu} + \varepsilon_t^m$$

Where $|\rho_m| < 1$ and ε_t^m is a white noise with zero means and variance of σ_m^2 ; $\overline{mu}$ stands for the steady-state level of real balances.

The net profit gain of household pr_t is:

$$pr_t = \frac{(1-\gamma_t) f_t}{s_{t-1}} = \frac{f_t}{k_{t-1}} \quad \text{(Equation 3)}$$

Where f_t is the total profit of an intermediate firm; γ_t and $(1 - \gamma_t)$ are define as the profit-shares of government and households for participating in firm capital financing, respectively:

$$1-\gamma_t = \frac{s_{t-1}}{k_{t-1}}$$

A household's choice variables are consumption, labour, money, and share of *Musharakah* in the capital financing. The Lagrangian function can be formulated as follows:

$$L = \max \sum_{t=0}^{\infty} E_t \beta^t \left[\begin{array}{l} u(c_t, l_t) + \lambda_t (m_t - c_t) + \mu_t \\ \left(w_t l_t + pr_t \dfrac{s_{t-1}}{1+\pi_t} + (1-\delta)\dfrac{s_{t-1}}{1+\pi_t} - m_t - s_t - \tau_t \right) \end{array} \right] \quad \text{(Equation 4)}$$

The optimality conditions for this problem can be written as follows:

$$\frac{-u_2(c_t, l_t)}{u_1(c_t, l_t)} = w_t$$

$$\frac{u_1(c_t, l_t)}{E_t u_1(c_{t+1}, l_{t+1})} = \beta \frac{1-\delta + pr_{t+1}}{1+\pi_{t+1}}$$

From which we can derive two main equations of the model: labour supply and the Euler equation. Then, after some manipulations and log linearizing, we derive the IS equation as follows:

$$\tilde{y}_t = \tilde{y}_{t+1} + \frac{(c_{ss} / y_{ss})}{\varphi} \tilde{\pi}_{t+1} + \zeta_t \quad \text{(Equation 5)}$$

The difference between the aforementioned IS and a conventional one is that IS no longer depends on the interest rate.

Final goods producer: The final product market works in a competitive market where the continuous amounts of intermediate products $f \in [0,1]$ aggregate through a CES function:

$$Y_t = \left(\int_0^1 y_t(f)^{1-\theta} \, df \right)^{\frac{\theta}{\theta-1}} \quad \text{(Equation 6)}$$

Here, $\theta > 1$ shows the elasticity of substitution for intermediate goods. The final firm buys the input at a price of $p_t(f)$ and sell the final goods at the price of the p_t (Juilliard, 2010, 2011). The demand for intermediate products is derived by solving the following profit-maximization problem:

$$\max \pi = P_t Y_t - \int_0^1 p_t(f) y_t(f) \, df \quad \text{(Equation 7)}$$

By replacing y_t from (Equation 6), we will have:

$$\max \pi = P_t \left(\int_0^1 y_t(f)^{1-\frac{1}{\theta}} \, df \right)^{\frac{\theta}{\theta-1}} - \int_0^1 p_t(f) y_t(f) \, df$$

The solution to the FOC problem yields the demand for final goods:

$$y_t(f) = \left(\frac{p_t(f)}{P_t}\right)^{-\eta} Y_t \qquad \text{(Equation 8)}$$

Where

$$P_t = \left(\int_0^1 p_t(f)^{-\frac{1}{\theta}} df\right)^{-\theta} \qquad \text{(Equation 9)}$$

Intermediate good producer: It is assumed that the economy consists of a continuous number of intermediate goods producers acting in a monopolistic competitive market indexed by $f \in [\circ, 1]$. These producers adjust their prices according to the Calvo process and rent labour in a competitive market. The producers operate through a Cobb-Douglas production function:

$$y(f)_t = A_t k(f)_t^{1-\eta} l(f)_t^{\eta} \qquad \text{(Equation 10)}$$

A_t is a static productivity shock, $k_t(f)$ and $l_t(f)$ are the capital and labour inputs. Technology shock follows from an AR (1) process:

$$logA_t = \rho_A logA_{t-1} + \varepsilon_t^A$$

Where ε_t^A is a white noise process with zero mean and variance σ_A^2 and $< |\rho_A| < 1$

In this model, the firm's capital is funded by the government and households. In each period, the required capital is financed by the participation of the household's savings s_t and government *Musharakah* in capital funding (x_t). The total capital can be written as:

$$k_t = x_t + s_t$$

In each period, the equation for the motion of capital can be written as follows:

$$k_{t+1} = (1-\delta)k_t + i_t$$

Intermediate goods firms set the prices based on the Calvo process with a probability of $1 - \xi$. Finally, firms supply the demanded product at $p_t(f)$ and rent labour at $l_t(f)$. The maximization problem of the firm can be formalized as follows:

$$\max_{p_t(f)} E_t \sum_{j=0}^{\infty} \xi^j \lambda_t \left[p_t(f) y_t(f) - w_t l_t - \gamma_t f_t\right] \qquad \text{(Equation 11)}$$

Where λ_t is the marginal utility of consumption. The phrase in the parentheses is the distributed profit between households and the government.

$$\text{s.t. } y_t(f) = \left(\frac{p_t(f)}{p_t}\right)^{-\left(\frac{1+\theta}{\theta}\right)}$$

The first-order condition of the above problem yields:

$$p_t(f) = \frac{(1+\theta)\sum_j \xi^j \lambda_{t+j}\left[mc_t(f).y_t(f)\right]}{\sum_j \xi^j \lambda_{t+j}\left[y_t(f)\right]} \qquad \text{(Equation 12)}$$

The marginal cost, $mc_t(f)$, can be found as follows: The total cost can be defined as:

$$CC_t = w_t l_t + \gamma_t f_t$$

Where f is defined as:

$$f_t = p_t(f)y_t(f) - w_t l_t$$

The optimization problem of the firm can be formalized as follows:

$$\text{Min } CC_t = w_t l_t + \gamma_t f_t$$

$$\gamma_t f_t = pr_t \frac{x_{t-1}}{\pi_t} = pr_t \frac{\gamma_t k_t}{\pi_t}$$

Where, subject to the production function

$$\text{s.t. } y_t(f) = a_t k_t^{1-\eta} l_t^{\eta}$$

Then differentiating with respect to l_t and k_t, yields:

$$\frac{\partial CC_t}{\partial l_t} = w_t - \lambda_t \eta \frac{y_t(f)}{l_t} \quad \Rightarrow \quad \lambda_t = \frac{w_t}{\eta \frac{y_t(f)}{l_t}}$$

$$\frac{\partial CC_t}{\partial k_t} = pr_t \frac{\gamma_t}{\pi_t} - \lambda_t (1-\eta) \frac{y_t(f)}{k_t} \quad \Rightarrow \quad \lambda_t = \frac{pr_t \gamma_t}{(1-\eta)\frac{y_t(f)}{k_t}}$$

Then, by substituting in CC and after rearrangements, the cost function can be yielded, as follows:

$$CC_t = A_t^{-1}\left(\frac{w_t}{\eta}\right)^{\eta}\left(\frac{pr_t}{1-\eta}\right)^{1-\eta} y_t(f) \qquad \text{(Equation 13)}$$

Where $mc_t(f)$ shows the marginal cost of firm f in t time:

$$mc_t(f) = A_t^{-1}\left(\frac{w_t}{\eta}\right)^{\eta}\left(\frac{pr_t}{1-\eta}\right)^{1-\eta}$$

The firm's optimization problem yields the Phillips curve as follows:[1]

$$\tilde{\pi}_t = \text{o}\tilde{y}_t + \vartheta\tilde{\gamma}_t + \beta E_t\tilde{\pi}_{t+1} + \varepsilon_t \qquad \text{(Equation 14)}$$

The Phillips curve indicates that inflation is a function of output, the share of government *Musharakah*, and expected inflation. By removing the government *Musharakah* from the model, the standard Phillips will obtain. It is noticeable that $\tilde{\gamma}$ is affected by the economy through the supply side.

Oil sector: Oil production has not been modelled as a separate productive sector because oil revenue is exogenous and only changes with the oil prices. The oil revenue shock follows an AR (1) process *as follows:*

$$or_t = \rho_{or} or_{t-1} + (1-\rho_{or})\overline{or} + \varepsilon_t^{or} \qquad \text{(Equation 15)}$$

Where $<|\rho_{or}|<1$ and ε_t^{or} is white noise process with zero mean and σ_{or}^2 variance. Moreover, $\overline{or}$ is the steady-state value of the oil revenues and or_t is the real flow of oil revenues. It is assumed that oil revenue is a part of government income.

Government and the central bank: It is assumed that the government is in charge of both monetary and fiscal policies. The real government budget constraint is defined as follows:

$$g_t + x_t = or_t + \tau_t + \gamma_t f_t + (1-\delta)x_{t-1} \qquad \text{(Equation 16)}$$

Where g_t is the real government expenditure, τ_t is the lump sum tax revenue, or_t is real oil income, and x_t is the participation share of government in capital funding. It is assumed that the government real expenditures follow an AR (1) process:

$$g_t = \rho_g g_{t-1} + (1-\rho_g)\overline{g} + \varepsilon_t^g$$

Where, $<|\rho_g|<1$, ε_t^g is a white noise process with zero mean and σ_g^2 variance, and $\overline{g}$ is a steady level of government expenditures.

As a monetary authority, the government implements the monetary policy to close the inflation and output gaps. In this chapter, the monetary policy instrument is the government's share of *Musharakah* (γ_t) instead of the interest rate. The policy rule that monetary authority applies to close the gaps is formulated as follows:

$$\left(\frac{\gamma_t}{\gamma}\right) = \left(\frac{\pi_t}{\pi}\right)^{g_\pi} \left(\frac{y_t}{y}\right)^{g_y} \left(\frac{\gamma_{t-1}}{\gamma}\right)^{g_\gamma} e_t \qquad \text{(Equation 17)}$$

Equilibrium:[2] The equilibrium can be reached by solving the system of equations, non-policy bloc equations IS (5), Phillips curves (14) and policy bloc equation *Musharakah* Rule (17).

Data, methods and results

Estimating the parameters of the model is one of the important stages of empirical measurement in general equilibrium models. The required ratios for the calibration are derived from the Central Bank of Iran's annual data. Some of the variables are calibrated according to recent studies, as follows (Table 5.1).

Table 5.2 shows the steady-state ratios of the variable of the Iranian economy by using the Hedrick Prescott method for the 2000–2016 period.

Table 5.1 The calibrated parameters

Symbol	*Parameter explanation*	*Calibrated value*	*Resource*
φ	Substitution elasticity of consumption	1.5	Bahatarchi and Tuneinson (2005)
η	The share of labour supply in production	0.656	Research findings
β	Subjective discount rate	0.976	Research findings (Basian method)
$\frac{1+\theta}{\theta}$	Demand elasticity of intermediate products	4.33	Based on 30% mark up
$\frac{1-l_{ss}}{\chi l_{ss}}$	The elasticity of labour supply subject to wage (Frisch)	0.46	Taei (2006)
δ	Depreciation rate	0.07	Research findings
ρ_i	Government participation weight in the monetary policy	0.3	Research findings
g_y	Production weight in the monetary policy	1.37	Research findings (Basian method)
g_π	Inflation weight in the monetary policy	0.3	Research findings (Basian method)

Source: Research findings

Table 5.2 The steady-state ratios gained from the time series of Iran's economy

The ratio of steady states	*Explanation of ratios*	*Estimated value*
$\frac{c_{ss}}{y_{ss}}$	The steady ratio of consumption of private sector to non-oil production	0.58
$\frac{or_{ss}}{y_{ss}}$	The steady ratio of oil incomes to non-oil production	0.104
$\frac{g_{ss}}{y_{ss}}$	The steady ratio of government expenditures to non-oil production	0.195
$\frac{T_{ss}}{y_{ss}}$	The steady-state ratio of government tax incomes to non-oil production	0.048
γ_{ss}	The steady-state level of government participation rate to investment	0.28

Source: Research findings

Second-order moments of variables

In order to complete the quantitative analysis, Table 5.3 reports the standard deviations of key variables of the model. The results indicate that the volatility (standard deviation) of consumption is the highest for both real and simulated data. The simulated standard deviations of real and simulated variables are close together. It means that the estimated model represented the Iranian economy

Four shocks are introduced to the model: technology shocks, government expenditure shocks, oil revenue shocks, and monetary policy shocks. Two models are estimated, the Islamic and the conventional. Then the dynamic responses of the macro variables to the shocks are compared in Islamic and conventional models. The impulse response functions are shown in Figures 5.1 to 5.4. Shocks impact the macro variables through two channels: direct and indirect effects. A positive demand shock (monetary, oil revenue,[3] and fiscal shocks) directly increases the output gap in period t. Then the government, by increasing $\tilde{\gamma}_t$, reacts through the policy rule to close the gap. In the case of a fiscal shock, in order to crowd out private investment, the government increases $\tilde{\gamma}_t$ (the crowding-out effect). Then, through the Phillips curve in an oscillating pattern, the inflation gap will be closed.

Immediately after a positive supply shock (technology shock), where the output increases and inflation decreases on impact, the government decreases $\tilde{\gamma}$ through the policy rule. As a result, output and other variables gradually converge to their steady-state levels. Therefore $\tilde{\gamma}$ decreases until the economy converges to the steady states. In both cases, $\tilde{\gamma}_t$ act as a countercyclical instrument.

Comparing the impulse response function of the Islamic (solid line) with the conventional (dashed lines) models indicates that the magnitude and persistence of all four shocks are different in Islamic and conventional models (Figures 5.1–5.4). The convergence time in the Islamic model is shorter than the conventional model, that is, the speed of adjustment in the Islamic economy is greater than the conventional economy. The magnitude of fluctuations of macroeconomic variables in the Islamic model is smaller than the conventional. It means that the *Musharekah* rate acts as a better countercyclical instrument than the interest rate.

Table 5.3 The second moments of simulated and real data variables comparison

Variable	*Standard Deviation (SD)*		*Correlation with non-oil production*		*Relative SD*	
	Model	*Real data*	*Model*	*Real data*	*Model*	*Real data*
Non-oil production	0.059	0.05	1	1	1	1
Consumption	0.062	0.07	0.70	0.83	1.05	1.4
Investment	0.159	0.13	0.69	0.73	2.69	2.6

Source: Research findings

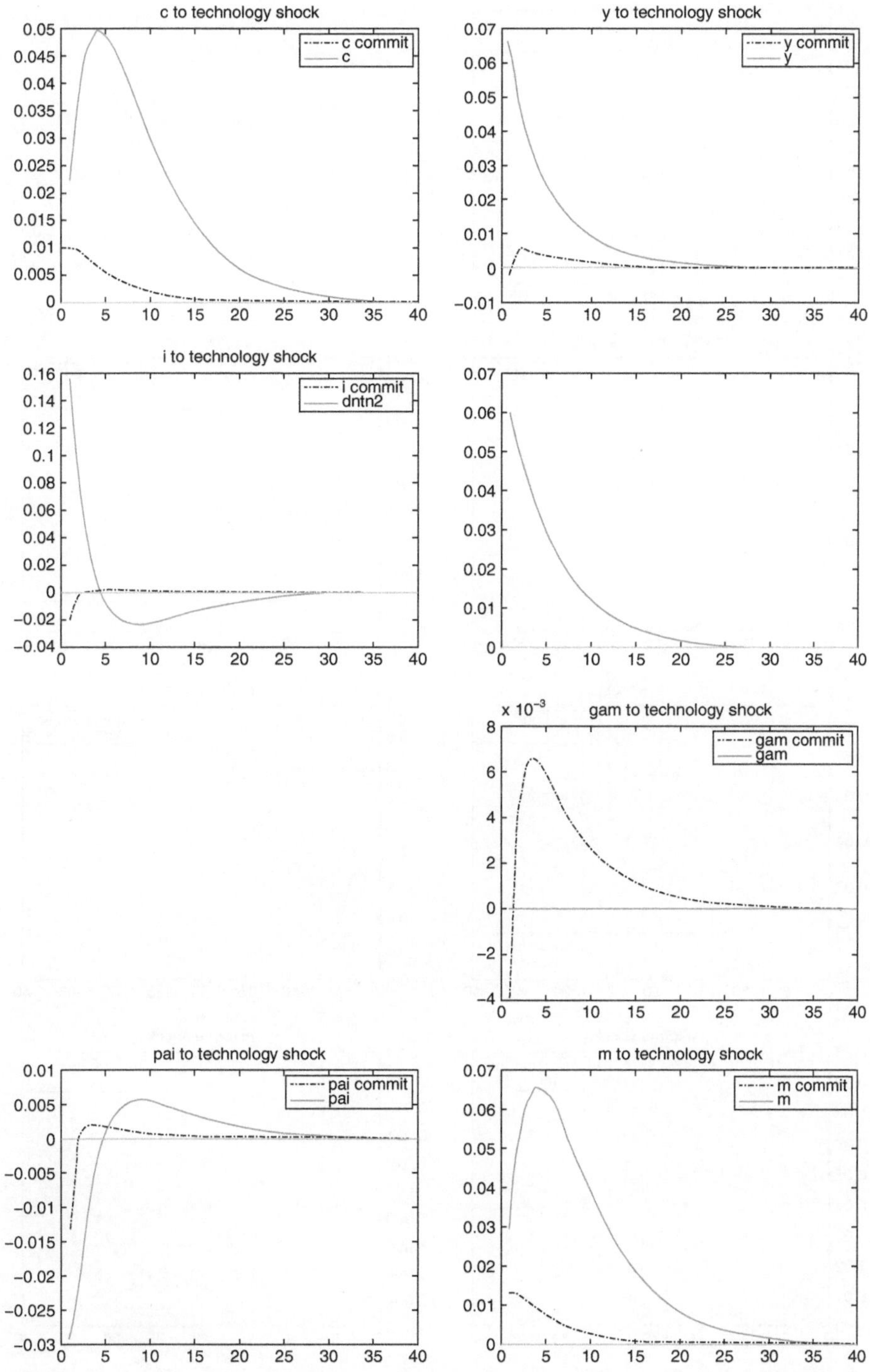

Figure 5.1 Dynamic responses of the macro variables to a technology shock (Islamic vs conventional)

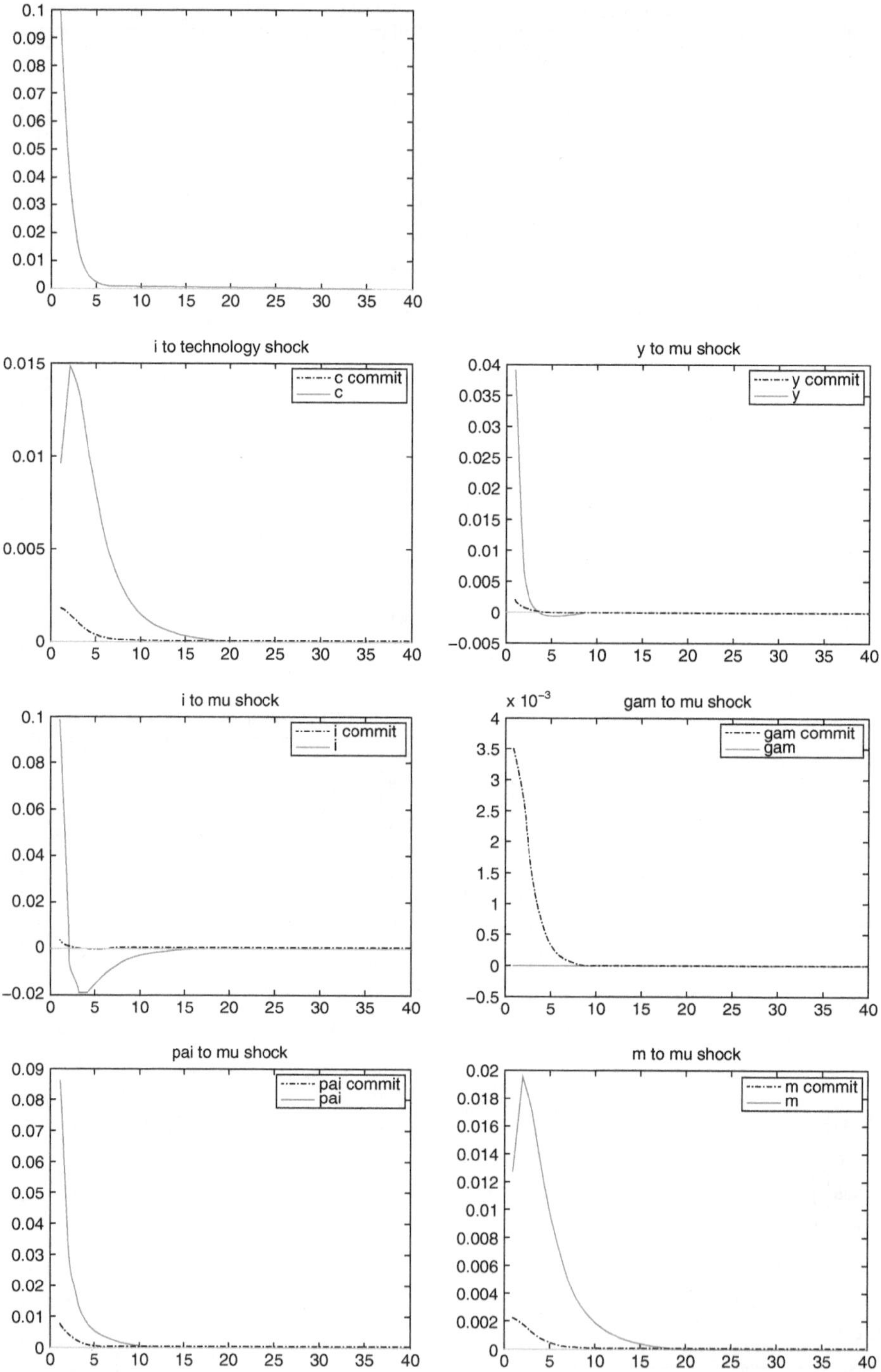

Figure 5.2 Dynamic responses of the macro variables to a monetary shock (Islamic vs conventional)

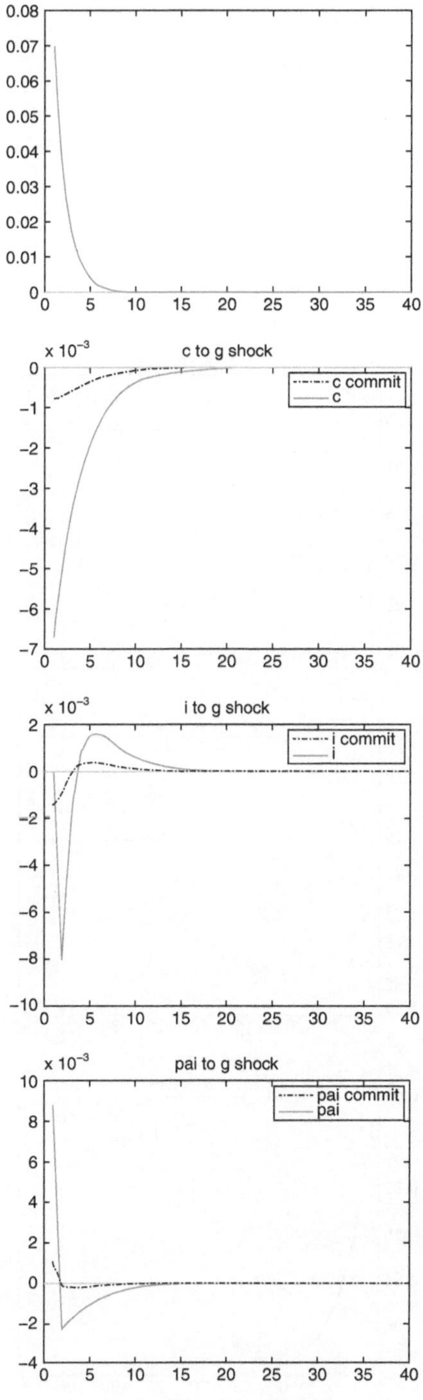

Figure 5.3 Dynamic responses of the macro variables to a government expenditure shock (Islamic vs conventional)

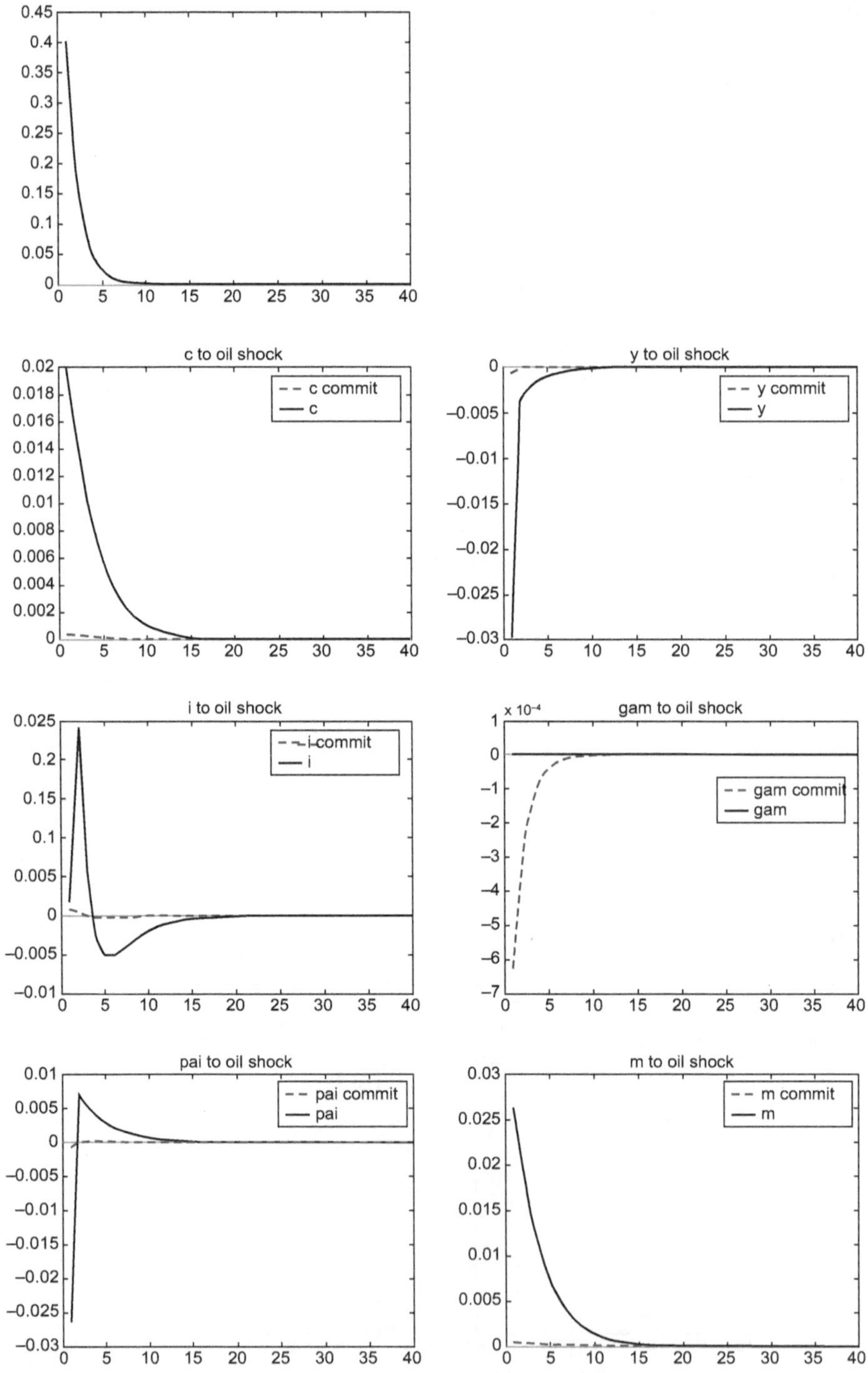

Figure 5.4 Dynamic responses of the macro variables to an oil revenue shock (Islamic vs conventional)

The optimal policy coefficients

According to Woodford (2003), the quadratic welfare loss function is derived from the model as follows:

$$W = \lambda_1 \tilde{y}_t^2 + \lambda_2 \tilde{\pi}_t^2 + \lambda_3 \widetilde{\Delta\gamma}_t^2$$

The loss function equation indicates the cost or loss to society associated with twin "evils" of deviations of inflation from equilibrium (desired) rate and deviations of output from potential (full employment) levels. One of the methods for analyzing the optimal policy results in the model is finding the coefficients that maximize (minimize) social welfare (central bank's loss function). For this purpose, different weights for output, inflation, and share of government *Musharakah* in the objective function are estimated for the optimal and non-optimal rules by Dinar software. Two kinds of targeting rules are introduced, and then their impact on welfare is evaluated: The Ramsey optimal and empirical non-optimal rules. Two strict rules—the flexible Inflation rule (zero price inflation target for all times) and the output rule (zero output gap)—are introduced. Furthermore, targeting rules are examined, that is, *Musharekah* reacts to both output and inflation gaps. Then the results are compared with optimal Ramsey rules. Table 5.3 compares the results for the optimal and non-optimal rules. The scenarios with the least welfare loss and the least gaps are preferred policies. The results imply that the minimum loss occurs when the authorities respond equally to the inflation and output gaps.

Table 5.4 shows that in the case of implementing non-optimal rules, the maximum loss occurs when policy instrument responds strictly to the inflation gap.

Table 5.4 The optimal coefficients of *Musharekah* rule

	ρ_i^*	g_y^*	g_p^*	W	V_r	V_Y	V_r
Ramsey Optimal Rules under $\lambda_1 = 1, \lambda_2 = 0, \lambda_3 = 0.25$							
	–	–	–	.458	.416	.0178	,084
$g_y = 3$ $g_\Pi = 1$ $\rho_i = .3$	.648	.366	1.067	.0514	.016	.0246	.0878
$g_y = 0$ $g_\Pi = 1$ $\rho_i = .3$	.722	.315	1.311	.0512	.0181	.0245	.0879
$g_y = 1$ $g_\Pi = 1$ $\rho_i = .3$	.707	.936	.934	.0246	.0237	.0241	.0876
$g_y = 1$ $g_\Pi = .3$ $\rho_i = .3$	.644	1.062	.364	.0514	.0156	.0247	.0878
$g_y = 1$ $g_\Pi = 0$ $\rho_i = .3$	.713	1.272	.272	.05136	.0159	.0246	.088

(*Continued*)

Table 5.4 (Continued)

	ρ_i^*	g_y^*	g_p^*	W	V_r	V_Y	V_r
Empirical Non-optimal Rules							
Smoothing Rules	.3	1.37	.3	.0198	.0458	.0234	.0858
Non-smoothing Rules	–	1.37	.3	.1996	.0485	.0236	.0852
Simple Policy Rule	–	–	.3	.221	.0005	.0324	.0940

Table 5.5 Real gaps, empirical gaps, and optimized gaps in the model

	Real Data%	*Empirical rules%*	*Optimal policy%*
Inflation Gap	18.7	0.3	0
Output Gap	9.1	6.4	1.6

Source: Research findings

The welfare losses in optimal rules are less than non-optimal rules. Furthermore, in the case of optimal rules, less government response is required to close the gaps. Finally, in optimal rules, the volatility of both output and inflation is less than non-optimal rules.

Table 5.5 shows that, on the basis of the real data of the Iranian economy, the output gap is 9.1 percent of potential output, while this ratio is 6.4 percent and 1.6 percent in empirical and optimal rules respectively. The inflation gap is 18.7 percent, .3 percent, and 0 percent for real data, empirical rules, and optimal rules, respectively. These results indicate that the simulated optimal and empirical models have the ability to converge the economy to their targeted values.

Concluding remarks

The purpose of this study is to provide a dynamic stochastic general equilibrium model, by introducing an Islamic instrument, that is, the *Musharakah* contracts in Iran. In this model, the interest rate is no longer acts as a monetary policy instrument. Then the impact of economic shocks on the dynamics of macroeconomic variables is considered. Finally, a policy rule based on *Musharakah* is introduced, and optimal policy and empirical coefficients are derived. Using data from the Iranian economy, the empirical results indicate that the magnitude and persistence of the shocks are not the same in Islamic and conventional models. The convergence time in the Islamic model is shorter than the conventional model; that is, the speed of adjustment in the Islamic economy is greater than the conventional economy. The magnitude of macroeconomic variables in the Islamic model is smaller than the conventional. It means that the *Musharekah* rate acts as a better countercyclical instrument than the interest rate. Moreover, the results reveal that the optimal policy rules indicate that the minimum loss occurs when the authorities respond equally to the inflation and output gaps, while in non-optimal empirical rules, the maximum loss occurs when policy instruments respond strictly to the inflation gap. Finally, the results confirm that the new policy rule introduced in this chapter could be a good substitute for the Taylor rule in conventional models to stabilize the economy.

It is suggested that in order to reach more realistic results, building models based on more realistic assumptions, several changes to the model are required: First, we should assume heterogeneous agents instead of homogeneous ones. Second, we should replace the assumptions of perfect rationality and foresight with those of bounded rationality and adaptive behaviour. As a result, we should substitute the rationality assumption with insights coming from behavioural economics (Islamic economics). Finally, we should introduce more aspects of Islamic economics in the model. One way to reach these goals is by integrating the DSGE model with agent-based models.

Notes

1 See Appendices for the proof.
2 See Appendices.
3 It is noticeable that in Iran, in contrast to oil importer countries, oil revenues go directly to the monetary base.

References

Adjemian, S., Paries, M. D. and Moyen, S. (2007) *Optimal monetary policy in an estimated DSGE for the Euro area*, European Central Bank Working Paper Series, No. 803, Germany.

Afshari, Zahra (2020) *A retrospective look at Islamic banking in Iran*, IRAN, F. I. IKAM Reports 13 | Country Reports 7, Istanbul, Turkey.

Ahmad, A., Rahman, Ashfaq, Kashif-ur and Asad Afzal, Humayoun (2011, March 4) Islamic banking and prohibition of Riba/interest, *African Journal of Business Management*, Vol. 5, No. 5, pp. 1763–7.

Anvari and others (2011) Determining the optimal monetary rule in a DSGE model by using the control theory, *The Quantitative Journal of Economics*, No. 3, pp. 129–58.

Ball, L. (1997). Efficient rules for monetary policy, *International Finance*, Vol. 2, No. 1, pp. 63–83.

Ball, L. M. (1999). Policy rules for open economies, in *Monetary policy rules* (pp. 127–156). Chicago, IL: University of Chicago Press.

Ben Daoud, K. (2012) L'intermediation financier participative des Banquets Islamiques. *Etudes en Economie Islamique*, Vol. 06–1, pp. 29–56.

Central Bank of the Islamic Republic of Iran (1997) https://cbi.ir/simplelist/1418.aspx

Chapra, M. Umer (1992) *Islam and the economic challenge*, Leicester, UK: The Islamic Foundation.

Clarida, R., Gali, J. and Gertler, M. (1999) The science of monetary policy: A new Keynesian perspective, *Journal of Economic Literature*, Vol. 37, pp. 1661–707.

Dahani, Khawla and Aboulaich, Rajae (2018) Dynamic stochastic general equilibrium model for the Islamic economy, *Investment Management and Financial Innovations*, Vol. 15, No.3.

Feizi, M. (2008, December). A new Keynesian small open economy DSGE model in Islamic economic framework: The case of Iran. In Conference on Iran's Economy at University of Illinois at Urban Champaign (pp. 11–13).

Gan, P., Yee, K., Hadi, F. and Jalil, N. (2019) Monetary policy reaction function and external economic uncertainty: evidence from 30 selected countries, *Management Science Letters*, Vol. 9, No. 8, pp. 1207–20.

Gerali, Andrea, Stefano Neri, Luca Sessa and Federico M. Signoretti (2010) Credit and banking in a DSGE model of the Euro area, *Journal of Money, Credit and Banking*, Blackwell Publishing, Vol. 42, No. s1, pp. 107–41.

Grohe, Stephanie Schmitt and Martín Uribe (2004) *Optimal simple and implementable monetary and fiscal rules*, NBER Working Papers 10253. Cambridge, MA: National Bureau of Economic Research, Inc., pp. 43–50.

Iqbal, Z. (1997) Islamic financial system, *Finance and Development*, Vol. 43, pp. 42–5.

Jaaskela, J. P. (2005) Inflation, price level and hybrid rules under inflation uncertainty, *Scandinavian Journal of Economics*, Vol. 107, pp. 141–56.

Jensen, H. (2003) Targeting nominal income growth or inflation, *American Economic Review*, Vol. 92, pp. 928–56.

Jondeau, E. and Le Bihan, H. (2002) Evaluating monetary policy rules in estimated forward-looking models. A comparison of US and German monetary policies, *Annales d'économie et de statistique*, pp. 357–88.

Jondeau, E. and Sahuc, J.-G. (2008) Optimal monetary policy in an estimated DSGE model of the Euro area with cross-country heterogeneity, *International Journal of Central Banking*, Vol. 4, pp. 23–72.

Juilliard, M. (2010, 2011) *User manual for optimal policy package*, MONFISPOL FP7 project SSH-225149, Deliverable 1.1.1 & 1.1.2. https://www.monfispol.eu/reports/report_1.1.2.pdf

Khan, M. F. (1984) Macro consumption function in an Islamic framework, *Journal of Research Islamic Economics*, pp. 71–3.

Khan, M. S. and Mirakhor, A. (1989) *The financial system and monetary policy in an Islamic economy* (Vol. 1), Washington, DC: Islamic Economics.

Khan, M. S. and Mirakhor, A. (1990) Islamic banking: Experiences in the Islamic republic of Iran and in Pakistan, *Economic Development and Cultural Change*, Vol. 38, No. 2, pp. 353–75.

Mills, P. S. and Presley, J. R. (1999) *Islamic finance: Theory and practice*, London: MacMillan.

Nili, F. (2014) *Islamic banking and finance. The Islamic finance handbook: A practitioner's guide to the global markets* (Vol. 175), Singapore: Wiley Finance Series, John Wiley & Sons.

OPEC, 2019 Annual Statistical Bulletin (2019) https://www.opec.org/opec_web/static_files_project/media/downloads/publications/OB012019.pdf

Parveen, T., Langari Zadeh, E. and Muzakkir Syed, A. (2015) Evolution of Islamic banking in IRAN: Prospects and problems, *IOSR Journal of Business and Management (IOSR-JBM)*, Vol. 17, No. 9. Ver. II, pp. 61–6.

Rasoulinezhad, E. (2012) The concept of Islamic dynamic stochastic general equilibrium method in the financial theme, *American Journal of Business and Management,* Vol. 1, No. 3, pp. 113–18.

Saymeh, A. A. F. and Orieqat, H. M. (2013) The global financial crisis: Is the Islamic system a potential solution?, *International Journal of Financial Economics*, Vol. 1, No. 3, pp. 76–87.

Sofia, B., Bulir, A. and Cihak, M. (2008) *Taylor rule under financial instability*, IMF Working Paper WP/08/18, Washington, DC.

Soleimani Movahed M., Afshari, Z. and Pedram, M. (2016) Optimal monetary policy in a dynamic stochastic general equilibrium model in an Islamic framework, *Journal of Economic Research and Policies 3*, Vol. 23, No. 76, pp. 115–44.

Svensson, L. (2000) Open-economy inflation targeting, *Journal of International Economics*, Vol. 50, pp. 155–83.

Taylor, J. B. (1993) Discretion versus policy rules in practical guide, *Carnegie-Rochester Conference Series on Public Policy*, Vol. 39, pp. 195–214.

Woodford, M. (2003) Optimal monetary policy inertia, *Review of Economic Studies*, Vol. 70, pp. 861–86.

World Bank; Islamic Development Bank Group (2017) *Global report on Islamic finance: Islamic finance – A catalyst for shared prosperity?* Washington, DC: World Bank. © Islamic Development Bank Group. https://openknowledge.worldbank.org/handle/10986/25738

Appendices

Log-linearized system equations

$$\chi\left(\frac{l_{ss}}{1-l_{ss}}\right)\tilde{l}_t + \varphi\tilde{c}_t = \tilde{w}_t \tag{1}$$

$$\tilde{c}_t = E_t\tilde{c}_{t+1} - \frac{1}{\varphi}E_t\left(\widetilde{pr}_{t+1} - \tilde{\pi}_{t+1}\right) \tag{2}$$

$$\widetilde{mc}_t = -\tilde{a}_t + \eta\tilde{w}_t + (1-\eta)\left(\widetilde{pr}_t + \tilde{\gamma}_t\right) \tag{3}$$

$$\tilde{\pi}_t = \frac{(1-\xi)(1-\xi\beta)}{\xi}\widetilde{mc}_t + \beta E_t\tilde{\pi}_{t+1} \tag{4}$$

$$E_t\tilde{k}_{t+1} = \tilde{k}_t + \delta\tilde{i}_t \tag{5}$$

$$\tilde{k}_t\left(\frac{k_{ss}}{y_{ss}}\right) = \tilde{s}_t\left(\frac{s_{ss}}{y_{ss}}\right) + \tilde{x}_t\left(\frac{x_{ss}}{y_{ss}}\right) \tag{6}$$

$$\widetilde{pr}_t = \tilde{f}_t - \tilde{k}_{t-1} + \tilde{\pi}_t \tag{7}$$

$$\tilde{x}_t = E_t\tilde{\gamma}_{t+1} + \tilde{k}_t \tag{8}$$

$$\tilde{y}_t = \tilde{a}_t + (1-\eta)\tilde{k}_t + \eta\tilde{l}_t \tag{9}$$

$$\begin{aligned}\tilde{g}_t\left(\frac{g_{ss}}{y_{ss}}\right) + \tilde{x}_t\left(\frac{x_{ss}}{y_{ss}}\right) &= \widetilde{or}_t\left(\frac{or_{ss}}{y_{ss}}\right) + \tilde{\tau}_t\left(\frac{\tau_{ss}}{y_{ss}}\right) \\ &+ \left(\tilde{\gamma}_t + \tilde{f}_t\right)\gamma_{ss}\left(\frac{f_{ss}}{y_{ss}}\right) + (1-\delta)\tilde{x}_{t-1}\left(\frac{x_{ss}}{y_{ss}}\right)\end{aligned} \tag{10}$$

$$\tilde{k}_t - \tilde{l}_t = \tilde{w}_t - \widetilde{pr}_t - \tilde{\gamma}_t \tag{11}$$

$$\widetilde{mu}_t = \tilde{m}_t - \tilde{m}_{t-1} + \tilde{\pi}_t \tag{12}$$

$$\tilde{\gamma}_t = \rho_i \tilde{\gamma}_{t-1} + (1-\rho_i)\left[g_y(\tilde{y}_t - \bar{y}) + g_\pi(\tilde{\pi}_t)\right] \tag{13}$$

$$\tilde{c}_t = \tilde{m}_t \tag{14}$$

$$\tilde{y}_t + \widetilde{or}_t\left(\frac{or_{ss}}{y_{ss}}\right) = \tilde{c}_t\left(\frac{c_{ss}}{y_{ss}}\right) + \tilde{i}_t\left(\frac{i_{ss}}{y_{ss}}\right) + \tilde{g}_t\left(\frac{g_{ss}}{y_{ss}}\right) \tag{15}$$

$$a_t = \rho_A a_{t-1} + (1-\rho_A)\bar{a} + \varepsilon_t^a \tag{16}$$

$$g_t = \rho_g g_{t-1} + (1-\rho_g)\bar{g} + \varepsilon_t^g \tag{17}$$

$$mu_t = \rho_m mu_{t-1} + (1-\rho_m)\overline{mu} + \varepsilon_t^m \tag{18}$$

$$or_t = \rho_{or} or_{t-1} + (1-\rho_{or})\overline{or} + \varepsilon_t^{or} \tag{19}$$

IS and Phillips curves derivation

IS derived from substituting:

$$\begin{aligned}
&\tilde{y}_t - (i_{ss}/y_{ss})\tilde{i}_t - (g_{ss}/y_{ss})\tilde{g}_t + (or_{ss}/y_{ss})\widetilde{or}_t \\
&= \tilde{y}_{t+1} - (i_{ss}/y_{ss})\tilde{i}_{t+1} - (g_{ss}/y_{ss})\tilde{g}_{t+1} + (or_{ss}/y_{ss})\widetilde{or}_{t+1} \\
&+ \frac{(c_{ss}/y_{ss})}{\varphi}\left(\tilde{\pi}_{t+1} - \widetilde{pr}_{t+1}\right)
\end{aligned}$$

Rearranging the parameters above property gives:

$$\begin{aligned}
&\tilde{y}_t = \tilde{y}_{t+1} + (i_{ss}/y_{ss})\widetilde{\Delta i}_t - (g_{ss}/y_{ss})\widetilde{\Delta g}_t + \\
&(or_{ss}/y_{ss})\Delta\widetilde{or}_t + \frac{(c_{ss}/y_{ss})}{\varphi}\left(\tilde{\pi}_{t+1} - \widetilde{pr}_{t+1}\right)
\end{aligned}$$

The second terms carry the demand-side variables which are independent of policy (*t.i.p.*) summarized as ζ_t:

$$\tilde{y}_t = \tilde{y}_{t+1} + \frac{(c_{ss}/y_{ss})}{\varphi}\tilde{\pi}_{t+1} + \zeta_t$$

Where ζ_t is a white noise, demand-side shocks with zero mean and variance of σ_t^2. The most important feature of this IS its independence to the interest rate as a policy instrument.

$$\begin{aligned}
\widetilde{mc}_t &= -\tilde{a}_t + \eta\left(\nu\tilde{l}_t + \varphi\tilde{c}_t\right) + (1-\eta)\left(\widetilde{pr}_t + \tilde{\gamma}_t\right)\widetilde{mc}_t \\
&= -\tilde{a}_t + \eta\left(\nu\tilde{l}_t + \varphi\tilde{c}_t\right) + (1-\eta)\left(\widetilde{pr}_t + \tilde{\gamma}_t\right)
\end{aligned}$$

Where $\nu = \chi\left(\frac{l_{ss}}{1-l_{ss}}\right)$. Knowing that the profit rate is *t.i.p.* substituting from

$$\widetilde{mc}_t = -\tilde{a}_t + \eta\left(\frac{\nu}{\eta}\left(\tilde{y}_t - \tilde{a}_t + (1-\eta)\tilde{k}_t\right) + \varphi\tilde{m}_t\right) + (1-\eta)\left(\widetilde{pr}_t + \tilde{\gamma}_t\right)$$

$$\widetilde{mc}_t = \nu\tilde{y}_t + (1-\eta)\tilde{\gamma}_t + (t.i.p)$$

Substituting the above equation in the Phillips curve, gained:

$$\tilde{\pi}_t = \frac{(1-\xi)(1-\xi\beta)}{\xi}\left(\nu\tilde{y}_t + (1-\eta)\tilde{\gamma}_t + (t.i.p)\right) + \beta E_t\tilde{\pi}_{t+1} : 0 = \lambda\nu$$

$$\vartheta = \lambda(1-\eta) \text{ where } \lambda = (1-\xi)(1-\xi\beta)/\xi$$

Phillips curve can be written as follows:

$$\tilde{\pi}_t = \text{o}\tilde{y}_t + \vartheta\tilde{\gamma}_t + \beta E_t\tilde{\pi}_{t+1} + \varepsilon_t$$

6 The problems with fractional reserve banking and proposing a shariah-compliant full reserve banking model

Ömer Faruk Tekdoğan and Mehmet Saraç

Introduction

Probably the most radical change in the money supply mechanism began with the adoption of fractional reserve banking and the abandonment of the gold standard. Facilitated by the general acceptance of goldsmith receipts as a circulating medium, fractional reserve was developed by the illegitimate action of goldsmiths, lending out the majority of the deposits which had to be held for safekeeping and cannot be used without the consent of depositors. The new convention in money creation has been rationalized on the ground that the gold-based monetary system was regarded incompetent to support the fast growth of the economies, whereas banknotes issued regardless of the gold reserves would do the job well. The simple yet wiser explanation behind the adoption of fractional reserve banking, however, is nothing but the greed of human beings. This new convention would serve much better to the very objective of homo economicus. A great deal of capital accumulation has been facilitated to a minority at the expense of unsustainable debt, unjust distribution of wealth, and the exploitation of millions of people.

In this chapter, we will first explain the role of fractional reserve banking in money creation and financial crises. Then, following the literature review of alternative approaches developed so far, an authentic full reserve banking model will be proposed along with a simulation exercise. We would like to draw more attention to the operating system of our banks and the problems arising from it and to show how these problems can be fixed with full reserve banking.

Theoretical background

Fractional reserve banking

The roots of modern banking practice can be traced back to the goldsmith bankers of the seventeenth century. The goldsmith would take the deposits from the customers in the form of precious metal coins and issue "bearer receipts" representing those coins. Initially, these bankers were nothing more than safe-keeping houses working for a fee. As time passed, these goldsmith receipts became like money used in all trade activities (Diwany, 2003, p. 35).

These bankers noticed that most customers would not withdraw their coins frequently and the coins in their vaults remained largely idle. The most obvious use of these idle reserves was to lend them at interest. However, the bankers had to be so careful that not too much of these reserves would be lent. They would need to keep sufficient quantities in reserve to meet the requests for redemption by their customers. The proportion of coins thus kept in reserve against receipts issued came to be known as the "cash reserve ratio". Because the net amount of receipts redeemed on any one day was usually small, only a small reserve ratio was seen sufficient under most circumstances. The lower the reserve ratio, the greater the risk of a bank collapse but also the more that could be lent out, meaning the greater the interest revenue. That is basically how fractional reserve banking began.

The bankers took a further, daring step towards making money out of lending at interest: They issued more receipts than the entire number of coins in their vaults and started to lend at interest. Since the receipts were equally regarded as money by the public and paper receipts could be manufactured at very little cost, such a policy had a great advantage. A typical bank would use its entire gold reserve as a ratio for receipts issued. For example, a banker with $100 coins in his vault and a 25 percent reserve ratio requirement could take the risk of issuing $400 in total.[1] Here, the depositors of the coins would receive receipts to the value of $100 and a further $300 could then be manufactured to lend at interest.

Banks, fuelled by the greed for higher interest revenue and backed by the governments, have provided huge amounts of loans. Though this credit expansion through fractional reserve banking accelerated economic growth at first, it resulted in bankruptcies of many banks due to economic crises and recessions (Huerta de Soto, 2009, p. 79).

The establishment of the Bank of England in 1694 is regarded as the official start of fractional reserve banking. The government bonds were used as reserves when the United States abandoned the gold standard. Since these bonds were perpetually redeemed by new ones, the debt has been accumulated and constitutes the US money supply today (Brown, 2008, p. 542–3). As transactions without the use of banknotes have become widespread, the definition of money has seriously changed, and money supply has been dominated by bank money (Ferguson, 2011, p. 47). A bank customer can immediately deposit his money borrowed from the bank. Because the customer can immediately use this money through checks or bank cards, money supply occurs just when the loan is extended.

Fundamentals of bank money production and control of money supply

Controlling the money supply is of crucial importance because it is a key element affecting interest rates and the economic process. Though central banks are responsible for this control function, there are other actors affecting the money supply including commercial banks, depositors, and creditors.

There are essentially two schools of thought as to who should produce money and control money supply: (a) the currency school and (b) the banking school.

According to the former, money production and the financial intermediary functions of banks should be separated. Advocating the full reserve banking system, this school argues that only the government can produce money. It is proposed that the money supply should be determined under a certain rule, such as the gold standard (Goodhart & Jensen, 2015, pp. 3–4). According to Mises, the currency school could not notice that the bank deposit and banknotes are the same; both are based on no assets. Therefore, those who adopted this school did not apply the same regulation to the deposits and banknotes. However, these two elements carry out the same functions (Mises, 1953, p. 370).

As for the banking school, it advocates that flexibility should be provided by leaving an assessment field because the rules would limit the mobility in the money supply needed for the economy. It proposes that the central bank should determine a policy interest rate following macroeconomic goals and provide the reserves needed by all commercial banks. Based on this rate, commercial banks would determine their own rules and conditions and provide loans to their customers. Bank money production is the basic linkage between money and the real economy (Goodhart & Jensen, 2015, pp. 9–10). As can easily be seen, fractional reserve banking is rationalized within the context of this school.

The money production through fractional reserve banking is measured by a "money multiplier", which is expressed as follows:

$$m = \frac{(1+c)}{(r+e+c)} \qquad \text{(Equation 1)}$$

m = Money multiplier
r = Reserve ratio required by central bank
e = Banks' optional reserve ratio
c = Currency drain ratio (cash to deposit ratio determined by customers' behaviours)

According to this formula, if, say, the required reserve ratio is 10 percent, banks' optional reserve ratio 5 percent and the drainage ratio is 25 percent, then the money multiplier is calculated as 3,125. This implies that an increase of 1 Turkish lira (TL) in deposits will result in a 3,125 TL increase in the total money supply.

Full reserve banking

Full reserve banking, which emerged as a structural solution against the instability and other problems caused by fractional reserve banking, assumes that banks are structured basically in two categories: (a) deposit (safekeeping) institutions and (b) lending institutions. However, there may be variations among the bank models proposed within the full reserve system.

In a full reserve system, deposit banks are required to back all deposits by fiat money (the currency that a government has declared to be legal tender) and prohibited from private money creation because of the separation of deposit-taking and lending functions of banks. The main goal here is to ensure the government's power in controlling the money supply.

Over the last two centuries, many different full reserve banking models have been proposed which can be classified under several categories. Laina (2015) provided a comprehensive chronological outlook on most of these proposals under six types of full reserve banking, beginning with David Ricardo and including many recent proposals which have been made, especially after the 2007-08 global crisis. He explains that full reserve banking has even been implemented as a solution for financial instability, such as the UK Bank Charter Act of 1844 which required banks to back their banknotes fully by government money. Bank deposits were exempted from this regulation, and eventually, they became the dominant means of payment (Laina 2015, p. 1).

We will briefly describe the most eminent full reserve banking proposals here which represent distinct types of models including (1) the Chicago plan, (2) sovereign money, (3) the pure commodity standard, (4) narrow banking, and (5) limited purpose banking.

After the Great Depression of 1929, a memorandum was signed by eight economists at the University of Chicago, which then came to be known as the Chicago plan. This plan proposed separating the deposit and the lending functions of commercial banks and requiring deposit banks to fully back their deposits with government money. Irving Fisher was a proponent of the Chicago plan. He asserted that this plan is the best one ever to solve the problem of depressions, for it would get at the root of the problem, which is the instability of demand deposit (Fisher, 1936, p. 8). Benes and Kumhof (2012) tested four major advantages of this plan, as described by Fisher (1936), and the results fully validated these claims. If implemented, the Chicago plan could reduce business cycle volatility by better control of credit cycles, eliminate bank runs, and lead to a substantial decrease in debt levels of both government and private sectors.

Sovereign money, proposed by Dyson (2012) and Dyson et al. (2016), is built on the Chicago plan and the works of Irving Fisher. Its originality comes from the idea of creating new account types and replacing the old ones within a rapid or gradual transition period and distributing newly created money in four alternative ways: (a) direct grants to citizens, (b) tax cuts and rebates, (c) increased government spending, and (d) indirect financing of business lending.

Ricardo's (1824) proposal for a pure commodity standard was implying stricter rules than other full reserve proposals. Bank deposits were to be backed by a commodity, such as gold, instead of government printed money; moreover, all money, including central bank reserves and paper money were to be fully backed by gold. It was later supported by economists of the Austrian school; some featured studies in this regard were Mises (1953), Hayek (1989), and Rothbard (2001).

Kay's (2009) proposal of narrow banking is often regarded as a type of full reserve banking model. In this model, only narrow banks can take deposits and can access the principal payments system. They can engage in lending activities along with other lending institutions. Kay's (2009) proposal did not put a 100 percent reserve requirement explicitly. However, Pennacchi (2012) counted a

100 percent reserve bank, which holds government money and keeps demand deposits, as one of the five types of narrow banks. Thus, we can infer from this that full reserve banking is accepted to be a subset of narrow banking.

Limited purpose banking was brought up by Kotlikoff (2012) and discussed later by Chamley et al. (2012). This model went beyond full reserve banking and suggests extra measures to reform the financial system. Various forms of mutual funds are designed for the new system. For instance, cash mutual funds would be the full reserve banking component of the model, and they would be permitted to hold cash only.

Debates about full reserve banking mainly revolve around a few topics. Dixhoorn (2013) provided a wider discussion. First, full reserve banking proponents advocate an independent monetary committee that would control the money and credit supply. This is a similar structure to the Federal Open Market Committee (FOMC) in the United States and the monetary policy committee of central banks in other countries. Opponents claim that this committee would not be totally independent and would not predict the agreeable amount of money supply smoothly and accurately. The second main argument is that there will be a sharp decrease in credit supply because banks will be prohibited from creating money through the lending channel. New lending institutions taking over this role does not seem to be a promising alternative for many economists. Third, it is believed that, after printing an enormous amount of government money to replace credit money during the transition, we would come up with high rates of inflation. This idea is based on the view that whenever the government prints more money, coupled with the multiplier effect, prices tend to rise rapidly. There are some other concerns related to the implementation of the new system, such as international issues, political conflicts, and transition costs, which have not yet been discussed comprehensively and need to be studied elaborately.

Full reserve banking is much more convenient for an Islamic monetary system. Akın and Dolgun (2015) asserted that the Chicago plan can be seen as a conventional version of Islamic precepts regarding banking and finance. In Ahmad and Ismail's (2017) view, full reserve banking could be useful to attain the *Maqaid al-Shariah*, since it would help to reach goals such as less poverty, more equitable distribution of wealth, and protection of wealth. We can, at least, argue that fractional reserve banking is incompatible with Islamic precepts, as it is based on creation of debt with the motivation of earning more interest income—in other words, earning something in return for nothing. Besides, increasing debt levels can reduce the number of potential *zakat* payers and lead to a decrease in the amount of *zakat* to be collected. As a result, full reserve banking would undoubtedly be a big step towards a just and Islamic economic system.

Superiority of full reserve over fractional system: empirical evidence through agent-based modelling

Agent-based modelling is a computer-aided computational method that is used for understanding complex social and economic issues by simulating the behaviours of heterogeneous agents. You can watch how simulations evolve step by step and change any parameter at any time to see the effects of policy changes on various variables. However, designing a model comes with a price: A balance between economic reality and simplicity must be observed to avoid misinterpretations regarding the outcomes of the interactions of agents. Since we do not have historical data on full reserve banking and we do not seek general equilibrium after changing our parameters, we decided to go with agent-based modelling rather than econometric models or general equilibrium models.

Previous studies

Fractional reserve banking has been simulated in some earlier models, which focused on different purposes but varied in designs. Monett and Navarro-Barrientos (2016) modelled a simple fractional reserve banking world which consists of three main groups of artificial entities represented by depositors or investors, debtors or borrowers, and banks. Depositors choose to deposit or withdraw money to/from a bank partially or entirely according to their confidence level about that bank. A bank becomes insolvent when its reserves are lower than the money one or more depositors want to withdraw back from their deposits. They simulated three scenarios by changing the values of both the minimum reserve rate and the average loss of confidence rate parameters. They found that the larger the minimum reserve rate, the fewer the cases where the bank is not able to pay the withdrawals of the depositors. As there were only five depositors defined in the model, they did not find the minimum reserve rate to be influential.

In his model, Chan-Lau (2017) analyzed the risks in the banking system by illustrating the effect of changes on regulatory requirements on solvency, liquidity, and interconnectedness risk. There are three types of agent in the banking system—savers, loans, and banks—and one type of interbank linkages—interbank loans. Savers receive interests on their deposits; however, they prefer to consume interest payments rather than keeping them in the bank account, leaving their account balance unchanged. Some attributes are defined for loans, including the loan amount, probability of default, risk weight, rating, and recovery rate in case of default. Banks offer rate quotes by staying compliant with capital and reserve requirements after adding the loan to the current loan portfolio. Borrowers compare the loan rate quote with their reservation interest rate and take the loan if the rate quote is smaller. Banks must satisfy minimum regulatory capital and reserve requirements.

Mallett's (2015) model was based on a double-entry bookkeeping implementation of the banking system's transactions. Interactions are performed via monetary transactions. The government is included in the model to set the base interest rate through the central bank, to make debt transactions, and to collect taxes. Two types of banks are defined in the model. One is a full-reserve bank that functions purely as a deposit holder. The other is a fractional-reserve bank that implements the Basel regulatory framework, with lending controlled by a risk-based weighting of its loan book and central bank reserve requirement. This model did not include interbank lending.

Lengnick (2011) built a stock-flow consistent agent-based model to analyze the impact of interbank lending on the stability of the financial sector. The three types of agents in the model are banks, households, and a central bank. Households represent the complete real sector where they both produce and buy goods and they both make savings and take loans. The central bank's assets are fixed because the model includes closing the system from an accounting point of view. All transactions have to be paid with cash. Each bank is required to deposit required reserves at the central bank. In the next step, they also introduced an interbank market in the model. They found that the interbank market stabilizes the economy during normal times but amplifies systemic instability, contagion, and bankruptcy cascades during crises.

Wilensky's (1998) model was the simplest. It modelled the creation of money in an economy through a private banking system. Two types of agents in the model are people and one mega-bank. People interact with each other to simulate everyday economic activity by exchanging money randomly. Then people sort out the balance of their wallet with the bank. People take out a loan if their savings account is empty and their wallet has a negative balance, as long as the bank has available funds to loan out. There is no interest introduced in the model. There are three categories of wealth defined—rich, middle, and poor—to see the effect of the minimum reserve rate on income distribution.

The model

General features

Our model not only incorporates different qualities of the aforementioned models but also introduces original elements like *waqf* to reflect Islamic considerations more in the simulation. Rather than mimicking the real world, we simulate an isolated world where we can see and explain the effects of different reserve requirement rates on various variables including production, wealth distribution, consumer demand, and bank viability. Our model is programmed in NetLogo software.

There are three types of agents: (1) households, (2) banks, and (3) the firm, which represents the real sector. The number of households and the firm is fixed at all times, as well as technology, which means that growth is not taken into consideration. The model does not include any type of government agent such as a central bank, as it envisages a free market economy that runs free of any interventions. The model follows a balance sheet approach in which each transaction changes either one or two agents' balance sheet items.

Basic assumptions and interactions

For simplicity, we assume that each household and the firm can only deposit into one given bank and only one bank can make a loan to them. In this way, we reflect the fact that most people are customers of a very limited subset of banks. We therefore matched each household and the firm with a random bank at the setup stage to deposit money and take out a loan.

Also for simplicity, we assumed a fixed deposit ratio (0.95) for households, which means at each round, households keep only 5 percent of their money in the form of cash and deposit the rest of it into their bank account.

M0 money supply is the total amount of cash of households and reserves of banks, whereas *M1* money supply is the total amount of cash of households, deposits of households and the firm (or total deposits kept at the banks), and the *waqf* (if available). To offset the nominal effect of credit expansion, we introduced the price level, defined as the division of *M1* by *M0*. Though it is a very simple way to assume that credit expansion will increase the price level identically, it is helpful to calculate the consumption in real terms and wages in nominal terms. In this way, however, we are constrained to ignore *Keynesian price stickiness theory and sticky wages.*[2]

Households

Households' balance sheet items are cash, deposits, and loans. There no balancing item is defined in coding, but we can assume that there is a net wealth item on the equity side. Net interest is the net of deposit interest paid and loan interest received.

Households have intrinsic attributes, such as a propensity to consume out of income (*Beta-inc*) and out of wealth (*Beta-wealth*), which change randomly at each round. These attributes are used for calculating the demand for consumption and the demand for loan for each household at each round.

There is no interaction between households. Households are divided into three income groups: rich, middle, and poor. Each income group has different consumption patterns. Households' consumption function (in nominal terms) is:

$$C_t = \frac{(\beta_{inc} \times W) + (\beta_{with} \times (Dep - L)) + C_{t-1}}{2} \qquad \text{(Equation 2)}$$

where

β_{inc}: propensity to consume out of income

β_{wlth}: propensity to consume out of wealth

W: Wage

Dep: Deposits

L: Loans

Consumption in real terms is calculated by dividing consumption demand to the price level. Wealth is defined as the difference between a household's deposits and loans. To have less volatility in demand, we included the household's demand from the previous round. Nevertheless, for assuring their sustenance, each household must demand at least two units in each round, which is met by the firm only if the quantity is available in the inventory.

Households' initial cash value is 100. Households are matched with a bank randomly to deposit cash and borrow loans. The initial consumption demand is two units.

Banks

Banks' balance sheet items are reserves, deposits, loans, interbank loans borrowed, and interbank loans received. Banks do not have cash, as for simplicity, we combined cash and reserves under the reserves item. Each bank has other attributes such as bank-to-loan, interbank supply, and interbank demand which are calculated at each round after each transaction, repeatedly.

Initially, banks' reserves are set to zero. Bank reserves are created in the first round, when households deposit 0.95 of their cash. Banks do not have equity in this model.

Bank-to-loan, a bank's available funds for lending, is simply calculated as:

$$\textit{Deposit Held} \times (1 - \textit{Reserve Ratio}) - \textit{Loans Lent} \qquad \text{(Equation 3)}$$

The firm

The firm's balance sheet items are deposits and loans only. The firm is matched with a bank randomly to carry out monetary transactions. The firm can take loans from its bank; however, the calibration of the model does not allow the firm to have a negative bank account balance. On the other hand, including a firm in the model allowed us to see the effects of changing reserve ratios on output and demand.

The firm makes production and puts the produced quantity into the inventory. The production is a function of the inventory, aggregate demand, and the produced amount in the previous round. The initial inventory value is four times the total number of households, which is 800. Half of it equals to the total demand in the first round.

The firm makes a regular and standard payment called "wage" to households. The minimum wage rate is twice as high as price level and the firm pays it even though it does not make production on that round. As the production increases the wage rate increases, not perpetually but to a certain limit. Wage helps to improve the resource allocation among households, as resources are allocated from overspending households to underspending households.

Interactions between agents

In each round, a household first checks if he deposited enough amount to stay in line with the deposit ratio; he either deposits or withdraws money to/from his account.

If a household has any loan balance, first, he wants to repay it in full. If he does not have enough deposits to do it, then he makes partial repayment with all his deposits. When this procedure is done, households check whether they can afford their demand for consumption. If not, then they will attempt to borrow from the

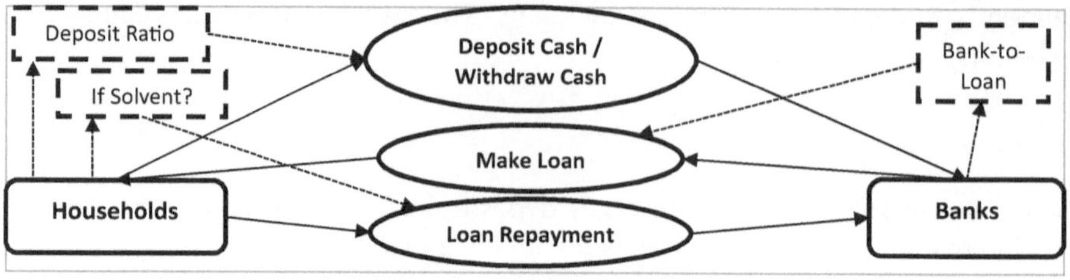

Figure 6.1 Interactions between households and banks

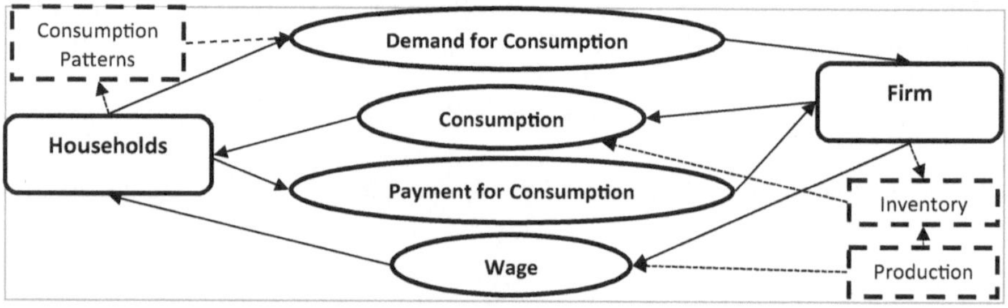

Figure 6.2 Interactions between households and firm

bank a random loan amount which is two to eight times larger than their consumption demand. However, loan demand is sensitive to loan interest rates; as the rate increases, households become less eager to borrow. If the bank has sufficient funds, it grants the requested amount; otherwise, it only gives its available amount. When a household borrows money from his bank, the bank credits the household's deposit account and debits its loans account, whereas the household credits his loans account and debits his deposits account. Higher reserve requirements would constrain banks' lending ability, as a single borrower could borrow the maximum amount allowed, which would make the entire loan book consist of a single loan. New loans could only be made if this loan would be repaid sufficiently to make the necessary loan capacity.

Households ask the firm if it has sufficient quantity in its inventory. If so, the household's demand is fully met by the firm; otherwise, it is met partially. After each transaction, the balance of the inventory is updated. To make the payment, households ask their banks to transfer the payment amount from their deposit accounts to the firm's deposit account. Accordingly, households adjust their deposit records, as the firm does. After this, the firm makes wage payments, and the related opposite transactions occur.

Interbank market

Banks with reserve deficit, which do not have the required level of reserves, have to reach a minimum reserve level and seek to borrow from banks with a reserve

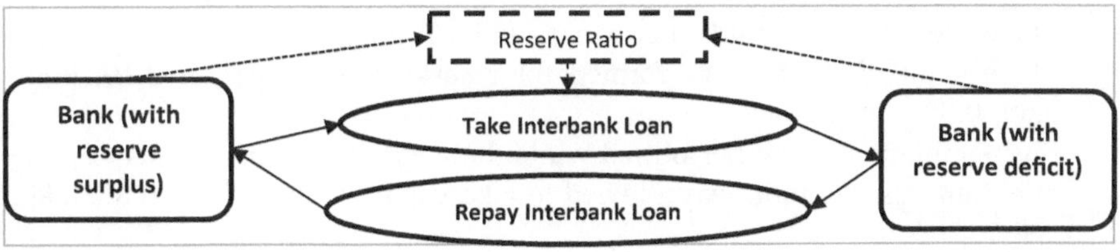

Figure 6.3 Interbank market

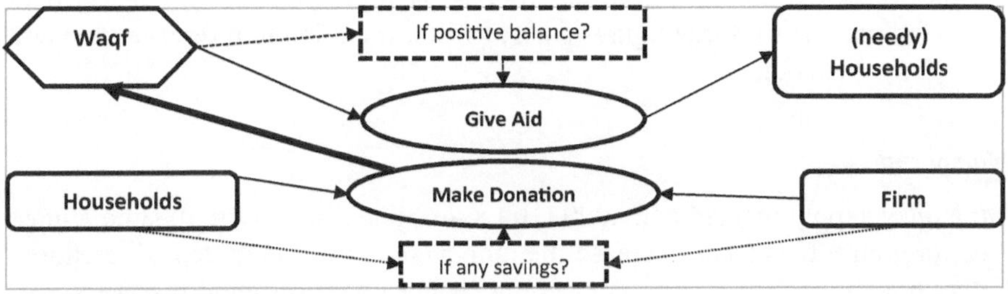

Figure 6.4 Benevolence mode

surplus in the interbank market. The surplus amount is the loanable amount in the market. Interbank loans have to be paid back completely in the next round. No interest is charged for interbank loans in the model.

Those banks that carry reserve deficits for 100 consecutive rounds, without any interruption, are allowed to go bankrupt. There are two alternative bankruptcy procedures programmed. According to the procedure used in this model, the bankrupt bank's balance sheet items and customers are transferred to one of other the banks, which is assigned randomly.

Benevolence mode

When this procedure is activated, the firm and rich and middle-income households donate money, which is a small portion of their wealth, to a pool called *waqf*. Being charitable makes households to into a state of contentment in which they change their consumption patterns and want to consume less. *Waqf* helps needy households as long as it holds a positive balance. *Waqf* is separate from the banking system; however, it reallocates resources. *Waqf* does not accept or pay cash; instead, donations and payments are all made by deposit transfers. We therefore included *waqf* in the *M1* money supply. If a household needs funding, he first asks the *waqf* if it can fulfil his request. If he is still in need, then he resorts to his bank.

Simulations and main results

- There are 200 households, ten banks, and a firm.
- Three simulations were performed for reserve ratio values of 0.10, 0.30, 0.60, 0.90, and 1.
- Five simulations were performed while the *waqf* procedure was active. The minimum reserve ratio was allowed to take values of 0.10, 0.30, 0.60, 0.90, and 1.
- Banks that could not fulfil the minimum reserve requirement for 100 consecutive rounds were allowed to go bankrupt. The interbank loan rate was set to zero.
- On the figures for this chapter, to save space, we did not add any label for the x-axis, which shows 1,000 rounds as time element. We used some abbreviations for these figures such as *rr* for the minimum reserve ratio and *w/o* for without.

Money supply

M0 money supply is fixed at 20,000 (100 × # of households) for all simulations; therefore, only banks can increase the money supply through deposit creation. Figure 6.5 shows how *M1* money supply changes with different reserve ratios. Expectedly, as the reserve ratio goes down, the money supply increases through private money creation and reaches a maximum of 87,000. For a 0.1 minimum reserve ratio, money supply booms and busts in the beginning, then draws a stable pattern. This sudden rise and fall arise from the decline of aggregate demand and thereby loan demand as a consequence of worsening income distribution. For 0.3 and 0.6 reserve ratios, the money supply keeps increasing and finds the balance after some banks go bankrupt, and therefore loan seekers get better access to available funds after being rematched with surviving banks.

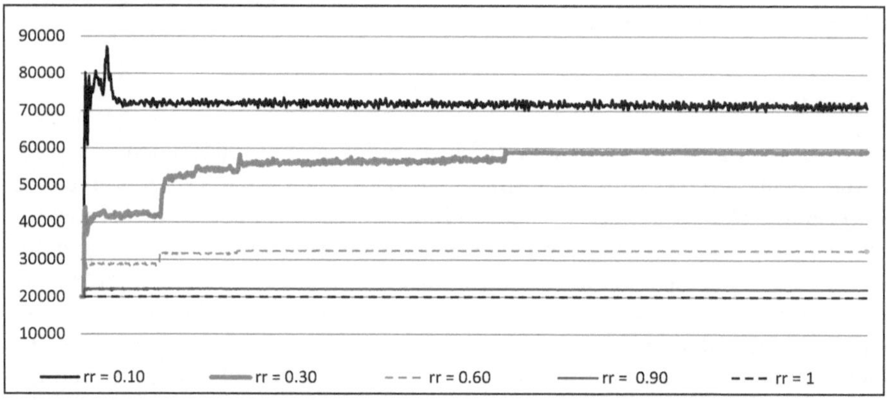

Figure 6.5 M1 money supply, banks only

Money multiplier

The theoretical value of the money multiplier is calculated by dividing (1 + cash ratio) by (reserve ratio + cash ratio). Remember, we fixed cash ratio at 5 percent; therefore, with respect to minimum reserve ratios of 0.1, 0.3, 0.6, and 0.9, theoretical values for the money multiplier are 7, 3, 1.615, and 1.105, respectively. However, cash ratio is an upper limit set for households for their cash holdings, and we found different cash holding ratios, fluctuating between 4.5 percent and 5.5 percent. Likewise, the minimum reserve ratio is the red line for banks. We can see it from Figure 6.6, in which most of the multiplier values, except for the 0.9 reserve ratio, are below the theoretical level. This is mainly from non-borrowed loans, which can be seen in the bank-to-loan column of Figure 6.7. However, we can say that available loans are almost fully utilized in cases with 0.3 and 0.6 reserve ratios.

We see that for the 0.9 reserve ratio, multiplier value exceeded the theoretical level by several times. This problem arises from the inefficiency of the interbank market, which constrains banks to find required funds to maintain reserves at required levels and makes the actual reserve ratio value less than 0.9.

Credit supply

A minimum reserve ratio and deposits at banks are the key parameters for banks' available funds for lending. In Figure 6.7, we can see total bank lending on the first column and the available amount left for lending on the second column. Bank-to-loan is an indicator showing how large the credit supply and thus the money supply can keep growing. There is a key fact that we need to understand. Lending 100 units of loan from bank-to-loan amount does not necessarily mean that a bank's loanable amount of funds decreased by 100. With this action, a bank creates deposit money, which in turn increases the loanable amount. For instance, in a banks-only case, the bank-to-loan amount for 0.10 reserve ratio reaches 17,000. After 35 rounds, loans hit 67,000, where bank-to-loan drops to 5,000. If banks could keep granting loans from this 5,000 loanable amount, theoretically, loans could reach 120,000 with a multiplier value of 7.

Looking from the demand side, households are more eager to spend money and seek loans as they get richer. When we look at Figure 6.8, as the reserve ratio rises, the number of poor households begin to decrease, whereas rich households increase in number. Therefore, loanable funds are utilized more and more as the reserve ratio gets higher. We can also see this effect when the benevolence mode is on, which makes income distribution better. In this mode, more loans are granted and bank-to-loan is almost fully utilized for all reserve ratios. As a consequence, we have greater money multiplier values in this mode.

Income distribution

Figure 6.8 is a summary comparison of income distribution with respect to minimum reserve ratio and benevolence mode. For all columns, when we look from up to down, as the reserve ratio increases, we can see that income distribution has

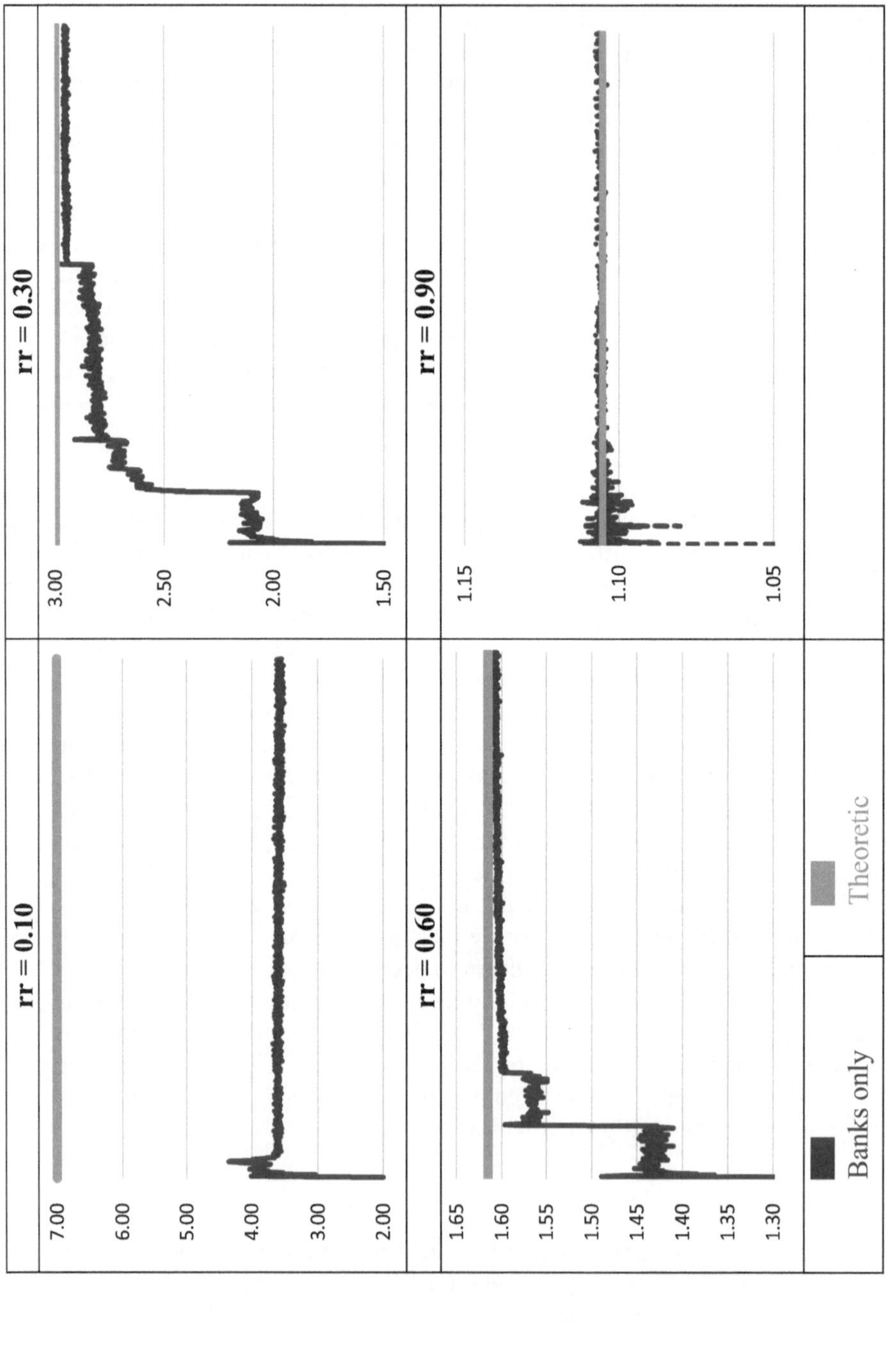

Figure 6.6 Changes in money multiplier values with respect to reserve ratio, banks only

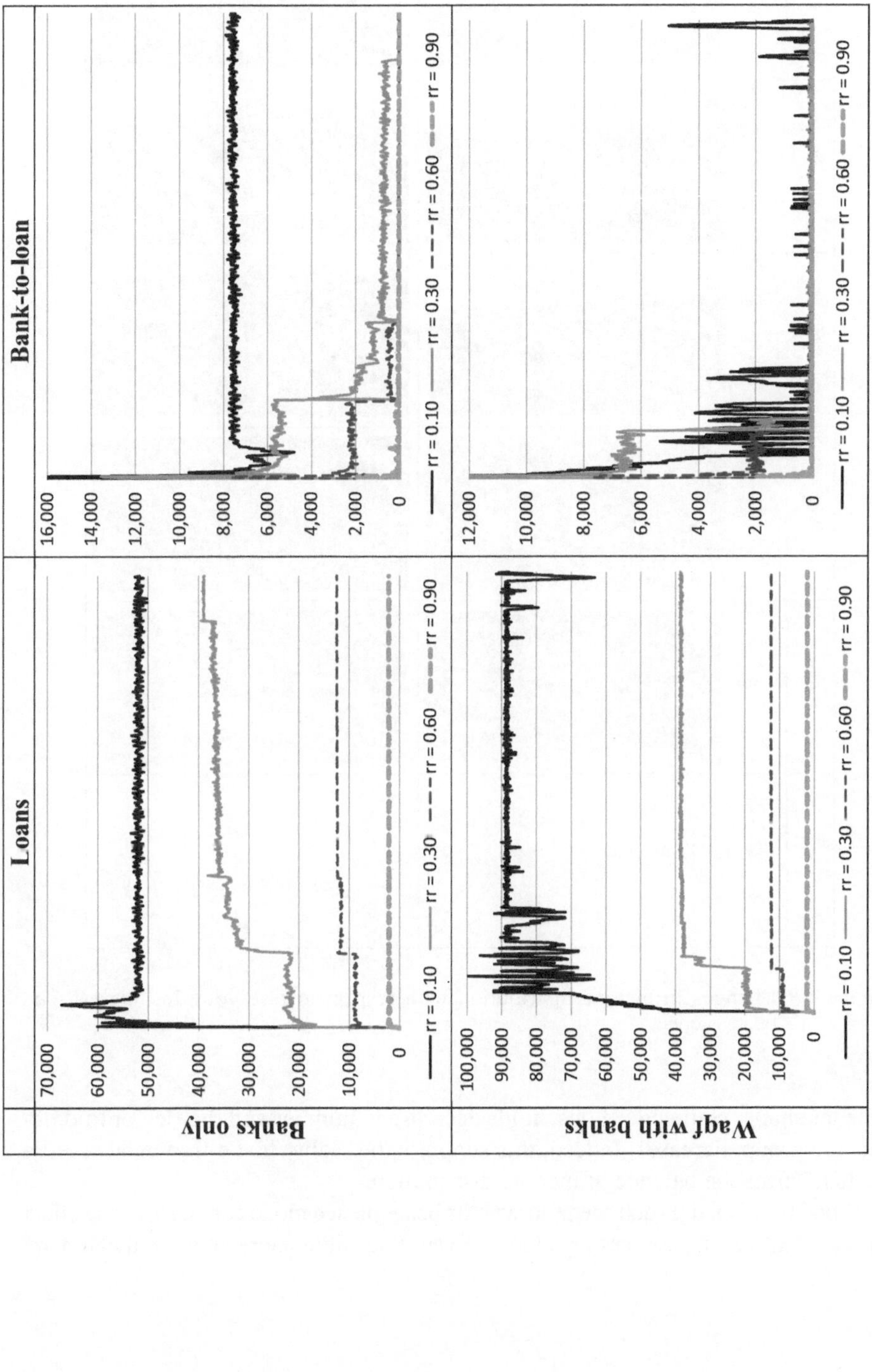

Figure 6.7 Total bank lending: loans granted vs. available funds

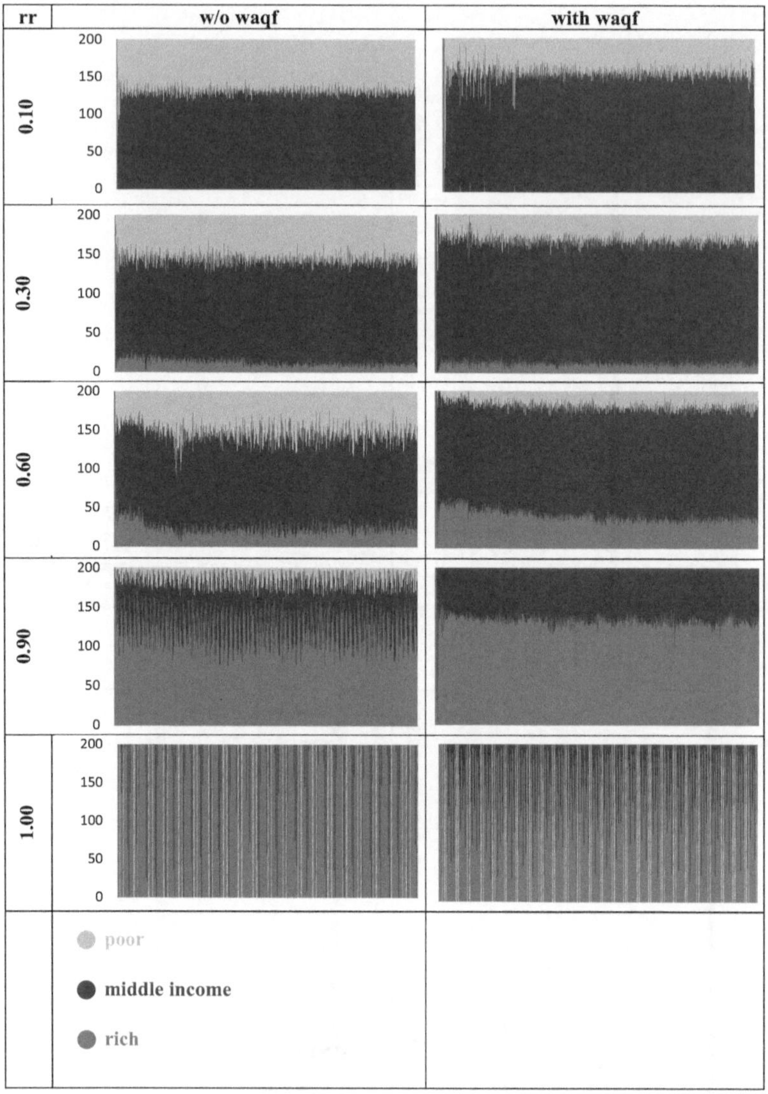

Figure 6.8 Changes in income distribution with respect to reserve ratio, interest, and benevolence

a better shape, while poor households decrease in number and the rich or middle-income group increases. Indeed, this supports the reality that a fractional reserve system harms the balance of income distribution.

When we compare each scenario with its benevolence mode counterpart, the effect of *waqf* reallocating sources is obvious. Even it has little intervention in the system, it has a larger impact on balancing income distribution. Benevolence mode tightens demand for consumption, and therefore for loans; on the supply side *waqf* partially satisfies the demand for loans, and consequently saves households from the debt burden.

In any case, we cannot see even a single poor household in full reserve banking. Income distribution is better as long as no private money creation is allowed through bank lending. Besides, the virtual tightness of money in a full reserve system in comparison with fractional reserve system does not affect total demand in real terms. This can be seen in Figure 6.10.

Bank failures

As stated in the beginning, we performed three simulations for each value of reserve ratio, and we assumed a bank that is not able to maintain the required reserve ratio for 100 consecutive rounds is failed and obliged to transfer its balance sheet with its customers to a randomly chosen bank. This assumption, however, is not capable of showing that the fractional reserve system is a fragile floor for the banking system, because we also assumed that households and the firm always have to keep deposits at banks, which means we did not define any bank run procedure as a threat to banks. Besides, we did not define equity as a balance sheet item for banks and the firm; therefore, the capital adequacy ratio is not applicable in our model. In addition, the interbank market is not efficient, because the seek and match procedure needs some minor improvements. For all these, the results in Table 6.1 seem to be questionable. For instance, a banking system with a 0.1 reserve ratio should have been the most fragile one; however, not even a single bank failed during all four simulations.

Nevertheless, these results prove to us how the model runs stochastically for each simulation. For 0.3, 0.6, and 0.9 reserve ratios, the number of surviving banks varies in each simulation. On the other hand, we did not define a bank failure procedure for a 100 percent reserve ratio scenario.

Output and demand

Production and loans are both dependent on demand. We can see this relationship in Figure 6.9. The amount of borrowed loans is always higher than consumption

Table 6.1 Number of surviving banks

Minimum Reserve Ratio	*Banks only*			Waqf *with banks*
	1st run	*2nd run*	*3rd run*	
0.10	10	10	10	10
0.30	6	5	6	7
0.60	7	5	3	6
0.90	4	7	6	5

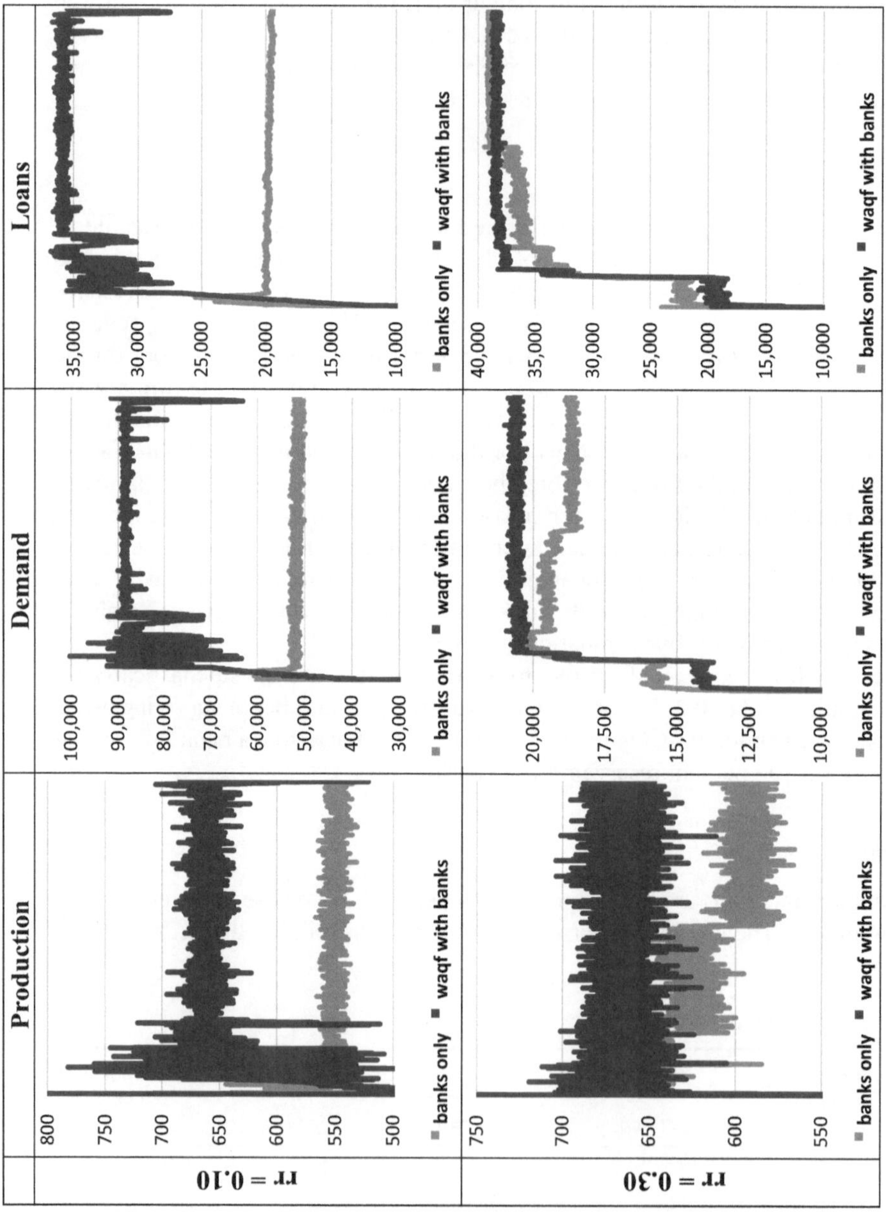

Figure 6.9 Production, total demand, and loans with respect to reserve ratio

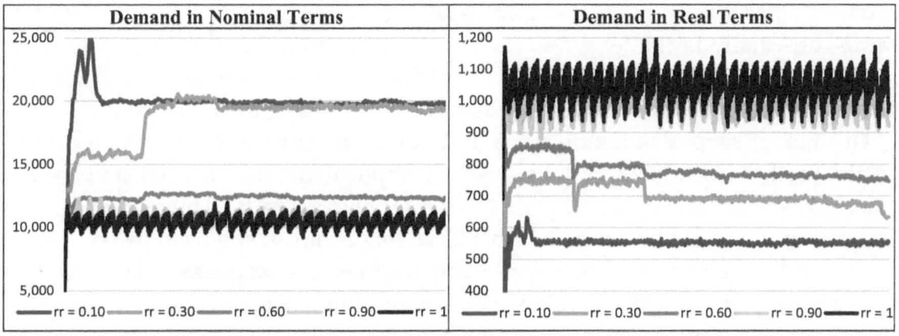

Figure 6.10 Demand in nominal and real terms

demand because the loan amount is a stock variable which shows previously borrowed and not yet repaid loans cumulatively. However, demand is a flow variable determined in each period repeatedly and does not cumulate.

The linear relationship between demand and production is more obvious when the reserve ratio is 0.1. Production stabilizes around 400 in quantity, because, as we said before, households need to have a demand of at least two quantities. This shows us a great majority of households are now poor.

We added benevolence results in 0.3 reserve ratio figures to make a comparison. Benevolence increases the demand both for consumption and loans. Though the total amounts of loans are equalized for with and without *waqf* around 500th round, demand goes down at the same time for non-*waqf* mode. The reason is that more people become poor as they borrow more, and they have to change their consumption patterns in a less spending way.

Figure 6.10 shows us how money illusion can lead us to misinterpretations. As the reserve ratio gets smaller, nominal demand gets larger, whereas reality is exactly the opposite. In the same direction with the right side of Figure 6.10, we expected less demand as the reserve ratio goes down and people get poorer.

Conclusion

We, in this empirical study, have simulated an agent-based model to show the superiority of full reserve banking over the fractional reserve banking system. Our model incorporated a credit market, interbank market, and market for consumption goods. We defined three types of agents with simple behavioural rules and added an alternative procedure, namely benevolence mode, to see how changing behaviours according to Islamic considerations affect the system.

The minimum reserve ratio is used as the key varying-parameter, assuming five different values. We found simulation results quite supportive of the case against the fractional reserve system. We showed how a fractional reserve banking system creates money without any costs while enjoying the interest gain through lending, and further, interest facilitates wealth transfer in the economy with no value creation. In other words, interest is a zero-sum game for the economy with serious harms, especially in the long run. In sum, it can be said that a fractional reserve system causes an imbalance in income distribution, a decrease in production and demand for consumption, and, consequently, destabilization in the economy.

This model is good at telling the story but may be criticized for being too simplistic. Further work incorporating a more complicated model is needed to have a more realistic setting. First, the price level might be determined by market forces. Second, equity might be defined for banks so that banks would be allowed to lend more, but they also would be constrained with capital adequacy rules. Third, a bank run procedure can be developed by determining the confidence level criteria for households. Finally, considering the situation of Islamic banks, interest rates (or profit rates) could take ex-post values instead of ex-ante values; that is, they can be determined endogenously from the interactions of the model itself.

Notes

1 Basically, the money multiplier is equal to the inverse of the reserve ratio value. Here, the money multiplier is the inverse of 0.25 (1/4), which is 4. That means $100 coins multiplied by 4; we would have $400 in total.
2 See: www.investopedia.com/terms/p/price_stickiness.asp

References

Ahmad, Z. & A.G. Ismail. (2017). Full reserve system and the Maqasid Shariah. *Journal of Emerging Economies & Islamic Research*, 5(2), pp. 58–66.

Akin, T. & M.H. Dolgun. (2015). The Chicago plan from the lenses of Islamic finance: Implications for financial stability and indebtedness. *International Journal of Islamic Economics and Finance Studies*, 1(2).

Benes, J. & M. Kumhof. (2012). The Chicago plan revisited. *IMF Working Paper*. Washington, DC.

Brown, E.H. (2008). *Web of Debt: The Shocking Truth about Our Money System and How We Can Break Free*. Baton Rouge, LA: Third Millennium Press.

Chamley, C. et al. (2012). Limited-purpose banking-moving from "trust me" to "show me" banking. Retrieved from www.aeaweb.org/aea/2012conference/program/retrieve.php?pdfid=568

Chan-Lau, J.A. (2017). ABBA: An agent-based model of the banking system. *IMF Working Paper*. WP/17/136. Retrieved from www.imf.org/en/Publications/WP/Issues/2017/06/09/ABBA-An-Agent-Based-Model-of-the-Banking-System-44916

Diwany, T. (2003). *The Problem with Interest*. London: Kreatoc

Dixhoorn, C. Van. (2013). *Full Reserve Banking: An Analysis of Four Monetary Reform Plans*. Utrecht, The Netherlands: A study for the Sustainable Finance Lab.

Dyson, B. (2012). *Full-Reserve Banking*. London: Positive Money.

Dyson, B. et al. (2016). *Sovereign Money: An Introduction*. London: Positive Money.

Ferguson, N. (2011). *The Ascent of Money: A Financial History of the World*. Trans. Barış Pala. İstanbul: Yapı Kredi Yayınları.

Fisher, I. (2009). *100% Money and the Public Debt*. Economic Forum. 1st ed. in 1936, rev. ed. Pakthongchai: ThaiSunset Publications. Digital Edition.

Goodhart, Charles & Meinhard Jensen. (2015). Currency school versus banking school: An ongoing confrontation. *Economic Thought*, 4(2). Retrieved from http://eprints.lse.ac.uk/id/eprint/64068

Hayek, F.A. (1989). *Monetary Nationalism and International Stability*. London: Longmans, 1937. Reprinted in Augustus M. Kelley: Fairfield, N.J.

Huerta de Soto, J. (2009). *Money, Bank Credit, and Economic Cycles*. 2nd ed. Alabama: Ludwig von Mises Institute.

Kay, J. (2009). Narrow banking: The reform of banking regulation. *CSFI Report*, London.

Kotlikoff, J. L. (2012). *The Economic Consequences of the Vickers Commission*. London: Civitas; Institute for the Study of Civil Society.

Laina, P. (2015). Proposals for full-reserve banking: A historical survey from David Ricardo to Martin Wolf. *Economic Thought, World Economics Association*, 4(2), pp. 1–19.

Lengnick, M. (2011). Agent-based macroeconomics: A baseline model. *Economics Working Paper, Christian-Albrechts-Universität Kiel. Department of Economics*. No: 2011-04. Retrieved from http://hdl.handle.net/10419/45012

Mallett, J. (2015). Threadneedle: An experimental tool for the simulation and analysis of fractional reserve banking systems. Retrieved from https://ideas.repec.org/p/arx/papers/1502.06163.html

Mises, L.V. (1953). *The Theory of Money and Credit*. Trans. H.E. Batson. North Haven: Yale University Press.

Monett, D. & J.E. Navarro-Barrientos. (2016). Simulating the fractional reserve banking using agent-based modelling with NetLogo. *2016 Federated Conference on Computer Science and Information Systems (FedCSIS)*, pp. 1467–1470. Retrieved from https://annals-csis.org/proceedings/2016/pliks/373.pdf

Pennacchi, G. (2012). Narrow banking. *Annual Review of Financial Economics*, 4, Retrieved from SSRN: https://ssrn.com/abstract=2170927 or http://dx.doi.org/10.1146/annurev-financial-110311-101758

Ricardo, D. (1824). *Plan for the Establishment of a National Bank*. London: John Murray.

Rothbard, M.N. (2001). *The Case for a 100 Percent Gold Dollar*. Cambridge, MA: Harvard University Press, 1962. Reprinted in Ludwig von Mises Institute: Auburn, Alabama.

Wilensky, U. (1998). *NetLogo Bank Reserves Model*. Center for Connected Learning and Computer-Based Modeling, Northwestern University, Evanston, IL. Retrieved from http://ccl.northwestern.edu/netlogo/models/BankReserves

7 Monetary policy and Islamic banking

Key challenges

Sajjad Zaheer

Introduction

Monetary policy refers to "the actions undertaken by a central bank to influence the availability and cost of money and credit to help promote national economic goals" (Federal Reserve Board).[1] These actions refer to using monetary policy instruments, namely the policy rate, reserve requirements, monetary base, etc. Through these actions total volume (monetary aggregates) and price (cost) of money and credit are controlled to achieve the final goals of the stabilization policy, specifically price stability, low unemployment, and economic growth. Figure 7.1 illustrates the mechanism of monetary policy.

The objectives of monetary policy in the Islamic financial system, as described by Islamic economists, are preservation of the value of money through ensuring price stability, economic well-being with full employment, an optimum rate of economic growth, and promotion of distributive justice. Al-Jarhi (1983) emphasizes saving the value of money as a policy objective and proposes expansion of the money supply only if it contributes to real growth. Chapra (1996) also points out that stability in the value of currency should be maintained to avoid the harmful socio-economic effects of inflation. Ariff (1982) comments that the number of objectives should be equal to the number of policy tools available (the Meade-Tinbergen principle) and distributive justice should be addressed through fiscal policy.[2]

Most Islamic economists agree that central banks in an Islamic framework need to perform all the main functions which are carried out in the conventional system. In this regard, the role of the central bank related to regulation and supervision of the financial sector in an Islamic financial system is performed mostly in the way it is done in conventional banking.

Central banks use various direct and indirect monetary policy tools to achieve their goals. Direct tools comprise price restrictions through limits on interest rate, quantity restrictions via credit ceilings, and moral suasion, whereas indirect or market-based instruments include open market operations, a reserve requirement, and use of interest rates. These tools are essential for the transmission of monetary stances. It is therefore important to have alternative tools which are congruent with an Islamic financial system. Direct tools of monetary policy can also be used

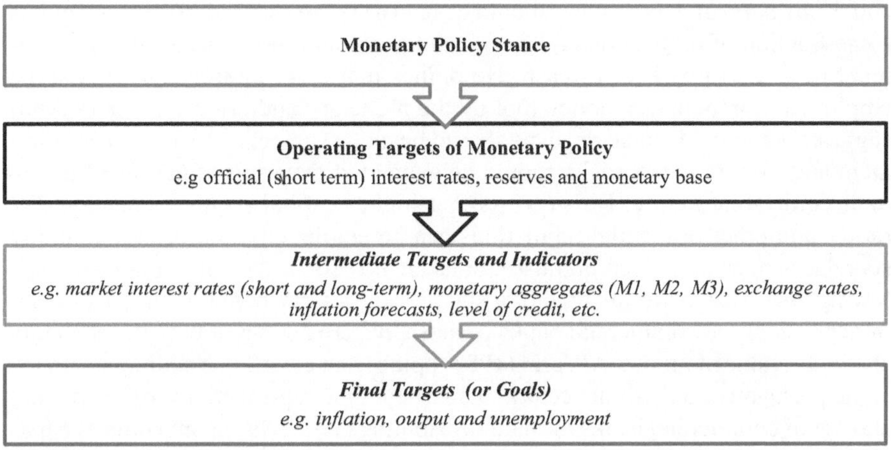

Figure 7.1 The mechanism of monetary policy

effectively in an Islamic financial system in the same manner these are employed in the conventional system. Some modifications, however, are needed in the contemporary system of open market operations and discount rate policy, as these are incompatible with shariah, mainly due to the involvement of interest and repurchase agreements (repos).

The aim of this chapter is to examine monetary policy in an interest-free system proposed by Islamic economists in theory and how it is practically implemented by the central banks of some Muslim countries. Moreover, it also suggests some policy tools for the implementation of monetary policy in an interest-free environment.

The rest of the chapter is organized as follows. The second section explains conventional monetary policy instruments and alternatives proposed by Islamic economists, the third notes the practice regarding use of monetary policy tools for an Islamic banking industry in various jurisdictions, and the fourth offers some potential solutions for interest-free monetary policy tools. Finally, the fifth section concludes the chapter.

Monetary policy tools

Statutory reserve requirement

Commercial banks are required to hold a certain fraction of their deposit as reserves at the central bank. Through this tool, a central bank ensures that banks maintain an adequate level of liquidity to meet their short-term obligations. The supply of money is also controlled by the central banks through manoeuvring required reserve ratios. There exists a difference of opinion among Islamic economists regarding the *types* of deposits that should be subject to the reserve requirement and the *fraction* of deposits that should be held as reserves. Siddiqi (1983) requires some fraction of both demand deposits and profit and loss sharing (PLS) investment deposits to be kept as cash. He opines that this requirement can also be employed as a monetary policy tool by the monetary authorities. Chapra (1983) suggests that only demand deposits should be made subject to the reserve requirement and investment deposits should be exempted from this requirement due to their equity-like nature. He suggests that higher capital requirement, liquidity ratios, and other prudential regulations can be employed to ensure the liquidity soundness of Islamic banking institutions (IBIs). Some Islamic economists, following the Chicago school, call for a 100 percent reserve requirement on all types of deposits of the commercial banks because this creates stability in the economy and in the value of money. Al-Jarhi (1983) opines that creation of additional money is the prerogative only of the central bank (being the representative of the public) and not of commercial banks through distributing credit. As in conventional banking, this stance is not followed by the central banks for the Islamic banking industry because in such a case commercial banking is reduced to safekeeping. Chapra (1983) proposes that a certain proportion (25 percent) of commercial bank demand deposits should be given to the government free of cost for socially beneficial projects, as it would benefit the whole society. Ariff (1982) also supports the idea, as it would shift the benefits of public money to the public in a broader perspective.

Open market operations

Conventionally, open market operations (OMOs) of a central bank refer to sale and purchase of interest-bearing government securities with an objective to affect money supply and interest rates.[3] In the case of a liquid market, the central bank absorbs the liquidity through an open market sale of government securities based on a repurchase agreement (repo). On the other hand, in the event of liquidity shortage, the central bank buys the securities from the market to inject liquidity using repo. In an Islamic financial system, a central bank cannot use the option of open market operations through repos since the institution of interest and sale and buy-back contract or repo is banned in IBF.

Uzair (1982), therefore, proposes that this monetary policy tool needs to be replaced to achieve the objectives of monetary policy. He suggests that central bank can use shares of public sector enterprises and corporations for trading related to open market auditions. The idea is criticized on the account that trading in the shares of public sector enterprises would cause instability in the prices of the shares of the relevant companies. Zangeneh and Salam (1993) present a similar idea with some additions: The central bank may use a "composite stock" which represents its ownership in public enterprises and shares in public banks instead of trading in shares of individual companies. Trading in composite stock, in their view, does not affect the prices of individual enterprises. However, the volume of these stocks may not be sufficient for required open market operations. Moreover, according to Uzair (1978), treasury bills may be continued only if "normal service charges" or "administrative costs" might be applied out of three components of interest, namely basic rate of interest, risk premium, and administrative expenses. But it may be difficult to decompose the three elements and may render a time inconsistency problem because the central bank can manipulate the said composition of interest to have some discretion. The author also suggests *weighted average of profitability* of government enterprises for the rate of return on the government securities. However, in developing countries, the public sector enterprises usually face governance issues and therefore are less efficient than the private sector, and mostly incur losses. Thus, to build the confidence of the investors, all the factors contributing to losses of these enterprises should be done away with.

Siddiqi (1967) proposes the idea of issuing commercial shares (of public enterprises) by the government, which can be used in OMOs. The holders of the stocks share profit/loss of the public enterprises and can sell these shares in a secondary market. The idea is similar to what is suggested by Uzair (1982). Chapra (1996) criticizes this proposal because of the limited depth of the commercial shares and significant movements in the prices of the commercial shares due to which holders of the shares may be affected.[4] Haque and Mirakhor (1998) presents the scheme of issuing a *National Participation Paper* (NPP) by the government which can be used to finance government operations and to conduct OMOs. The rate of return on NPP is the approximated payoff on underlying assets of the government. Al-Jarhi (1983) proposes issuance of central deposit certificates by the central bank to attract savings from the public on PLS basis. A central bank then invests these proceeds by opening deposits on a PLS basis in all commercial banks. Profits realized on these deposit would be shared with the holders of the certificates. Money supply can be controlled through variations in these PLS accounts of the central bank in commercial banks.

Discount rate

The discount rate is the rate at which commercial banks get collateralized, borrowing from the central bank on a relatively higher rate than the market. The discount rate is an important indicator of the monetary stance of the central bank: a high discount rate represents tight monetary policy and a low discount rate reflects a loose monetary stance. Through the discount rate policy, the central bank regulates the *credit supply* in the economy as well as performs its role as a *lender of last resort*. Developing an alternative to the discount rate is a major challenge in Islamic financial systems, as the same instrument cannot be used for monetary policy. Some alternatives are proposed by Islamic economists. Uzair (1982) suggests that to affect money supply a central bank may regulate the profit sharing ratio (PSR) of *mudarabah* contracts, both between the IBIs and their depositors (depositors' share ratio) and between IBIs and their clients (investors' share ratio). He elaborates that changes in the depositors' share ratio would affect the supply of money and adjustments in the investors' share ratio would affect economic activity. Credit can be reduced by decreasing the share in profit accruing to the entrepreneurs and eased by increasing the share. Also, he states that these ratios may differ across various sectors according to social preferences. According to the author, the authority of the central bank to control the PSR would be akin to controlling "bank rate". Siddiqi (1982) and Khan (1982) also support the suggestion. Chapra (1996), however, does not agree with the proposal and opines that profit-sharing ratios should be set by the bank and business enterprises bilaterally according to the market conditions. Ariff (1982) favours the idea of utilizing PSRs if these are applied to only new deposits that are opened after the policy announcement. Siddiqi (2006) suggests that PSRs can be used as a signal to the market about the monetary policy stance of the central bank. Uzair (1982) also suggests that the central bank may hold some equity share (25 percent) in commercial banks, in contrast to the Fed, where the capital of Fed is owned by the commercial banks.[5] He mentions three advantages of this proposal for a central bank: (i) it will have a permanent source of income to play its role as lender of last resort effectively, (ii) it will have its representation on the board of the commercial banks, which increases their compliance to the regulations of a central bank, and (iii) it will have a stake in the development of commercial banks. Although he does not explain the link between this provision and the central bank's role as lender of last resort, he might have a view that a central bank can increase equity stake in the banks or provide interest-free loans with some service charges if they need liquidity. Zangeneh and Salam (1993) criticize this idea because of the potential conflict of interest between a central bank's role as a regulator and as an owner of commercial banks.

Zangneh and Salam (1993) recommend charging a *weighted average rate of return* of various sectors of the economy, with some discretionary premium to discourage borrowing from the central bank if the economy is facing inflation. For easy monetary policy, they suggest, the central bank could provide a subsidy (discretionary discount) to the banks to boost the economy in a recession. They defend their argument for fixed policy rate because even though the central bank and the borrowing commercial bank know exactly what the policy premium or discount is, since the profit rate of the economy is not known at the time, the overall rate is uncertain, therefore shari'ah is not violated.

However, shariah also requires that return should be attached to the performance of the underlying real assets or stocks in some venture. Moreover, charging a *fixed* premium above the GDP growth may not be acceptable to the Islamic economists due to its similarity to an interest rate. On the other hand, Ahmad (2000) suggests that loans may be provided to commercial banks to face a liquidity shortage on *Qard-e-Hasana* (interest-free loans) basis with or without a service charge.

Siddiqi (1982) proposes that the central bank may refinance some ratio of the interest-free loans given by the IBIs. This ratio, called the *refinance ratio*, can be used to affect the volume of short-term loans. In case of expansionary monetary policy, the refinance ratio may be increased, and the opposite may be done in case of tight monetary policy. He further suggests that banks should be obliged to lend some ratio, called a lending ratio, of their demand deposits as interest-free loans. This ratio can be manipulated by the central bank to affect the credit supply in various circumstances. Similar thoughts are presented by Ariff (1982) and Khan (1982). Chapra (1996) recommends mobilizing government deposits in banks to or from the banks to influence money supply, and he cited the example of Saudi Arabia. Moreover, he also proposes to make a "common pool" for the commercial banks at the central bank level and using the same to meet the liquidity requirement of the banks based on "cooperative arrangements". Net use of this facility by any bank over a given period is zero.

Othman and Mirakhor (2014) suggest that government could issue macro-market instruments such as equity shares in some projects to get non-interest rate-based financing while promoting risk sharing. *Equity participation shares* provide participation in financing of government expenditure, such as in *development projects*. The authors propose that these securities must have low denominations and be traded in secondary markets so that ordinary citizens—not just institutional investors—can have access to them. Mirakhor (2012) thinks that these instruments can hedge the idiosyncratic risks of households and firms provided that the same are issued in low denominations and sold in the retail market. They recommend that the rate of return on these shares can be benchmarked against the average rate of return of the stock exchange or the return on the real sector of the economy.

Askari and Krichene (2014) propose that governments may opt for equity financing of infrastructure projects in the form of public-private partnerships (PPP). They also consider investment deposits/certificates to be traded in the secondary market, such as certificates of deposit (CDs), and the central bank can buy and sell these deposits from the investors to affect the liquidity, apart from purchase and sale of the bank's equity. Thus, the authors think that the central bank, by buying and selling risk sharing securities/deposits or equity of the IBIs, can directly affect the financial portfolio of the private sector, and indirectly by affecting the holdings of banks that in turn affect real economic activity. The authors also suggest that for lender of last resort facility the central bank could charge an Islamic bank the rate of return equivalent to the rate of return of the real sector. Alternatively, they opine, the central bank may also buy the assets of the Islamic bank that needs financing.

Practice of central banks regarding interest-free monetary policy

Like Islamic commercial banking, central banking practice is also different from what is suggested in theory. A number of amendments are needed in the legal framework of a country to develop shariah-compliant monetary policy instruments. International Islamic Financial Markets (2009) notice the lack of shariah-compliant monetary policy framework in the countries experiencing rapid growth in Islamic banking. This scarcity of monetary policy instruments limits the monetary policy operations for the Islamic banking segment of a country having a significant share of Islamic banking. Also, there is no clear mechanism for interest-free standing credit facilities for the IBIs. This situation creates difficulties in the liquidity management of IBIs. Consequently, IBIs keep excess reserves to meet any unanticipated liquidity shock.

To solve liquidity management issue, one popular method adopted by the IBIs is commodity *murabahah* combined with *tawarruq* (monetization) in interbank transactions. This mechanism can be understood through a simple hypothetical example. Bank A needs US$100 million and approaches Bank B, which has excess liquidity. Bank B buys a commodity, platinum, for instance,[6] of US$100 million from the broker and sells it to Bank A on deferred payment, charging some markup, say, a price of US$110 million. The amount is generally paid by Bank A to Bank B in periodic instalments. To liquefy the commodity, Bank A sells the same to the broker at US$100 million. The net result is the creation of debt obligation of Bank A in favour of Bank B. However, the complex structure of the transaction makes it more costly than simple interest-based lending in conventional banks. The practice has been condemned by various scholars, who believe that commodity *murabahah* is merely an avoidance of shariah.

IBIs also use interbank placement of funds on *mudarabah (*cum *musharakah)* and *wakalah* basis to meet liquidity requirements. In this method, a liquidity abundant Islamic bank places its funds as an investor with an illiquid Islamic bank on *mudarabah* basis that acts as a *mudarib*. The *mudarib* invests these funds in some profitable avenue, for example, purchase of government *sukuk*. Both the banks share in profit of the business depending on the profit-sharing ratios which are set ex-ante. The loss is borne proportionally if the *mudarib* also mingles its own funds in the investment pool. The profit-sharing ratio among banks may vary subject to the credibility of the illiquid banks.[7] *Wakalah* is an agency agreement in which one person appoints the other to perform a certain task on her behalf with mutually agreed terms and conditions, generally against a certain *wakalah* (agency) fee.

In resolving liquidity problem, the emergence of *sukuk* in money markets has been an important innovation. Fixed return instruments like *ijarah*, *murabahah*, and *salam sukuk* are issued by central banks and governments. In *ijarah sukuk*, government sells an identified asset to financial institutions and in another agreement takes the same asset back on lease. Rentals are paid to the *sukuk* holders periodically. On maturity of the *sukuk*, investors receive the amount equal to the face value of the *sukuk*.[8] In *salam* the central bank buys some commodity in forward (through advance payment and deferred delivery) and then sells the same commodity in forward to the IBIs. As the maturity date approaches, the central bank sells the same commodity on behalf of the banks with a promise to pay a higher price than their purchase price, which becomes an obligation on the part of the central bank/ government.

The mechanism for *murabahah sukuk* is the same as described for interbank transactions earlier. As the sale of debt is prohibited in *shariah*, *murabahah* and *salam sukuk* are not eligible for the secondary market transactions being debt securities. *Ijarah sukuk*, therefore, have gained popularity due to their eligibility for secondary market trading. However, the lack of *sukuk* issuance renders liquidity management by the IBIs inefficient. This scenario limits the transmission mechanism of monetary policy through IBIs because they keep excess reserves to avoid liquidity shortage in the contractionary phase of monetary policy (Zaheer, Ongena and van Wijnbergen (2013).

Sudan and Iran transformed their entire financial system according to Islamic principles, whereas South-East Asian and Gulf Cooperation Council (GCC) states introduced Islamic banking side by side with conventional banking. The countries mentioned later chose a market-based approach for Islamic banking and let the market forces decide the future prospects of Islamic banking through demonstration of their preferences. The Central Bank of Sudan (CBOS) introduced an *interest-free overdraft* facility for banks in liquidity problems *for 10 days*, but after that period CBOS would share in the profit of the banks. In November 1997, the first Islamic security was approved in Sudan, called the Central Bank *Musharakah* Certificate (CMC), which is an equity instrument and issued against ownership of the central bank *ownership in nine commercial banks and public sector enterprises* (Elhiraika, 2004). Holders of the CMC share the profit of the central bank derived from its operations, such as clearance fees, foreign exchange operations, dividend income from its share in commercial banks, and profits from credit to banks and public. For its monetary operations, CBOS currently uses Central Bank *Ijarah* Certificates (*Shihab*), Government *Musharaka* Certificates (*Shahama*), and Government Investment *Sukuk* (GIS) based on *ijarah*, *musharakah*, and *mudarabah*, respectively. *Shahama sukuk* are based on a *musharakah* contract, issued to investors against a financial pool that consists of government ownership in certain companies. These *sukuk* are also traded on the Khartoum Stock Exchange. The CBOS also provides financial support to IBIs facing temporary liquidity difficulties through purchase of financial papers (*sukuk*). The holders of *shahama* are entitled to the share in profit of the underlying corporations. Suggestions were also made to raise funds for the government through issuing *sukuk* that promise a return to the investor, which is associated with the (tax) revenue of the government against providing public goods such as security, foreign relations, legal, and arbitration. It can also be stated that government securities in the conventional financial system also show claims to future revenues of the government. However, the key difference lies in how claims are defined in the relevant documents of the underlying instrument. Government Musharakah Certificates is currently not practiced in Sudan.

The Central Bank of Iran (CBI) developed a National Participation Paper (NPP) to finance the state expenditure to be used in open market operations. Also, CBI controls the volume of money by issuing NPP backed by state-funded projects. These papers are based on *musharakah*, and their return is tied to the performance of a composite of stock market securities. Moreover, CBI is allowed to intervene in determining the profit rates of banks for investment projects or partnerships. The provisional profit rate of CBI's participation papers is determined up to two percentage points higher than the provisional profit rate of other deposits. Regarding the discount rate policy, banks are allowed to open a special deposit account (ODA) with the CBI in which they deposit their *excess* liquidity for a specific profit determined by CBI.

In late 1983, Bank Negara Malaysia (BNM) took the initiative and issued the first *sukuk* called Government Investment Certificates (GIC). Holders of GIC give interest-free loans (*Qard-e-Hasana*) to the government. However, the government would give some return to them unilaterally as a gift or as an act of benevolence. In 2001, Government Investment Issue (GII) was issued on the basis of a sell and buy back agreement (SBBA), which is akin to a repo agreement. According to this contract, the Malaysian government sells its specific asset on a pre-agreed cash price to the financial institutions and then buys back the same assets from them at a higher price to be paid in future. The purchase price is securitized in the form of GII issued to financial institutions. At maturity, government pays the purchase price to GII holders in exchange for securities.[9] Further, to address the demand for Islamic instruments, BNM issued the first asset-backed *ijarah sukuk* in February 2006 using a securitization-type structure for the amount of about US$110 million (Bank Negara Malesia, 2006). Moreover, to meet the liquidity requirements of IBIs, an Islamic Interbank Money Market (IIMM) was introduced in 1994. Deficit banks can get funds from surplus banks on the basis of *mudarabah*.

In 2012, to add diversity to the existing liquidity management and promote greater liquidity in the Islamic financial market, BNM introduced a new Islamic money market instrument called collateralized *murabahah*. The instrument was initially launched by the central bank of the UAE. The instrument is a shariah-compliant financing secured by some assets. It is a hybrid of *murabahah* financing and *sukuk* as pledged assets to back the transaction to get a *murabahah* financing facility from the BNM.[10] The mechanism can be used by IBIs to obtain funds from the BNM under the standing facility and from the interbank money market as well. The financier has an option to sell the asset if the issuer defaults. For standing facility, BNM uses short-term instrument commodity *murbahah* and *wadiah* placements to control the liquidity in the market. In the latter, BNM absorbs liquidity by taking deposits from IBIs as a trustee. The principle amount is guaranteed by the BNM. For intraday credit facility, BNM gives a credit line to the member IBIs for a period less than one day. The facility can be availed by pledging eligible securities as collateral. There is no cost involved other than very minimal administrative charges.

The Central Bank of Bahrain (CBB) is empowered to issue securities on behalf of the government through a special law called CBB Law 2006. Mainly two types of *sukuk* are issued, *salam sukuk* and *ijarah sukuk*. The former securities are issued on a monthly basis for a three-month maturity period, whereas the latter are issued for maturity of six months or longer, on a fixed return basis. In *salam* structure, the government of Bahrain, being a seller of the underlying commodity (aluminium), undertakes to deliver the commodity to the investors at the maturity of the *sukuk* period (three months). Since *sukuk* are issued on the basis of a *salam* (advance payment) contract, the investors pay the *sukuk* amount in advance. As the maturity date arrives, the government, being an agent of investors, sells the same commodity on behalf of the banks to some brokers in the market. As an agent, the government guarantees a purchase price plus some markup that is initially disclosed to the investors.

In Indonesia, IBIs can obtain financing from Bank Indonesia through a short-term shariah-compliant financing (FPJPS). This facility is based on a *mudarabah* contract and is typically used as a last resort facility, where an Islamic bank may obtain short-term financing against collateral. The return of this financing is linked to the *mudarabah* deposit rate of the recipient bank.

The State Bank of Pakistan held the first auction of long-awaited government *ijarah sukuk* in 2008 to cater to the demand for a liquidity instrument by the Islamic banking industry. To date, *ijarah sukuk* has been proven a successful alternative to interest-based government securities. During the first phase of Islamic banking in 1980, SBP was allowed to buy and sell Partnership Term Certificates (PTA) issued by the Investment Corporation of Pakistan, a public enterprise, and banker's equity limited. An alternative to discount rate policy has yet to be developed for Islamic banking. In October 2014, to facilitate the liquidity management of the Islamic banking industry, the SBP started outright purchase of the Government of *Pakistan Ijara Sukuk* (GIS) on a deferred payment (*Bai-Muajjal*) basis. Subsequently, SBP sells these *sukuk* through auction-based OMOs in the ready market. This mechanism of outright purchase on a deferred payment basis helps the IBIs increase the duration of their investment in GIS even after the maturity of these *sukuk*. Efforts are being made to provide a financier of last resort solution to the Islamic banking industry of Pakistan.

Some potential solutions

This section offers some potential solutions to monetary management by the central bank. Option 1 is relatively easier to be implemented by a central bank with a dual banking system such as Malaysia, GCC countries, Turkey, Pakistan, etc.

1 **Open Market Operations:** The most common *sukuk* that pay a fixed return and are also tradable in the secondary market are *ijarah sukuk*. However, the supply of these *sukuk* is not adequate relative to the market appetite. Naturally, the suggestion is to the volume and frequency of issuing *ijarah sukuk*. In this connection, the main task is identification of government-owned assets that can be used for leasing purpose. Consequently, interbank money markets would also become efficient, as the *ijarah sukuk* can also be used as reliable collateral. Since every *ijarah sukuk* should be backed by a specific underlying asset, there is a maximum limit to the assets to be used for *sukuk* issuance, constraining the budget deficit in affordable limits.

   As repo is not allowed in IBF, it is suggested that outright sale and purchase of government *ijarah sukuk* can be employed for open market operations that may be called Islamic open market operations (IOMO). The Federal Reserve (Fed) also uses this mechanism and conducts outright sale and purchase of government securities.[11] However, in contrast to repos, outright transactions are employed to inject or absorb liquidity for longer time periods. Following the example of BNM, *Wadiah* deposits can also be accepted by the central bank to absorb liquidity from the IBIs.

2 **Profit-sharing Ratio**: So far, the proposal for PSR has been discussed in the framework suggested by Uzair (1982), in the context of depositors' share ratio and investors' share ratio and considered as analogous to changing bank rate. It is suggested that PSR of the *mudarabah* (cum *musharakah*)

contract between the central bank and the IBIs may be used as a policy stance and monetary policy tool. For example, if the central bank wants to pursue a tight monetary policy, the PSR ratio between the central bank and the IBIs for *mudarabah*-based financing to the IBIs can be set high, say 80:20. On the other hand, the central bank can decrease PSR to follow an expansionary monetary policy. These stances would be transmitted to the real economy through its impact on PSR set between the IBIs and the depositors and investors and their clients. As the financer of last resort, the central bank may also provide funds to the IBI by investing in the general *mudarabah* pool of the IBI. Special weightages may be given to the central bank's investment while calculating its return in the general pool.

3 **Equity Shares in Government Projects:** One possibility to fund the government budget deficit owing to various developmental projects for the government can be to issue securities which do not offer fixed interest rate but instead offer return linked to the annual growth rate of nominal gross domestic product (Karsten, 1982; Buiter, 2009).[12] It is proposed that these securities should represent the equity participation in the infrastructural projects of the government such as roads, dams, power plants, schools, and hospitals. Since the rate of return for most of these projects is difficult to determine precisely, at least in initial stages, the nominal GDP growth rate can be a reasonable proxy for the rate of return on these projects. Usmani (2007) also discusses this proposal to finance public debt. Othman and Mirakhor (2014) float the idea of issuing equity participation for deficit financing. These shares provide participation in the financing of government expenditure, such as development projects. Mirakhor (2012) thinks that these instruments can hedge the idiosyncratic risks of households and firms provided that the same are issued in low denominations and sold in the retail market. They suggest the rate of return on these shares can be benchmarked against the average rate of return of the stock exchange or the return on the real sector of the economy. Askari and Krichene (2014) propose that governments may opt for equity financing of infrastructure projects in the form of public-private partnerships (PPP). In this mechanism, the rate of remuneration for security holders would not be fixed and predetermined but variable, as Islamic principles require. Moreover, since the return on government security corresponds to the performance of the overall economy, the same is therefore more justified than a fixed interest rate. The return on these securities, which is a cost of financing for the government, increases in the expansionary phase of the business cycle and decreases in recession. GDP-linked debt thus has a countercyclical impact (i.e., it dampens the cyclical movements in GDP) by entailing a smaller amount for interest payments when the economy performs poorly, offering space for higher government spending and fewer taxes. Moreover, the probability of financial distress through issuing these *sukuk* is minimized by letting the debt-service ratio to fall during the recessionary phase of business cycle. The aforesaid pricing criterion can also be used as a benchmark for other government *sukuk* as well.

A requisite for these securities is the accuracy and transparency in calculation of the GDP growth rate.[13] Issues related to revisions in the GDP estimates can be resolved by creating a reserve account which can be used to settle differences in various GDP estimates. This pricing mechanism would also discipline the government to keep inflation within reasonable limits, because otherwise it has to pay a high return to the holders of that instrument. Argentina in 2002 and Greece during the recent sovereign debt crisis issued a GDP-indexed bond which is also in accordance with IBF doctrines because returns on any general government security should correspond to the performance of the overall economy.

Since accuracy and transparency is needed in calculating the GDP growth rate, the idea is more suitable for advanced and well-documented economies. Moreover, since these *sukuk* have equity-like features, the same can be traded in the secondary market and can be used for open market operations and collateral purposes. A financial system based on equity and thus a risk-sharing basis has more potential to absorb cyclical and external shocks because the losses of the banks can be passed on to the depositors.

Conclusion

Islamic banking coexist in many jurisdictions with conventional banks. Although the share of Islamic banking in these countries is still low, it is increasing with a brisk growth. Despite rapid growth, the Islamic banking industry faces problems related to liquidity management, monetary policy instruments, standardization of financial products, cost inefficiencies, shariah-compliance, and development of interbank and money markets. The lack of monetary management framework for the Islamic segment of the financial industry may hamper the monetary policy transmission through the Islamic banking industry.

The most important job to be done is to ensure the ample issuance of suitable interest-free government securities (*sukuk*) in which IBIs can invest their excess liquidity. Second, there is demand for developing a mechanism for standing credit facilities by the central bank which can be drawn on in a distress situation. Absence of these facilities along with inefficient Islamic interbank and money markets creates liquidity management problems for IBIs. Thus, to meet any unforeseen liquidity shock, these banks hold costly excess reserves which render IBIs inefficient. IBIs, in turn, include these costs while pricing their financing products. Therefore, a higher markup rate on Islamic financing may render IBIs less competitive vis-à-vis other market players. Some countries like Malaysia and Bahrain have addressed the issue of liquidity management by developing an Islamic interbank money market. However, their main instruments are not accepted in other regions from the shariah viewpoint.

The study offers some potential solutions for the issues related to liquidity and monetary management of the Islamic banking industry. The problems related to instruments can be resolved through increasing the volume and frequency of *ijarah sukuk* to match the demand for these instruments. Since these *sukuk* are also eligible for trading in the secondary market, the same will help in developing an efficient interbank market and open market operation mechanism. *Musharakah* and *Mudarabah sukuk* may be issued against infrastructural projects of the government such as roads, dams, power plants, schools, and hospitals; the return on these *sukuk* can be linked to the GDP of the country. Similarly, *salam* can be issued against the agriculture products employing the services of government procurement organizations. A national mutual fund can be created which can act as a special purpose vehicle.

More deliberations of shariah scholars, practitioners, and economists are needed on the issue of the central bank role as a financer of last resort.

Notes

1 The Federal Reserve System, United States, Monetary Policy. www.federalreserve.gov/monetarypolicy/fomc.htm
2 Indirectly, instability in the value of money also affects distributive justice in the sense that it deteriorates the purchasing power of the poor relative to the rich.
3 These operations are based on a sale and repurchase (repo) basis to absorb the liquidity and purchase and resale (reverse repo) to inject liquidity into the market.
4 The market for a stock is "deep" if there is enough volume of pending orders for the buying (bid) and selling (ask) side, preventing large movements in the price.
5 Also see section 5 of the Federal Reserve Act.
6 Government *Ijarah sukuk* are also used for this purpose. In that case, an illiquid bank buys the *sukuk* from a liquid bank on deferred payment basis and sells the same in a ready market.
7 There are practical difficulties to calculate overnight profit rates of the IBIs if the funds are invested on a *musharakah* or *mudarabah* basis in some venture. Since profits are generally not known ex-ante, some proxies for current returns would have to be found, or the lenders could be compensated retroactively (Ingo Karsten, "Islam and Financial Intermediation," in *Staff Papers-International Monetary Fund* (Washington DC1982)).
8 In principle, investors should get the market price of *sukuk* in accordance with the market price of the underlying *sukuk* assets. However, there is no pricing mechanism for the underlying assets. In fact, no market exists for the *sukuk* assets in which these assets are bought and sold. However, the value of the underlying assets can be determined only through valuation by a third party, which is not practiced for sovereign *sukuk* in which the underlying assets are public.
9 The scholars from Gulf Cooperation Council and other countries consider the buy-back contract prohibited in Islam because it is two contracts in one contract.
10 BNM (2012). Introduction of Collateralised Murabahah. www.bnm.gov.my/index.php?ch=en_press&pg=en_press_all&ac=2468
11 For details see www.newyorkfed.org/aboutthefed/fedpoint/fed32.html. In 2012, the European Central Bank (ECB) started outright monetary transactions (OMT). Through this program the ECB makes outright purchases of the bonds issued in member states of the Eurozone. This program started after the recent financial crisis for quantitative easing.
12 Kamstra and Shiller (2009) suggest a security that would represent a permanent fraction of the issuer country's nominal GDP. It would pay, for instance, one-trillionth of a nation's nominal GDP, thus being named as "trill". Argentina in 2002 and Greece in the 2012 sovereign debt crisis issued similar GDP-indexed bonds.
13 There are generally some upward or downward revisions in GDP figures after some time lag. Therefore, provisional rates may be used for the GDP-linked securities.

References

Ahmad, A. (2000). *Instruments of Regulation and Control of Islamic Banks by the Central Banks*. Jeddah: IRTI, Islamic Development Bank.

Al-Jarhi, Ma'bid AU. (1983). A monetary and financial structure for an interest-free economy: Institutions, mechanism and policy. In Ahmed, Z., Iqbal, M., & Khan, M. F. (Eds.), *Money and Banking in Islam*. Islamabad: Institute of Policies Studies.

Ariff, M. (Eds.). (1982). *Monetary and Fiscal Economics of Islam*. Jeddah: International Centre for Research in Islamic Economics.

Askari, H., & Krichene, N. (2014). Islamic finance: An alternative financial system for stability, equity, and growth. *PSL Quarterly Review*, 67(268), 9–54.

BNM (2006). *Issuance of sukuk bank negara Malaysia based on ijarah concept*. Available at: https://www.bnm.gov.my/index.php?ch=en_press&pg=en_press&ac=841&lang=en (accessed on September 26, 2020).

BNM (2012). *Introduction of collateralised Murabahah*. Available at: https://www.bnm.gov.my/index.php?ch=en_press&pg=en_press&ac=84&lang=en (accessed on August 2020).

Buiter, W. (2009). Islamic finance principles to restore policy effectiveness. *Financial Times*, 22.

Chapra, M. U. (1983). Monetary policy in an Islamic economy. In Ahmed, Z., Iqbal, M., & Khan, M. F. (Eds.), *Money and Banking in Islam*. Islamabad: Institute of Policies Studies.

———. (1996). Monetary management in an Islamic economy. *Islamic Economics Studies*, 4(1).

Elhiraika, A. B. (2004). *On the design and effects of monetary policy in an Islamic framework: The experience of Sudan*. Jeddah: Islamic Research and Training Institute.

The Federal Reserve System, United States, Monetary Policy. Available at: https://www.federalreserve.gov/monetarypolicy/fomc.htm (assessed on September 26, 2020)

Haque, N., & Mirakhor, A. (1998). *The design of instruments for government finance in an Islamic economy*. IMF Working Paper 54, Washington, DC.

International Islamic Financial Market. (2009). A comprehensive study of the international sukuk market. *Sukuk Report*. International Islamic Financial Market, Manama.

Kamstra, M. J., & Shiller, R. J. (2009). *The case for trills: Giving the people and their pension funds a stake in the wealth of the nation*. Cowles Foundation Discussion Paper No. 1717, Yale ICF Working Paper No. 16. Available at SSRN: https://ssrn.com/abstract=1444351 or http://dx.doi.org/10.2139/ssrn.1444351

Karsten, I. (1982). Islam and financial intermediation. *Staff Papers*, 29(1), 108–42.

Khan, M. A. (1982). *Inflation and the Islamic economy: A closed economy model*. International Centre for Research in Islamic Economics, Jeddah.

Mirakhor, A. (2012). *Islamic finance, risk sharing and macroeconomic policies*. MPRA Paper No. 56338. Available at: https://mpra.ub.uni-muenchen.de/56338/ (accessed on September 26, 2020).

Othman, A., & Mirakhor, A. (2014). Risk sharing and public finance. *Journal of Islamic Business and Management*, *219*(2621), 1–18.

Siddiqi, M. N. (1967). *Banking without Interest* (in Urdu). Lahore: The Islamic Publications Ltd.

———. (1982). Islamic approach to money, banking and monetary policy. In Ariff, M. (Ed.), *A Review. Monetary and Fiscal Economics of Islam*. Jeddah: International Centre for Research in Islamic Economics.

———. (1983). *Issues in Islamic Banking*. Leicester, London, UK: The Islamic Foundation.

———. (2006). Islamic banking and finance in theory and practice: A survey of state of the art. *Islamic Economic Studies*, 13(2).

Usmani, M. M. T. (2007). *Sukuk and their contemporary applications*. AAOIFI Shari'a Council Meeting, Saudi Arabia.

Uzair, M. (1978). *Interest Free Banking*. Karachi, Pakistan: Royal Book Company.

———. (1982). Central banking operations in an interest-free banking system. In *Monetary and Fiscal Economics of Islam* (pp. 211–236). Jeddah: International Centre for Research in Islamic Economics.

Zaheer, S., Ongena, S., & van Wijnbergenc, S. J. (2013). The transmission of monetary policy through conventional and Islamic banks. *International Journal of Central Banking*, 9(4), pp. 175-224.

Zangeneh, H., & Salam, A. (1993). Central banking in an interest-free banking system. *Journal of King Abdulaziz University: Islamic Economics*, 5.

8 Impacts of monetary policy on credit supply of Islamic banks

An empirical study of Pakistan versus Malaysia

Syed Muhammad Abdul Rehman Shah and Abdul Rashid

Introduction

The recent financial crises have raised several questions on the role financial intermediaries played in an economy, especially during economic downturns. No doubt, the authorities design monetary policies to monitor and put the efforts of these intermediaries in the right direction to achieve stability in price levels and sustainable higher economic growth. However, the choice and effectiveness of different policy instruments in this regard critically depend on the way the monetary policy transmission mechanism occurs in the economy. In principle, monetary policy works through different transmission channels including the interest rate channel, exchange rate channel, asset price channel, and credit supply channel to affect both the real and nominal sectors of an economy. Further, these channels behave quite differently in different countries depending on the institutional structure and functioning of an economic system.

By reviewing the theoretical literature, we find that the traditional monetary policy theories have mainly emphasized the control of money supply to make changes in the interest rate and levels of spending in the economy (Friedman and Schwartz, 1963; King and Plosser, 1984; Sim, 1992), although the importance of financial intermediaries, particularly banks, is highly highlighted by new theories of monetary policy (Bernanke and Gertler, 1995). The role of the banking sector in the monetary policy transmission process depends on how much banks rely on deposits, how much consumers and business firms are bank dependent, and how much bank credit expansion is affected by monetary policy shocks.

Mishkin (1996) is the first one who seems to be dissatisfied with the performance of conventional interest rate channels and, perhaps for the first time, systematically introduced the role of asymmetric information in financial markets, which led to the credit channel in two different ways in credit markets. The first one is the balance sheet channel, and the second one is the bank-lending channel, which is also known as the credit supply channel of banks. By reviewing a vast amount of empirical literature, we find that several well-known scholars have provided strong evidence confirming the transmission process of monetary policy through these two channels for different economies across the globe. Examples of these researchers include, among several others, Kashyap and Stein (1994), Bernanke and Gertler (1995), and Cecchetti (1999).

After the 2007–08 financial crisis, the credit supply channel of banks, which is known as the "bank-centric view of monetary transmission", came to the forefront because the banking sector was affected badly. According to the bank-centric view of monetary policy transmission mechanism, money, bonds, and bank loans are assumed to be three important financial assets in the economy. The functioning of the credit supply channel of monetary transmission mechanism mainly relies on the assumption that during periods of monetary tightening policy, the aggregate lending by banks slows down, and non-banking financing such as commercial papers increases. A monetary tightening drains reserves from the banking sector, which in turn weakens banks' deposit base. Hence, banks are expected to be unable to issue new loans and even perhaps to continue with their existing lending projects without using external sources of finance such as equity, debt, or commercial paper issuance (Gertler and Gilchrist, 1993; Kashyap and Stein, 1994; Cecchetti, 1999).

Given that banks have an important role to play in the monetary policy transmission mechanism and Islamic banking is growing across the world (Rashid, Riaz, and Zaffar, 2017), one fundamental question arises: Do Islamic banks respond differently to a monetary tightening? Answering this question is very essential for the effectiveness of monetary policy for achieving higher economic growth and stability of the whole financial system. The basic purpose of this chapter, therefore, is to empirically examine the role of Islamic banks in the monetary policy transmission mechanism in the case of Pakistan and Malaysia.

In principle, the structure of Islamic banks is quite different in terms of composition of assets and liabilities as compared to their conventional counterparts. The fundamental feature that differentiates the Islamic banking from conventional banking is the prohibition of interest. Profit and loss sharing (PLS) and risk-sharing principles are instrumental features that further differentiate Islamic banks from their conventional peers. In Islamic banking, fund providers do not transfer their risk to the users. Rather, they share profits and losses as well as the risk associated with the business. Another notable feature of Islamic banking is that its transactions are fully backed by real assets. Finally, avoiding speculative activities such as financial derivatives, doing ethical and socially responsible investments, and linking the financial sector to the real economy are also the salient features of Islamic banking (Nosheen and Rashid, 2019). Due to these unique features of Islamic banking one can put forth the hypothesis that compared to conventional banks, Islamic banks respond quite differently to monetary policy shocks.

Indeed, based on the previously mentioned unique contractual and motivational features of Islamic financial institutions (IFIs), Hardianto (2004), Kaleem and Isa (2006), Sukmana and Kassim (2010), and Zaheer, Ongena, and Wijnbergen (2013), using aggregate data on the Islamic banking industry, have examined the response of Islamic financing to monetary policy shocks in different countries. However, one should note that the focus of these studies was on consolidated macroeconomic data of Islamic banks rather than the bank-level data. Empirical evidence on the occurrence of monetary policy transmission process based on microeconomic data of Islamic banks would definitely not only help understand the monetary policy transmission mechanism in the economy in depth but also achieve the macroeconomic objectives of monetary policy. In fact, if both Islamic and conventional banks are part of the financial system, then any instrument of monetary policy should have to affect the economy by affecting both types of banking. Thus, it is worth exploring empirically whether Islamic banks hinder or intensify the monetary policy transmission mechanism in the economy. Nevertheless, we so far know less about the empirical role of Islamic banking in the monetary policy transmission mechanism.

The potential gaps left in the empirical literature on the monetary policy transmission mechanism and the growing interest in Islamic banking and its ability to sustain financial crisis motivate us to explore the response of Islamic baking to monetary policy shocks. Specifically, this chapter contributes to the literature first by investigating the differential impact of monetary policy measures on the credit supply of Islamic banks in the case of Pakistan and Malaysia and second by investigating whether bank size and bank liquidity matter in formulating the effects of monetary policy shocks on bank credit expansion. The dynamic panel data (aka system-GMM) estimator is used to overcome the issue of endogeneity, heterogeneity, and inertia present in the data. While estimating the effects of three alternative measures of monetary policy on banks' credit supply, we have included several bank-specific variables in the model specification as control variables.

After having been provided strong empirical evidence on the significant role of Islamic banks in the monetary transmission in both Pakistan and Malaysia, we extend our baseline model by introducing the interaction terms between the monetary policy measure and bank size and bank liquidity. Estimation of the "interacted model" enables us to examine the role of the size of a bank and the liquidity position of a bank in articulating the effects of a tight monetary policy on banks' credit expansion. The results of the chapter suggest that the monetary policy indicators used in the empirical analysis affect the small-sized banks and the less-liquid banks more compared to the large-sized banks and the more-liquid banks in both Pakistan and Malaysia. The findings presented in this chapter strongly suggest that there is a vital need to take into account the nature of Islamic banks while devising monetary policy instruments to efficiently manage credit supply in the economy and to successfully achieve the overall macroeconomic objectives of monetary policy.

We select the data set of Pakistan and Malaysia to investigate and compare the response of Islamic banks to monetary policy measures for the following reasons. First, the economies of Pakistan and Malaysia are almost bank dependent, which increases the importance of the banks' credit channel of monetary policy transmission. Second, unlike most other countries, both Pakistan and Malaysia have a dual banking system: both Islamic and conventional banks are operating parallel in the same market with modern practices. Third, both countries are using accounting systems for their financial institutions in line with modern practices of international accounting standards. Moreover, Islamic banking operations are dealt with as per the modern practices proposed by the Accounting and Auditing Organization of Islamic Financial Institutions (AAOIFI) and Islamic Financial

Services Board (IFSB). The central banks of both countries, the State Bank of Pakistan (SBP) in Pakistan and Bank Negara Malaysia (BNM) in Malaysia, ensure the implementation of these rules and regulations along with some additional *Shari'ah* compliance requirements to be regulated through *Shari'ah* governance framework. Fourth, the accounting differences of both banking strands are harmonized to make them comparable for further analysis in the same framework. Lastly, data for Islamic banks are available and managed by the central banks of both countries.

The rest of the chapter is structured as follows. The second section reviews the empirical literature on monetary policy transmission mechanism. The third section describes data and presents the empirical framework, and the fourth presents the empirical findings. Finally, the fifth section presents some conclusions and policy recommendations.

Review of empirical literature

The bank-lending channel works through the response of credit supply to the indicators of monetary policy such as interest rates and other policy instruments. Therefore, the credit channel can also be said to be an enhancement mechanism of the interest rate channel of monetary policy transmission mechanism. Bernanke and Gertler (1995) laid down the foundation for the roles of banks in monetary policy transmission. Bernanke and Gertler (1995), Kashyap and Stein (1995), and Kishan and Opiela (2000) have confirmed the presence of the lending channel of the monetary policy transmission mechanism in the United States. Most of the studies deal with the response of credit supplies of banks from distinct characteristics, like bank size, the level of liquidity, and bank capital. Bernanke, Gertler, and Gilchrist (1999) extend the New Keynesian model to account for the balance sheet channel of monetary transmission. Kashyap and Stein (1994) have documented that small-sized banks reduce their lending more than large-sized banks in response to a tight monetary policy in the United States. Similarly, Kashyap and Stein (1994), Cecchetti (1999), Ehrmann *et al.* (2001) and Santis and Surico (2013) have explored some descriptive evidence on credit supply channel for the EU countries. Several other studies including Aysun and Hepp (2013), Wong (2000), Kashyap and Stein (1995), Bernanke, Lown, and Friedman (1991), Evans, Fisher, Gourio, and Kran (2015), Jermann and Schmid (2016), Auclert (2017), Erdogdu (2017), and Anwar and Nguyend (2018) have also documented empirical evidence on the credit view of monetary transmission mechanism.

In Pakistan, Janjua, Rashid, and Qurrat-Ul-Ain (2014) empirically examined the presence of the bank-centric view of monetary transmission in Pakistan using annual bank-level data for the period 2006–2012. They found that there is a significant negative relationship between monetary measures and banks' loan supply. They also showed that small-sized banks are likely to be more affected by monetary policy tightening than large-sized banks. However, one should note that they do not explore the relative role of Islamic banks in the transmission mechanism of monetary policy in Pakistan, which is the core theme of this chapter.

Islamic banking is an emerging market across the globe, and this industry holds a substantial share of credit supply in countries like Pakistan, with a dual banking system wherein Islamic and conventional banks are running parallel. In Pakistan and Malaysia, Islamic banking is recorded at 11.6 percent and 35.4 percent, respectively, as the market share of total banking assets and Islamic deposits are recorded at 13.7 percent and 38.7 percent, respectively, of the banking industry at the end of June 2017. Further, the capital structure decisions of Islamic banks operating in Pakistan are also found empirically with unique features (Shah, Rashid, and Khaleequzzaman, 2017). Zaheer, Ongena, and Wijnbergen (2013), using aggregate data on Islamic banking, have examined the response of Islamic financing to monetary policy and found that Islamic financing continues to grow even in periods of tight monetary policy, irrespective of their size and liquidity. Recently, Rashid, Riaz, and Zaffar (2017) have documented that Islamic and conventional banks are significantly different from each other in respect of operating leverage, insolvency, credit risk, and efficiency. More recently, Nosheen and Rashid (2019) have provided evidence that although Islamic banks are relatively less cost-efficient, they have higher credit quality and capitalization as compared to their conventional counterparts. They also showed that the outperformance of Islamic banks in terms of credit quality and financial stability holds even during periods of business cycle troughs.

In Malaysia, Sanrego and Rusydiana (2013) and Alaro and Hakeem (2011) explained that an economic agent substitutes loan-based credit with available profit-loss sharing credit in Islamic banks. As a result, this *Shari'ah* mechanism creates a balance between the monetary and real sector of economy along with controlling the rate of inflation. Similarly, Majid and Hasin (2012) differentiated Islamic banks and their conventional counterparts on the basis of alternate products on both sides of balance sheet, despite meeting the same demand of market. These products of Islamic banking are based upon a variety of underlying contracts. Their findings revealed that Islamic banks significantly differ from conventional banks. Sukmana and Kassim (2010) also explored the idea that Islamic banks play a vital role in the transmission process of monetary policy through a credit supply channel in Malaysia. Specifically, they suggested that the policy makers should consider fundamental differences of the dual banking system (Islamic and conventional banks) in the same economy; otherwise there may appear quandaries for monetary policy (Chapra, 1985; Chaudary and Mirakhor, 1997; Farahani and Dastan, 2013).

On basis of unique contractual and motivational features of IFIs, Hardianto (2004), Kaleem and Isa (2006), Sukmana and Kassim (2010) and Zaheer, Ongena, and Wijnbergen (2013) have identified the potential gaps in the existing literature on the role of Islamic banks in the monetary policy transmission mechanism. There is a dire need to empirically explore the presence of credit supply channel through *Shari'ah*-based financing instruments. Empirical evidence on the response of Islamic banks' credit supply to a tight monetary policy will not only help to understand the transmission mechanism of monetary policy in a better way but also to achieve the macroeconomic objectives of monetary policy more effectively and efficiently. Indeed, recently, studies by Shah, Rashid, and Mansoori (2018), Akhatova, Zainal, and Ibrahim (2016), and Stepanchuk and Tsyrennikov (2015) have comparatively evaluated the credit channel of Islamic banks and conventional banks by examining the effects of monetary policy measures such as the lending rate, the deposit rate, and the interest rate spread on bank credit expansion. Yet we know less about the relative role of Islamic banking in the monetary policy transmission mechanism. Specifically, we do not know the differential response of large- and small-sized banks and less- and more-liquid Islamic banks to tight monetary policy. Therefore, this chapter contributes to the literature on the monetary policy transmission mechanism by exploring the Islamic bank-centric view of monetary policy in Pakistan and Malaysia from the perspective of their responses to monetary tightening. Furthermore, the chapter examines how tight monetary policy affects the Islamic banks' credit supply in Pakistan and Malaysia by taking into account the moderator role of bank size and bank liquidity.

Research design

This chapter uses an unbalanced annual panel data set of Islamic banks along with selected macroeconomic variables and monetary policy indicators for Pakistan and Malaysia. Specifically, we construct an unbalanced annual panel data set for banking sector of both countries through various sources. Data on policy variables are also collected from central banks of Pakistan and Malaysia to observe the impact of monetary policy stances on the credit supply of Islamic banks of both countries.

The chapter uses a sample of five full-fledged Islamic banks and six Islamic branches/divisions of conventional banks of Pakistan. For Malaysia, we select 11 Islamic banks for empirical analysis. Overall, the data on bank-specific and macroeconomic variables are collected from financial statements of banks available on their websites. We also collect some data from the publications of the State Bank of Pakistan (SBP) and Bank Nagara Malaysia (BNM), the World Development Index (WDI), International Financial Statistics (IFS) of the IMF, and Orbis Bank Focus (Bankscope). Some data of Islamic branches/divisions of conventional banks are taken from Thomson Reuters Datastream.

We estimate three empirical models separately for Pakistan and Malaysia with several different specifications of bank size and liquidity to achieve the objectives of this chapter. Specifically, following Kashyap and Stein (1994), Janjua, Rashid, and Qurrat-Ul-Ain (2014) and Shah, Rashid, and Mansoori (2018), these models are estimated to explore the impact of different monetary measures on credit supply of Islamic banks with some additional specifications. While estimating the effects of monetary policy measures on bank credit supply, several bank-specific and macroeconomic variables are included in the specification as control variables. We start our empirical analysis by estimating the following model.

$$Y_{it} = \beta_i + X_{it}\alpha + Z_t\theta + \rho M_t + \lambda Y_{it-1} + \mu_t + \varepsilon_{it} \qquad \text{(Equation 1)}$$

where

Y_{it} = the credit supply of *i*th Islamic bank in *t* year.

β_i = Individual-specific effect.

μ_t = Year-specific effect.
ε_{it} = Error term.
X_{it} = A vector of bank-specific variables that include size, liquidity, capital, coverage ratio, credit risk, profitability, and debt-to-equity ratio.
Z_t = A group of macroeconomic variables that include the growth of gross domestic product (GDP) and the rate of inflation.
M_t = A monetary policy indicator: the lending interest rate, the deposit interest rate, and the interest rate spread.

The main idea behind the baseline model is to analyze the impact of tight monetary policy on credit expansion of banks. It is notable that we have included several bank-specific and macroeconomic variables in the specification as control variables for maximum explanation of the dependant variable in line with existing literature. This baseline model works as a reference in the next models, which explains how the tightening of monetary policy differently affects the credit supply decisions of small-sized banks and less-liquid banks as compared to large-sized and more-liquid banks in both countries.

The baseline model presented in equation 1 is extended by adding the interaction terms between monetary policy measures and bank size dummy as well as bank liquidity dummy. Specifically, we interact small-sized bank dummy (D_{it}^{Small}) and large-sized bank dummy (D_{it}^{Large}) with the monetary policy indicator to examine the differential impact of tight monetary policy on bank credit supply across small- and large-sized banks. The model takes the following form. Analogously, in order to examine whether more- and less-liquid Islamic banks respond differently to monetary tightening, we use the interaction terms between monetary measures and bank liquidity dummies. Specifically, the extended model, which is named the "interacted model", takes the following form.

$$\begin{aligned} Y_{it} = \beta_i + \beta_1 X_{it} + \beta_2 Z_t + \beta_3 M_t \times D_{it}^{Small} + \beta_4 M_t \times D_{it}^{Large} \\ + \beta_5 M_t \times D_{it}^{Less} + \beta_6 M_t \times D_{it}^{More} + \lambda Y_{it-1} + \mu_t + \varepsilon_{it} \end{aligned} \quad \text{(Equation 2)}$$

In equation 2 all the variables are defined as in equation 1. The small (large)-sized bank dummy takes value one if the log value of total assets of a bank for a particular year is less (greater) than the average value of log of total assets of all sample Islamic banks over the sample period and zero otherwise. The less-liquid bank dummy (D_{it}^{Less}) takes value one if the ratio of cash and cash equivalent to total assets for a bank in a particular year is less than the average value of all Islamic banks included in the sample and zero otherwise. Similarly, the more-liquid bank dummy (D_{it}^{More}) takes value one if the ratio of cash and cash equivalent to total assets for a bank in a particular year is greater than the average value of all Islamic banks included in the sample and zero otherwise.

We use the bank-specific variables, the macroeconomic factors, and the monetary policy variables to examine the existence credit view of monetary policy in Pakistan and Malaysia. The rationale for the selection of these specific variables is discussed in detail. First, we begin with the dependent variable that is banks' credit supply. The banks' credit supply is defined as the ratio of total financing to total assets according to the financial statements of Islamic banks in line with Akhatova, Zainal, and Ibrahim (2016) for Malaysia and Shah, Rashid, and Mansoori (2018) for Pakistan. This chapter intends to investigate the effects of monetary policy indicators on credit supply decisions of banks. The decline in credit supply of banks due to an increase in policy interest rate implies the existence of the bank-centric view (credit supply channel) of monetary transmission mechanism (Alper, Hulagu, and Keles, 2012; Sukmana and Kassim, 2010). The bank-specific independent variables are described in Table 8.1. Following Janjua, Rashid, and Qurrat-Ul-Ain (2014) and Shah, Rashid, and Mansoori (2018), three different monetary policy measures, namely the lending interest rate, the deposit interest rate, and the interest rate spread that is taken as the difference between the lending and the deposit interest rate, are used in this chapter to carry out the empirical analysis.

The bank characteristics, macroeconomic variables, and policy variables are selected in line with the existing literature. Bank credit supply is measured through the ratio of gross financing (loan) to total assets because it is assumed that a bank reacts to a change in the monetary policy indicator by adjusting the new loans. A one-period lagged credit supply is selected to manage the individual effects that are assumed to be stochastic. It also expresses the historical trend of bank credit supply, that especially those banks which offer more credit previously continue to supply more credit in the current period and vice versa. Bank size is measured by the log of total assets, which reflects the total value of bank assets. Similarly, different investment decisions, risk management techniques, information asymmetries, and credit supply decisions are strongly lined with banks' size. The inclusion of bank liquidity for Islamic banks is an indicator about socially acceptable and *Shari'ah*-compliant investment projects. If Islamic banks hold more cash and equivalent securities in their tills and are not rushing to investment, they may face difficulty in finding opportunity in compliance with the previously mentioned opportunities. Similarly, capital is measured by calculating total shareholder equity to total assets. It is notable that appreciation usually comes along with an improvement of the capital balance, which can therefore extend the asset side of banks' balance sheets.

Table 8.1 Bank-specific variables

Variables	*Description*
Bank credit supply	Ratio of gross financing to total assets
Bank size	Log of total assets
Liquidity	Cash and cash equivalent divided by total assets
Capital	(Total shareholder equity/total assets) × 100
Coverage ratio	(EBIT/interest expense) × 100
Credit risk	Ratio of classified loans to total loans
Profitability	(Profit after tax/total assets) × 100
Debt to equity ratio	Debt/equity ratio

The bank-specific variables are included in the specification to capture the degree to which a bank suffers from informational friction in financial markets. Specifically, we select coverage ratio because it reflects the immediate impact of tightening the monetary policy on the financial position of banks, as the coverage ratio is a ratio of earning before distribution of interest and taxes to interest expenses. Credit risk is defined by the ratio of classified loans to total loans. It is adopted as a proxy against the internal measure of risk. If its sign is found negative in relationship with banks' lending, it means an increase in the loan portfolio riskiness may weigh on banks' ability to resume lending. This implies that as credit risk increases, bank credit supply decreases, implying that a decrease in proportion of classified loans leads to an increase in banks' credit supply. Profitability is measured by the ratio of profit after tax to total assets of banks. Banks ensure that they will have profitability by their business activities for their shareholders to secure for them non-discriminatory returns and for their managers because they pledge more flexible capital ratios to enhance the business, even in the setting of an uncertain business environment. For banks' characteristics, we have defined the leverage of banks through the ratio of debt to banks' equity capital. Similarly, the leverage ratio growth has a significant impact whether organization is in financial turmoil or in tranquil periods. We consider the macroeconomic factors because of the developing economies where the banking sector is affected due to uneven patterns of the macroeconomic conditions. Investors rely a lot on research when macroeconomic conditions are entertained in econometric models.

These empirical models are dynamic in nature because they include a one-period lagged dependent variable as an explanatory variable to control the inertia/persistence in credit supply decisions of banks. It is very likely that the lagged dependent variable is correlated with the error term, which creates the problem of endogeneity. Therefore, we apply the robust two-step system-generalized method of moments (GMM) estimator, which is also called the dynamic panel data estimator. This estimator was initially proposed by Arellano and Bover (1995) and then was fully developed by Blundell and Bond (1998). Although this estimator has several of its own merits, the robustness of estimation results critically depends on whether the selected instruments satisfy the orthogonality condition. Therefore, to test the validity of the instruments, we use two diagnostic tests. The first one is Arellano and Bond's (1991) AR (2), which is used to test the existence of serial correlation in the residuals. The second one is the J-test of Hansen (1982), which is employed to test whether the instruments used in the estimation are orthogonal to the estimated residuals.

Empirical findings

Impact of monetary policy on credit supply of Islamic banks in Pakistan

The results for Pakistan are presented in Table 8.2. Panel A and Panel B present the empirical results of three different models and diagnostic tests, respectively. In Panel A of Table 8.2, all three monetary policy indicators—the lending interest rate, the interest rate spread, and the deposit rate—are negatively and significantly related to the credit supply of Islamic banks. This finding implies that Islamic banks reduce their financing on average during periods of monetary tightening. Said differently, a tightening in monetary policy by raising interest rates has an adverse effect on the credit expansion of Islamic banks in Pakistan. The estimated value of the coefficient implies that Islamic banks decrease their financing as a percentage of total assets by 2.5 percent, on average, in response to a 1 percent increase in the lending rate. This rate of decline in credit expansion is even higher during periods of an increased interest rate-spread. This finding suggests that when the State Bank of Pakistan tightens the monetary policy by raising either the lending or the deposit rate, Islamic banks face difficulties and cut back their lending. During periods of monetary contractions, banks may have limited financing. This is because the central bank drains reserves out of the banking system, and so it

Table 8.2 Impact of monetary policy indicators on Islamic banks' credit supply in Pakistan

Panel A: Estimation Results						
Variables	*Model (a)*		*Model (b)*		*Model (c)*	
	Coefficient	*Std. Error*	*Coefficient*	*Std. Error*	*Coefficient*	*Std. Error*
Lagged Credit Supply	0.628***	0.117	0.728***	0.035	0.751***	0.059
Bank Size	0.049***	0.017	0.025***	0.011	0.029**	0.015
Bank Liquidity	−0.296	0.343	−0.150	0.142	−0.239	0.111
Bank Capital	0.005***	0.002	0.005***	0.001	0.005***	0.001
Coverage Ratio	0.007**	0.003	0.001**	0.001	0.000***	0.001
Credit Risk	−0.178**	0.155	−0.442***	0.168	−0.514***	0.172
Bank Profitability	0.014***	0.004	0.011***	0.003	0.024***	0.007
Debt-to-Equity Ratio	0.012**	0.001	0.002***	0.002	0.001***	0.001
Lending Rate	−0.025***	0.006				
Interest Rate Spread			−0.027***	0.003		
Deposit Rate					−0.024***	0.003
GDP Growth	12.564**	7.654	7.123***	2.435	3.543***	1.654
Inflation	0.069***	0.023	0.027***	0.009	0.013**	0.008
Constants	45.449**	15.483	27.818***	8.875	15.798***	5.783
Panel B: Diagnostic Tests						
Observations	103		103		103	
Banks	11		11		11	
AR (2)	0.60		1.16		−0.50	
***p*- value**	0.550		0.244		0.621	
***J*- statistic**	14.15		15.69		15.04	
***p*- value**	1.000		1.000		1.000	

reduces the monetary base of the banks. As a result, banks become unable to offer more financing and so reduce their credit supply. The results given in Table 8.2 also reveal that all the three measures of monetary policy are negatively and statistically significantly related to the credit supply of Islamic banks, ensuring the robustness of the negative influence of monetary tightening.

The strong empirical evidence on the negative impact of monetary measures on bank credit expansion supports the presence of the bank-centric view of monetary policy transmission mechanism in Islamic banks of Pakistan. This finding also suggests that although the structure of Islamic banks is quite different from that of conventional banks, any monetary tightening by the SPB in terms of increasing interest rate would have an adverse impact on the credit supply decisions of Islamic banks. One of the possible explanations for such finding is that although Islamic banks do interest-free and *Shari'ah*-compliant financings/investments, they share the same interbank mark and work under the same laws and regulations governing their conventional counterparts. Thus, it is expected that the increased interest rates negatively affect Islamic banks' credit supply. The presence of the bank-centric view in the case of Islamic banks suggests that while devising monetary policy instruments to achieve the macroeconomic objective of monetary policy, authorities should also take into account Islamic banks along with conventional banks. Finally, the finding of the negative effects of tight monetary policy on Islamic banks' credit supply is consistent with several prior studies in the literature that have documented the same effect for conventional banks (see, for instance, among several others, Kashyap and Stein, 1994; Sharpe, 1995; Majid and Hasin, 2012; Janjua, Rashid, and Qurrat-ul-Ain, 2014).

Turning to bank-specific variables, we observe that in Model (a) of Table 8.2, Islamic banks' credit supply is significantly and positively related to one-period lagged credit supply. This finding implies that those Islamic banks offering more credit previously continue to supply more credit in the current period. Inspecting the coefficient of banks' size, we find that banks' credit supply increases significantly with an increase in bank size. This finding suggests that larger banks may do more financing to harvest the benefits of economies of scale. Larger banks are generally financially sound and face less financial distress and so offer more financing. This result is also consistent with several previous empirical studies that have reported the positive relationship between bank size and the credit supply of banks (Alper, Hulagu, and Keles, 2012; Köhler, Hommel, and Grote, 2006; Schmitz, 2004). However, one should note that this result is contrary to the findings of Pruteanu (2004) and Janjua, Rashid, and Qurrat-Ul-Ain (2014), which indicate a negative association between bank size and the credit supply decisions of conventional banks.

The coefficient of banks' liquidity is negative but appears statistically insignificant, suggesting that although bank liquidity is negatively related to the credit supply of banks, this effect is statistically weak. One possible explanation of the negative effect of bank liquidity is that Islamic banks may hold more cash and equivalent securities in their tills and do not do investment as they may face difficulty in finding socially acceptable and *Shari'ah*-compliant investment projects.

Consistent with our result, some prior studies such as Janjua, Rashid, and Qurrat-Ul-Ain (2014), Alper, Hulagu, and Keles (2012), and Köhler, Hommel, and Grote (2006) have also found negative and significant effects of liquidity on banks' loan supply. However, some other studies such as Schmitz (2004) and Majid and Hasin (2012) have found evidence of a positive and significant relationship between bank liquidity and loan growth.

The results given in the table also suggest that both bank capital and coverage ratio are positively and significantly related to banks' credit expansion decisions. Specifically, we find that the variable bank capital appears with the coefficient value of 0.005, indicating it is positively and significantly related to the credit supply of banks. This finding suggests that Islamic banks with more capitalization are expected to issue more credit. Several studies in the literature such as Girardin and Moussa (2011), Schmitz (2004), Bernanke, Lown, and Friedman (1991) have also reported the positive impact of bank capital on the credit supply of banks. Further, our finding on the positive impact of bank capital supports the prediction of monetarists that well-capitalized banks survive more in periods of contractions of monetary policy and offer more financing.

The coefficient of coverage ratio is positive and statistically significant in all three estimated models, suggesting that banks with higher earnings before taxes relative to rent paid to participants increase their supply of credit. Likewise, Kaleem and Isa (2006), Sanrego and Nikmawati (2010), and Alaro and Hakeem (2011) have also documented the positive relationship between coverage ratio and banks' credit supply. Nevertheless, this finding is inconsistent with Janjua, Rashid, and Qurrat-Ul-Ain (2014), who found a negative and statistically insignificant effect of coverage ratio on bank credit supply in the case of conventional banks in Pakistan.

Credit risk appears to be negatively related to banks' credit supply, suggesting that when the credit risk of a bank increases, the bank becomes cautious in issuing new loans, and so declines its investment financing. This finding holds in the three-estimated models. Further, this finding is consistent with Janjua, Rashid, and Qurrat-Ul-Ain (2014) and Pruteanu (2004), who have also reported the negative impact on bank credit expansion of the increased credit risk.

Another variable that is positively and significantly related to bank credit supply is the profitability of banks. Specifically, the estimated value of the coefficient of bank profitability suggests that the higher the profitability of an Islamic bank, the higher the credit supply of the bank. More profitable Islamic banks may have more internally generated funds, and thus they may issue more credits. The variable related to the capital structure of banks, namely the debt to equity ratio, appears to affect banks' credit supply positively and significantly. This finding implies that banks having more debt relative to equity in the composition of assets structure supply more credit to market. This finding is consistent with the finding of Janjua, Rashid, and Qurrat-Ul-Ain (2014). Last but not least, the estimated coefficients of the variable GDP growth and the rate of inflation are positive and appear statistically significant at any acceptable level of significance. Following the existing literature on bank credit supply we use the growth of GDP as a proxy for demand for loanable funds. The positive effect of GDP growth on the bank credit supply suggests that Islamic banks do more investment financing during periods when economic growth is higher. During periods of high economic growth, since Islamic banks may face less financial distress and since both consumers and business firms may be willing to pay higher returns, Islamic banks expand their investment financing. Further, in periods of good macroeconomic conditions, investment projects may yield relatively higher returns, which motive Islamic banks to supply more credits. The results also suggest that Islamic banks increase their investment financing with the rate of inflation.

In Model (b) and Model (c) of Table 8.2, we use the interest rate spread and the deposit rate as a measure of monetary policy instead of the lending rate. Both the interest rate spread and the deposit rate are negatively and statistically significantly related to Islamic banks' credit supply. This result testifies the presence of the bank-centric view of the monetary policy transmission mechanism in the case of Islamic banks in Pakistan. The empirical results presented in Table 8.2 confirm the robustness of our finding on the existence of bank credit supply channel of the monetary transmission because our finding holds for different measures of monetary policy used in the analysis. The results in the table also reveal that the effects of the control variables in Model (b) and Model (c) are similar, in terms of both sign and statistically significance, to those in Model (a). Therefore, in order to economize we do not interpret them again.

Panel B of Table 8.2 reports number of observations, number of banks, statistics of diagnostic tests, and their *p*-values. The estimated statistics of the AR(2) test provide strong evidence that in case of all three-estimated models, the estimated residuals are free from the second order serial correlation. Analogously, the estimated statistics of the *J*-test suggest that the instrument set used in the estimation fulfils the orthogonality condition, ensuring the robustness of estimation results.

Impact of monetary policy on basis of Islamic banks' size and liquidity for Pakistan

After having confirmed the presence of the credit supply channel of the monetary policy transmission process in the case of Islamic banks in Pakistan, we investigate the asymmetric effects of monetary policy tightening across small and large Islamic banks and across less and more liquid Islamic banks. For this purpose, we estimate the "interacted model" presented in equation 2. One should note that we present here first-hand empirical evidence on the asymmetric effects of tight monetary policy in the case of Islamic banks. Nevertheless, in the case of conventional banks, there is a vast body of literature that has already presented strong evidence of the asymmetric influence of monetary policy tightening on banks' credit supply across small-sized and large-sized banks for both developing and developed countries (see, for instance, Bernanke and Gertler, 1995; Gertler and Gilchrist, 1993; Kashyap and Stein, 1995; Janjua, Rashid, and Qurrat-Ul-Ain, 2014).

Following the existing literature, we hypothesize that monetary tightening has a greater adverse influence on the lending behaviour of small-sized and less-liquid banks as compared to large-sized and more-liquid banks, respectively. To test the hypothesis, the baseline model in equation 1 is extended after categorizing banks on the basis of their size and liquidity positions. There are two dummies included in the specification on the basis of bank size: small-bank dummy and large-bank dummy. Similarly, two dummies are included in the specification on the basis of banks' liquidity position. To ensure our estimation results do not suffer from any specification bias, we include all the four interaction terms in the specification at a time.

The analysis of the effects of tight monetary policy on the lending behaviour of small-sized versus large-sized banks and less-liquid versus more-liquid banks enables us to understand further the role of Islamic banking in the transmission mechanism of monetary policy. As in Table 8.2, we use the same set of control variables. Further, we estimate three specifications of equation 2 by using three different monetary measures. The results are given in Table 8.3. Panel A of the table reports the estimated coefficient and standard errors, whereas Panel B of the table presents the diagnostic tests. In all three estimated models, the instruments used in the system-GMM estimation pass the orthogonality condition, and the estimated residuals appear from the problem of the second-order serial correlation. In sum, the diagnostic tests ensure the robustness of our results.

The results reveal that all the three monetary policy indicators are negatively and statistically significantly related to the credit supply of both small and large banks. However, we observe that the adverse impact of monetary policy tightening on credit supply is higher at small-sized banks than at large-sized banks. For instance, the estimated value of the coefficient of the lending rate suggests that when the lending rate increases by a 1 percent, small-sized Islamic banks decrease their investment financing by 2.7 percent of their total assets, whereas large-sized banks cut back their financing by 2.3 percent. This difference appears even more profound when the interest rate spread and the deposit rate are used as monetary policy measures. For instance, in response to a 1 percent increase in the deposit rate, small-sized Islamic banks decrease their credit supply by 4.0 percent, whereas the corresponding decline in the credit supply of large-sized Islamic banks is only by 2.9 percent.

These findings confirm the asymmetric effects of tight monetary policy across bank size. Further, these findings suggest that the credit supply of small-sized Islamic banks is more adversely affected during episodes of monetary tightening. The stronger impact of monetary tightening on credit supply at small-sized Islamic banks is consistent with our hypothesis that tight monetary policy has more of a burden on small-sized banks as compared to large-sized banks. The asymmetric effect of monetary policy on the credit supply of small-sized and large-sized Islamic banks is also in line with the results for conventional banks reported by several existing empirical studies including Bernanke and Gertler (1995), Gertler and Gilchrist (1993), Kashyap and Stein (1995, 1997), and Janjua, Rashid, and Qurrat-Ul-Ain (2014). Specifically, these studies have noted the differential effects of monetary policy on credit supply across small and large conventional banks.

Table 8.3 Asymmetric impact of monetary policy across bank size and bank liquidity for Pakistan

Panel A: Estimation Results						
Variables	*Model (a)*		*Model (b)*		*Model (c)*	
	Coefficient	*SE*	*Coefficient*	*SE*	*Coefficient*	*SE*
Lagged Credit Supply	0.716***	0.084	0.828***	0.075	0.745***	0.082
Bank Size	0.017**	0.008	0.024**	0.012	0.036***	0.017
Bank Liquidity	−0.477***	0.228	−0.617**	0.317	−0.02*	0.164
Bank Capital	0.002**	0.001	0.002*	0.002	0.003***	0.001
Coverage Ratio	0.002***	0.001	0.002**	0.001	−0.001	0.001
Credit Risk	−0.205**	0.090	−0.212**	0.114	−0.537***	0.191
Bank Profitability	0.014***	0.004	0.013**	0.008	0.004**	0.004
Debt to Equity Ratio	0.002***	0.001	0.002***	0.001	0.001*	0.001
Lending Rate × $D^{Small\ bank}$	−0.027***	0.007				
Lending Rate × $D^{Large\ bank}$	−0.023***	0.006				
Interest Rate Spread × $D^{Small\ bank}$			−0.045***	0.006		
Interest Rate Spread × $D^{Large\ bank}$			−0.035***	0.005		
Deposit Rate × $D^{Small\ bank}$					−0.040***	0.006
Deposit Rate × $D^{Large\ bank}$					−0.029***	0.009
Lending Rate × $D^{Less\ liquid}$	−0.021***	0.005				
Lending Rate × $D^{More\ liquid}$	−0.019***	0.005				
Interest Rate Spread × $D^{Less\ liquid}$			−0.034***	0.006		
Interest Rate Spread × $D^{More\ liquid}$			−0.025***	0.006		
Deposit Rate × $D^{D^{Less\ liquid}}$					−0.021***	0.003
Deposit Rate × $D^{More\ liquid}$					−0.015***	0.004
GDP Growth	0.132 ***	0.052	3.491	2.621	12.527***	4.502
Inflation	0.119***	0.027	0.109***	0.022	0.031**	0.018
Constants	12.346**	7.807	−11.377***	8.872	43.607***	15.404
Panel B: Diagnostic Tests						
Observations	103		103		103	
Banks	11		11		11	
AR (2)	0.60		1.16		−0.50	
p-value	0.550		0.244		0.621	
J-statistic	14.15		15.69		15.04	
p-value	1.000		1.000		1.000	

Note: The *J*-statistic is a test of the over-identifying restrictions and distributed as chi-squared under the null of instrument validity, and the AR (2) Arellano-Bond is the test of second-order autocorrelation in the first-differenced residuals.

*** $p < 0.01$, ** $p < 0.05$, * $p < 0.1$

Finally, these results suggest that the large banks are more able to absorb the effects of tightening monetary policy because they may have enough internally generated funds, and if they need external financing they can easily get funding from external sources of finance by issuing commercial papers, issuing equity, borrowing from capital markets, etc. Thus, large-sized banks are more likely to neutralize the influence of tight monetary policy. On the other hand, the small banks are affected more during the monetary policy tightening. The small banks may not have enough internally generated funds and may not find feasible external financing because of the increased cost of external financing. Thus, they are more affected by any tightening of monetary policy in terms of increased interest rates.

Turning to the asymmetric effect of tight monetary policy on less- and more-liquid banks, we find that the credit supply of more-liquid banks is less adversely affected by monetary policy contractions. This result holds in the case of all three monetary policy measures we use in our empirical analysis. The estimated value of coefficient suggests that a 1 percent increase in the deposit rate causes less- and more-liquid banks to decrease their credit supply by 2.1 percent and 1.5 percent of total assets, respectively. This difference in the response of less- and more-liquid banks to monetary tightening even becomes more substantial in the case of the interest rate spread. However, it becomes relatively narrow when the lending rate is utilized as a proxy for monetary measure. These results confirming our prediction suggest that the liquidity position of a bank has a significant role to play in formulating the effects of tight monetary policy on the lending behaviour of the bank. They also suggest that bank liquidity can be used as a safeguard to lessen the adverse effects of monetary tightening. Since the results for control variables are generally similar, in terms of both sign and statistically, to those given in Table 8.2, we do not do any commentary on them.

Impact of monetary policy on credit supply of Islamic banks in Malaysia

Similar to the case of Pakistan, we begin empirical examination for Malaysia by estimating the baseline model. Next, we estimate the "interacted model", which enables us to examine the asymmetric effect of monetary tightening for Malaysian Islamic banks. The results of the baseline model are presented in Table 8.4. Panel A of the table presents estimated coefficients along with their standard errors, whereas Panel B presents the diagnostic tests along with number of observation and number of banks included in the sample. Three different specifications of the baseline model—Model (a), Model (b), and Model (c)—are estimated to examine the effects of three different measures of monetary policy: the lending rate, the interest rate spread, and the deposit rate.

The estimated coefficients provide strong evidence that all the measures of monetary policy are negatively and statistically significantly related to the credit supply of Islamic banks in Malaysia. These results suggest that Malaysian Islamic banks cut back their investment financing during periods of monetary policy tightening. According to the estimated value of the coefficient, Islamic banks of Malaysia

Table 8.4 Impact of monetary policy indicators on Islamic banks' credit supply in Malaysia

Panel A: Estimation Results

Variables	*Model (a)*		*Model (b)*		*Model (c)*	
	Coefficient	*SE*	*Coefficient*	*SE*	*Coefficient*	*SE*
Lagged Credit Supply	0.685***	0.114	0.861***	0.093	0.693***	0.077
Bank Size	0.007**	0.015	0 .009**	0.050	0.003**	0.006
Bank Liquidity	−0.496***	0.138	−0.331***	0.064	−0.307***	0.085
Bank Capital	0.469**	0.014	0.288***	0.098	0.005***	0.001
Coverage Ratio	0.044	0.567	0.440	0.784	0.477	0.563
Credit Risk	−0.110***	0.043	−0.030***	0.007	−0.022***	0.003
Bank Profitability	0.021***	0.007	0.011***	0.003	0.024***	0.007
Debt to Equity Ratio	−0.002***	0.001	0.001	0.001	−0.003***	0.002
Lending Rate	−0.045***	0.012				
Interest Rate Spread			−0.043***	0.002		
Deposit Rate					−0.045***	0.003
GDP Growth	0.278**	0.156	0.009**	0.020	0.089 *	0.093
Inflation	0.004*	0.016	0.004**	0.015	0.014**	0.006
Constants	−0.566	0.648	0.285**	0.039	−0.088*	0.080

Panel B: Diagnostic Tests

Observations	107	107	107
Banks	11	11	11
AR (2)	0.41	0.40	0.84
p-value	0.684	0.690	0.401
J-statistic	15.05	13.20	15.24
p-value	1.000	1.000	1.000

Note: The *J*-statistic is a test of the over identifying restrictions and distributed as chi-squared under the null of instrument validity, and the AR (2) Arellano-Bond is the test of second-order autocorrelation in the first-differenced residuals.

*** $p < 0.01$, ** $p < 0.05$, * $p < 0.1$

decline their credit by 4.5 percent of their total assets as a result of a 1 percent increase in the lending rate. The results also suggest that the amount of decline in Islamic bank credit supply is almost the same when either the interest rate spread or deposit rate increases by a 1 percent. These findings provide strong evidence of the existence of the bank-centric view in Islamic banks of Malaysia. Further, these results are in accordance with the existing literature for conventional banks (Kashyap and Stein, 1994; Sharpe, 1995; Majid and Hasin, 2012; Janjua, Rashid, and Qurrat-Ul-Ain, 2014).

Turning to bank-specific and macroeconomic variables, we find that in all three estimated regressions the coefficient of one-period lagged credit supply is positive and statistically significance, suggesting that banks that supply more credit in the previous year continue to supply more credit in the current year as well. The results also reveal that bank size, bank capital, the coverage ratio, and the profitability of banks all are positively and significantly related to the credit supply of Islamic banks in Malaysia. These findings suggest that large-sized banks, more capitalized banks, banks with higher earnings before taxes relative to fixed rent expenses, and more profitable banks issue more credit supply to the market. These findings are not only consistent to those for Pakistan but also to the existing empirical literature for conventional banks.

The results given in the table also suggest that the variable bank liquidity, credit risk, and the debt to equity ratio are negatively and significantly related to the credit supply of Islamic banks in Malaysia. These findings imply that more liquid banks, banks facing higher credit risk, and banks having more debt financing in their capital structure supply less credits in the market. These findings hold in all the three estimated regressions in terms of their sign and statistical significance. Only the estimated coefficient of the debt to equity ratio changes its sign from negative to positive and becomes statistically insignificant when it is regressed with the interest rate spread as a monetary policy measure. These findings are consistent with the findings of prior studies on conventional banks. Finally, we find that similar to the case of Pakistan, both the growth of GDP and the rate of inflation have a positive and statistically significant impact on the credit supply of Islamic banks in Malaysia. These results suggest that Islamic banks in Malaysia expand their credit supply in periods of higher economic growth and heightened inflation in the economy.

In Panel B of Table 8.4, the diagnostic tests reveal that our instruments are robust. Especially, the estimates of *J*-test do not provide any significant evidence in favour of rejecting the null hypothesis that the instruments are orthogonal to the residuals. Similarly, based on the estimated value of the AR(2) test, we do not find any significant evidence of the existence of the second-order serial correlation in the residuals. Overall, these diagnostic tests ascertain the validity of the instruments used in the system-GMM estimation.

Impact of monetary policy on basis of Islamic banks' size and liquidity for Malaysia

After having found the significant empirical evidence of the presence of a credit supply channel in Islamic banks of Malaysia, we scrutinize the asymmetric effect of monetary policy tightening on credit supply at small-sized versus large-sized banks as well as at less-liquid versus more-liquid banks. As we do in the case of Pakistan, three different versions of the "interacted model" are estimated, and the results are reported in Table 8.5. The diagnostic tests given in Panel B of the table do not provide any significant evidence in favour of rejecting the null hypothesis that the instruments are orthogonal to the residuals. Similarly, we do not find any significant evidence of the existence of the second-order serial correlation in the residuals. Thus, we can conclude that our sets of instruments are valid and uncorrelated with the estimated results, suggesting the robustness of the system-GMM estimation results.

Table 8.5 Asymmetric impact of monetary policy across bank size and bank liquidity for Malaysia

Panel A: Estimation Results						
Variables	*Model (a)*		*Model (b)*		*Model (c)*	
	Coefficient	*SE*	*Coefficient*	*SE*	*Coefficient*	*SE*
Lagged Credit Supply	0.345***	0.161	0.398***	0.190	0.679***	0.114
Bans Size	0.065**	0.038	0.047**	0.027	0.236**	0.018
Bans Liquidity	−0.845***	0.293	−0.749***	0.204	−0.472***	0.134
Bans Capital	0.499**	0.130	0.131*	0.783	0.903**	0.466
Coverage Ratio	0.008	0.261	−0.140	0.095	−0.380	0.764
Credit Risk	0.005***	0.020	0.079**	0.041	0.226**	0.139
Bans Profitability	0.365	0.317	0.276**	0.150	0.424***	0.187
Debt to Equity Ratio	−0.068	0.398	−0.275	0.199	−0.237	0.167
Lending Rate × $D^{Small\ banks}$	−0.035***	0.010				
Lending Rate × $D^{Large\ banks}$	−0.029***	0.007				
Interest Rate Spread × $D^{Small\ banks}$			−0.052***	0.006		
Interest Rate Spread × $D^{Large\ banks}$			−0.036***	0.005		
Deposit Rate × $D^{Small\ banks}$					−0.098**	0.059
Deposit Rate ×$D^{Large\ banks}$					−0.063**	0.009
Lending Rate ×$D^{Less\ liquid}$	−0.049***	0.005				
Lending Rate ×$D^{More\ liquid}$	−0.046***	0.005				
Interest Rate Spread × $D^{Less\ liquid}$			−0.047***	0.006		
Interest Rate Spread × $D^{More\ liquid}$			−0.040***	0.006		
Deposit Rate × $D^{D^{Less\ liquid}}$					−0.068***	0.003
Deposit Rate × $D^{More\ liquid}$					−0.028***	0.004
GDP Growth	0.116**	0.027	0.222*	0.174	0.062*	0.057
Inflation	0.028***	0.011	0.026***	0.011	0.037***	0.014
Constants	1.929**	0.898	0.732**	0.308	0.696*	0.540
Panel B: Diagnostic Tests						
Observations	107		107		107	
Banks	11		11		11	
AR (2)	0.41		0.40		0.84	
p-value	0.684		0.690		0.401	
J-statistic	15.05		13.20		15.24	
p-value	1.000		1.000		1.000	

Note The *J*-statistic is a test of the over-identifying restrictions and distributed as chi-squared under the null of instrument validity and the AR (2) Arellano-Bond is the test of second-order autocorrelation in the first-differenced residuals.

*** $p < 0.01$, ** $p < 0.05$, * $p < 0.1$

Since the effects of bank-specific variables and macroeconomic indicators are similar to those in Table 8.4, we only discuss the coefficients of interaction terms of bank size dummy and bank liquidity dummy with measures of monetary policy. The estimated value of the coefficients of the interaction term between bank size and monetary measures suggest that although both small-sized and larger-sized Islamic banks decrease their lending as a result of the increased interest rate, small-sized Islamic banks reduce their investment financing by higher amounts in all the three estimated regressions. For instance, when the lending rate increases by a 1 percent, small-sized Islamic banks cut their financing back by 3.5 percent of their total assets, whereas, the corresponding figure for large-sized Islamic banks is 2.9 percent. This behaviour of small-sized Islamic banks might be attributed to the increased costs of external financing due to monetary tightening.

Another possible explanation for this finding is that small-sized banks face more financial distress as they become more financially constrained during periods of tight monetary policy, and thus they become more cautious in expanding credits to their customers. Finally, one can expect that small-sized banks generally have less internally generated funds and face more difficulties in raising non-borrowing funds such as issuance of equity and commercial papers. These barriers become serious in periods of monetary tightening, and hence small-sized Islamic banks are affected more than large-sized Islamic banks. In contrast, larger Islamic banks have more capability to absorb the adverse effects of tightening monetary policy, whereas small-sized banks have less such ability and thus are affected more by contractions of monetary policy. Several prior studies (see, for instance, Kashyap and Stein, 1994; Sharpe, 1995; Bernanke and Gertler, 1995; Gertler and Gilchrist, 1993; Kashyap and Stein, 1995; Majid and Hasin, 2012; Alper, Hulagu, and Keles, 2012) have documented similar findings for conventional banks of different countries across the globe.

The estimates of the interaction terms between the bank liquidity dummy and monetary policy measures suggest that the tightening of monetary policy has a significant asymmetric effect on credit supply of less- and more-liquid Islamic banks in Malaysia. Specifically, we show that the credit supply of more-liquid banks is less adversely affected by tight monetary policy. This result holds in all the three estimated regressions.

The estimated value of coefficient suggests that due to a 1 percent increase in the deposit rate, less-liquid banks decline their investment financing by 9.8 percent of their total assets, whereas more-liquid banks decrease their credit supply by only 2.8 percent. However, this difference in the response of less- and more-liquid banks to monetary tightening becomes narrow in the regressions where we use the lending rate and the interest rate spread as monetary policy measures. These results suggest that the asymmetric impact of monetary tightening on credit supply at less-liquid banks versus more-liquid banks is more profound when it is measured in terms of the spending rate instead of the lending rate. These results confirming our prediction suggest that the liquidity position of a bank has a significant role to play in formulating the effects of tight monetary policy on the lending behaviour of the bank. These results suggest that bank liquidity can be used as a safeguard to lessen the adverse effects of monetary tightening.

Differential impact of monetary policy Islamic banks' credit supply in Pakistan versus Malaysia

In Table 8.6, we re-present the estimated coefficients of the monetary measures to compare the effects of monetary tightening for Pakistan and Malaysia. The values of monetary policy measures are taken for the bassline model of Pakistan from Table 8.2 and for the baseline model of Malaysia from Table 8.4. Similarly, we find that the monetary policy indicators affect small-sized banks and less-liquid banks more as compared to large-sized banks and more-liquid banks in Table 8.3 for Pakistan and in Table 8.5 for Malaysia. Furthermore, we scrutinize how tight monetary policy affects Islamic banks' credit supply in Pakistan as compared to that of Malaysia by taking into account Islamic banks' size and liquidity stocks. Based on the estimated size of coefficients, we find that the credit supply channel of the monetary policy transmission mechanism is more effective in Malaysia than Pakistan.

The Malaysian Islamic banking sector is found to be efficient and working smoothly. In Malaysia, the banking sector documents 4.7 percent of GDP, boasting

Table 8.6 Impacts of monetary policy on Islamic banks' credit supply in Pakistan versus Malaysia

Panel A: Effects of monetary tightening on Islamic banks' credit supply					
		Lending Interest Rate	*Interest Rate Spread*	*Deposit Interest Rate*	
Baseline Models	Model 1 (Pakistan)	−0.025***	−0.027***	−0.024***	
	Model 4 (Malaysia)	−0.045***	−0.043***	−0.045***	
Panel B: Asymmetric effects of monetary tightening across bank size					
Small versus Large Banks	Model 2 (Pakistan)	−0.027***	−0.045***	−0.040***	Small Banks
		−0.023***	−0.035***	−0.029***	Large Banks
	Model 5 (Malaysia)	−0.035***	−0.052***	−0.098**	Small Banks
		−0.029***	−0.036***	−0.063**	Large Banks
Panel C: Asymmetric effects of monetary tightening across bank liquidity					
Less Liquid versus More Liquid	Model 3 (Pakistan)	−0.021***	−0.034***	−0.021***	Less-Liquid Banks
		−0.019***	−0.025***	−0.015***	More-Liquid Banks
	Model 6 (Malaysia)	−0.049***	−0.047***	−0.068***	Less-Liquid Banks
		−0.046***	−0.040***	−0.028***	More-Liquid Banks

assets worth 198.8 percent of GDP, and holds 3 percent of the total employed force of the country as in 2016. Comparatively more effective monetary policy of Malaysia is because of the professional commitment of the central bank of Malaysia. BNM's monetary policy actions are conducted to stabilize the prices through keeping an eye on the economic growth of the country. In addition, BNM plays a vital role in development of a progressive, sound, and diversified financial sector, which leads to financial system stability. It also takes initiatives to deepen the financial markets' role in the development of real economy, including the foreign exchange market. Similarly, BNM also supervises the framework of the nation's payment systems, which ensures the efficiency of financial markets and security of the financial systems. Moreover, it has played an important role in developing the infrastructure for financial inclusion through easing the public access to financial services. BNM advices the government, as a banker and an adviser, on the macroeconomic public policies and the management of public debt. It is also an independent authority with a sole right to issue the national currency and to manage the international reserves of Malaysia. These functions of BNM provide a conducive environment for working credit supply channel of banks more efficiently in Malaysia as compared to Pakistan.

In Malaysia, the Islamic banking sector is also found more effective as compared to that of Pakistan because of well-developed infrastructure. The Islamic banks are not entirely based on the interest rate; rather, there is the IBOR (Islamic Banking Offered Rate) determined by the Islamic Inter-Bank Money Market (IIMM) in Malaysia. There are a variety of monetary instruments on the basis of a number of Islamic contracts. These instruments of IIMM include Government Investment Issue (GII), *Mudarabah* Interbank Investment (MII), *Wadiah* Acceptance (WA), Islamic Accepted Bills (IAB), Islamic Negotiable Instruments (INI), Bank Negara Monetary Notes-i (BNMN-i), Sell and Buy Back Agreement (SBBA), *Cagamas Mudharabah* Bonds (SMC), *Sukuk* BNM *Ijarah* (SBNMI), When Issue (WI), Islamic Private Debt Securities, and *Ar Rahnu* Agreement-I (RA-i). Pakistan and other countries may need to get benefits from the successful experience of Malaysia, especially in developing Islamic financial market and improving institutions quality, which will definitely help transmit the monetary policy through the credit supply channel more efficiently.

Conclusion and policy implication

The bank credit supply channel of monetary policy has recently received increased attention by both researchers and policy makers. In fact, we have a vast body of literature on the effects of monetary policy on the credit supply decisions of conventional banks. Yet we know less about the behaviour of Islamic banks during periods of monetary tightening. In this chapter, we examine the existing of an Islamic bank-centric view of the monetary policy transmission mechanism by quantifying the impact of three different measures of monetary policy on the credit supply of Islamic banks in Pakistan and Malaysia.

Estimating the models for both countries separately, we provide strong evidence on the existence of the credit supply channel of monetary policy through Islamic banks in both countries. Similarly, the results indicate that Islamic banks respond more to the tightening of monetary policy in Malaysia as compared to Pakistan. The results from the extended model indicate that large-sized and more-liquid Islamic banks respond less to monetary policy tightening as compared to small-sized and less-liquid counterparts. The relatively lesser response of larger and more liquid banks to the tightening of monetary policy may make it difficult for the central bank to achieve the desired objectives of the monetary policy.

There are several policy implications emerging from the empirical results of this chapter for monetary policy authorities of both countries. First, the central bank should manage the interest rate to stabilize the credit supply through Islamic banks, because we present strong evidence of the present of Islamic bank-centric view in Pakistan and Malaysia. Second, our findings suggest that for an effective monetary policy, there is a vital need to consider the unique nature of Islamic banks while devising the instruments to manage credit supply in the economy. Otherwise, there may appear quandaries to monetary policy actions. Third, our findings suggest that for an effective monetary policy, there is a vital need to consider the size and liquidity stocks of Islamic banks while devising the instruments to manage credit supply in the economy. Fourth, policy makers should keep in preference the microeconomic aspects of banks' credit supply behaviour in formulating monetary policy, because we find that small-sized and less-liquid banks are affected more as compared to their large-sized and more-liquid counterparts in both Pakistan and Malaysia. Lack of adequate monetary instruments will lead to high intermediation cost and persistent inflationary pressures. This study suggests policymakers should consider Islamic financing as a complement channel to the monetary policy transmission mechanism because we find strong evidence of the presence of Islamic banks' credit supply channel in Pakistan and Malaysia.

We suggest that the authorities in Pakistan can get some benefits from a successful experience of Malaysia while designing Islamic financial products and devising monetary instruments to achieve higher economic growth and price stability, although a sound *Shari'ah* appraisal would be required, as a future research agenda, of Islamic monetary instruments that are based upon controversial vehicle contracts like *Bai-Inna*, commodity *Murabh'ah*, etc. This area of research is a challenge for researchers to find out ways to harmonize different juristic opinions in domain of Islamic monetary instruments, enabling the industry to move to the development of a global Islamic financial market.

References

Akhatova, M., Zainal, M. P., & Ibrahim, M. I. (2016). Banking Models and Monetary Transmission Mechanisms in Malaysia: Are Islamic Banks Different? *Economic Papers*, 35(2), 169–83.

Alaro, A. R., & Hakeem, M. (2011). Financial Engineering and Financial Stability: The Role of Islamic Financial System. *Journal of Islamic Economics, Banking and Finance*, 7(1), 34–55.

Alper, K., Hulagu, T., & Keles, G. (2012). An Empirical Study on Liquidity and Bank Lending. *Central Bank of the Republic of Turkey*, Working Paper No. 4, Turkey.

Anwar, S., & Nguyend, L. P., (2018). Channels of Monetary Policy Transmission in Vietnam. *Journal of Policy Modelling*, 23, 32.

Arellano, M., & Bond, S. (1991). Some Tests of Specification for Panel Data: Monte Carlo Evidence and an Application to Employment Equations. *Review of Economic Studies*, 58, 277–97.

Arellano, M., & Bover, O. (1995). Another Look at the Instrumental Variable Estimation of Error-Components Models. *Journal of Econometrics*, 68, 29–51.

Auclert, A. (2017). Monetary Policy and the Redistribution Channel. *NBER Working Paper Series*, Working Paper 23451, Cambridge, MA, 02138, 1–46.

Aysun, U., & Hepp, R. (2013). Identifying the Balance Sheet and the Lending Channels of Monetary Transmission: A Loan-Level Analysis. *Journal of Banking & Finance*, 37, 2812–22.

Bernanke, B. S., & Gertler, A. S. (1995). Inside the Black Box: The Credit Channel of Monetary Policy Transmission. *Journal of Economic Perspectives*, 9(4), 27–48.

Bernanke, B. S., Gertler, M., & Gilchrist, S. (1999). The Financial Accelerator in a Quantitative Business Cycle Framework. In *Handbook of Macroeconomics*. Amsterdam: Elsevier.

Bernanke, B. S., Lown, C. S., & Friedman, B. M. (1991). The Credit Crunch. *Brookings Papers on Economic Activity*, 205–247.

Blundell, R., & Bond, S. (1998). Initial Conditions and Moment Restrictions in Dynamic Panel Data Models. *Journal of Econometrics*, 87, 115–43.

Cecchetti, S. G. (1999). Legal Structure, Financial Structure, and the Monetary Policy Transmission Mechanism. *NBER*, Working Paper No. W 7151.

Chapra, M. U. (1985). Towards a Just Monetary System. *International Institute of Islamic Thought (IIIT)* and *The Islamic Foundation*, London Road, Leicester, UK, 223.

Chaudary, N. N., & Mirakhor, A. (1997). Indirect Instruments of Monetary Controlling an Islamic Financial System. *Islamic Economic Studies*, 4(2), 27–65.

Ehrmann, M., Gambacorta, L., Martínez-Pagés, J., Sevestre, P., & Worms, A. (2001). Financial Systems and the Role of Banks in Monetary Policy Transmission in the Euro Area. *ECB*, Working Paper No. 105, Germany.

Erdogdu, A. (2017). Functioning and Effectiveness of Monetary Transmission Mechanisms: Turkey Applications. *Journal of Finance and Bank Management, American Research Institute for Policy Development*, 5(1), 29–41.

Evans, C., Fisher, J., Gourio, F., & Kran, S. (2015). Risk Management for Monetary Policy Near the Zero Lower Bound. *Brookings Papers on Economic Activity*, 141–219.

Farahani, Y, G., & Dastan, M. (2013). Analysis of Islamic Banks' Financing and Economic Growth: A Panel Co-Integration Approach. *International Journal of Islamic and Middle Eastern Finance and Management*, 6(2), 156–72.

Gertler, M., & Gilchrist, S. (1993). The Role of Credit Market Imperfections in the Monetary Transmission Mechanism: Arguments and Evidence. *The Scandinavian Journal of Economics*, 95(1), 43–64.

Girardin, E., & Moussa, Z. (2011). Quantitative Easing Works: Lessons from the Unique Experience in Japan 2001–2006. *Journal of International Financial Markets, Institutions and Money*, 21, 461–95.

Hansen, L. P. (1982). Large Sample Properties of Generalized Method of Moments Estimators. *Econometrica*, 50(4), 1029–54.

Hardianto, E. (2004). Shariah Transmission Mechanism in Indonesia. *Journal of Economic Cooperation and Development*, 8(2), 20–38.

Janjua, P. Z., Rashid, A., & Qurrat-Ul-Ain. (2014). Impact of Monetary Policy on Bank' Balance Sheet in Pakistan. *International Journal of Economics and Finance*, 6(11), 187–96.

Jermann, U., & Schmid, J. (2016). Negative Swap Spreads and Limited Arbitrage. Available at SSRN.

Kaleem, A., & Isa, M. (2006). Islamic Banking and Money Demand Function in Malaysia: An Econometric Analysis. *Pakistan Economic and Social Review*, 44(2), 277–90.

Kashyap, A. K., & Stein, J. C. (1994). Monetary Policy and Bank Lending in Monetary Policy. *The University of Chicago Press*, 29(1).

Kashyap, A. K., & Stein, J. C. (1995). The Impact of Monetary Policy on Bank Balance Sheets. *NBER*, Working Paper No. 4821, USA.

Kashyap, A. K., & Stein, J. C. (1997). The Role of Banks in Monetary Policy: A Survey with Implications for the European Monetary Union. *Economic Perspectives-Federal Reserve Bank of Chicago*, 21, 2–18.

King, R. C., & Plosser, I. (1984). The Behavior of Money, Credit, and Prices in a Real Business Cycle. *National Bureau of Economic Research Cambridge*, 74(3), 363–80.

Kishan, R. P., & Opiela, T. P. (2000). Bank Size, Bank Capital, and the Bank Lending Channel. *Journal of Money, Credit and Banking*, 32(1), 121–41.

Köhler, M., Hommel, J., & Grote, M. (2006). The Role of Banks in the Transmission of Monetary Policy in the Baltics. *Centre for European Economic Research (ZEW)*, Discussion Paper, 06-005, Germany.

Majid, M. S., & Hasin, Z. (2012). Islamic Banks and Monetary Transmission Mechanism in Malaysia. *Journal of Economic Cooperation and Development*, 35(2), 137–66.

Mishkin, F. S. (1996). The Channels of Monetary Transmission: Lesson for Monetary Policy. *NBER*, Working Paper No. 5464.

Nosheen & Rashid, A. (2019). Business Orientation, Efficiency, and Credit Quality across Business Cycle: Islamic versus Conventional Banking: Are There Any Lessons for Europe and Baltic States? *Baltic Journal of Economics*, 19(1), 105–35.

Pruteanu, A. (2004). The Role of Banks in the Czech Monetary Policy Transmission Mechanism. *Czech National Bank*, Working Papers 2004/03.

Rashid, A., Riaz, M., & Zaffar, A. (2017). Are Islamic Banks Really Different from Conventional Banks? An Investigation using Classification Techniques. *Journal of Islamic Business and Management*, 8(1), 37–52.

Sanrego, Y. D., & Nikmawati, K. (2010). Transmission Mechanism of Sharia Financing in Malaysia. *The Journal of Muamalat& Islamic Finance, Research (JMIFR)*, 7(1).

Sanrego, Y. D., & Rusydiana, A. S. (2013). Transmission Mechanism in Dual Monetary System: Comparison between Shariah and Conventional Monetary System. *Journal of Islamic Economics, Banking and Finance*, 9(2).

Santis, R. A., & Surico, P. (2013). Bank Lending and Monetary Transmission in the Euro Area. *Economic Policy*, 28(75), 423–57.

Schmitz, B. (2004). What Role do Banks Play in Monetary Policy Transmission in EU New Member Countries? *Mimeo*, 4(2).

Shah, M. A. R., Rashid, A., & Mansoori, M. Tr. (2018). The Role of Islamic versus Conventional Banks in Monetary Policy Transmission: An Empirical Investigation for Pakistan. Unpublished manuscript, International Islamic University, Islamabad, Pakistan. *FWU Journal of Social Sciences*, 12(1).

Shah, M. A. R., Rashid, A., & Khaleequzzaman, M. K. (2017). Capital Structure Decisions in Islamic Banking: Empirical Evidence from Pakistan. *Journal of Islamic Banking and Finance*, 34(2), 88–103.

Sharpe, S. A. (1995). Bank Capitalization, Regulation, and the Credit Crunch: A Critical Review of the Research Findings. *Board of Governors of the Federal Reserve System*, Finance and Economics Discussion Series No. 95–20, USA.

Sims, C. (1992). Interpreting the Macroeconomic Time Series Facts: The Effects of Monetary Policy. *European Economic Review*, 36(5), 975–1011.

Stepanchuk, S., & Tsyrennikov, V. (2015). Portfolio and Welfare Consequences of Debt Market Dominance. *Journal of Monetary Economics*, 74(2), 89–101.

Sukmana, R., & Kassim, S. H. (2010). Roles of the Islamic Banks in the Monetary Transmission in Malaysia. *International Journal of Islamic and Middle Eastern Finance and Management*, 31(1).

Wong, K. (2000). Variability in the Effects of Monetary Policy on Economic Activity. *Journal of Money, Credit and Banking*, 32(2), 179–98.

Zaheer, S., Ongena, S., & Wijnbergen, S. J. G. (2013). The Transmission of Monetary Policy through Conventional and Islamic Banks. *International Journal of Central Banking Duha*, 8, 175–224.

9 Cryptocurrencies from the perspective of Islamic economics

Discussions and opportunities

Mücahit Özdemir, Zeyneb Hafsa Orhan, and Hüseyin Burgazoğlu

Introduction

The speed of technological developments is increasing day by day and transforming many areas, from everyday life to relations between countries. While there are many innovations and possibilities that make life easier, current or potential negativities of technology are also discussed from different perspectives. It is impossible that the economy and finance, which are at the centre of our lives, will not be affected by technological developments in both positive and negative ways. One of these developments is the cryptocurrencies, which are still debated as to whether or not they are money.

Thousands of cryptocurrencies, which first emerged with Bitcoin in 2008 and have increased their popularity in recent years, are among the essential subjects of the financial agenda. Systems based on blockchain and other similar cryptology techniques that are the base for cryptocurrencies are increasing, and they are expected to transform not only finance but also other areas such as health, law, the electoral system, and public records. Additionally, issues related to cryptocurrencies such as anonymity, decentralization, and extreme price fluctuations attract the attention of many stakeholders, from individuals to multinational companies and countries. Here, the position of governments and states against cryptocurrencies is particularly essential. There are many issues, such as risk management, taxing, and money laundering, that need to be addressed by public authorities in the context of cryptocurrencies.

Today, although the share of cryptocurrencies in the global financial system is meagre and can be considered as insignificant in a trillion-dollar financial market, the potential of them and the blockchain technology upon which they are built is making cryptocurrencies one of the most critical items on the financial agenda.

Blockchain technology and cryptocurrencies are also new phenomena for Muslims. Evaluation of the position of cryptocurrencies in Islamic economics and related views about them is a necessity in order to integrate such currencies in Islamic economics in an appropriate way. Because the nature of the cryptocurrencies is complex and evolving, it requires interdisciplinary study. So it is useful to consider and reconsider the developments in the cryptocurrencies and the approaches in the Islamic world. This section examines the cryptocurrencies within the framework of recent developments in Islamic economics and aims to contribute to the effort to understand the phenomenon. For this purpose, firstly, the technical features of blockchain technology and cryptocurrencies will be examined. Afterwards, the views of the leading scholars/religious authorities in the Islamic world regarding cryptocurrencies and practical initiatives will be mentioned. Finally, the potential that cryptocurrencies can offer to Islamic economics will be discussed, and some issues will be raised for further studies.

Blockchain technology and cryptocurrencies

Blockchain technology

Following the article titled "Bitcoin: A Peer-to-Peer Electronic Cash System" published by Satoshi Nakamoto (2008) on October 31, 2008, Bitcoin came into our lives with the creation of the necessary infrastructure by several software enthusiasts. Bitcoin is the first large-scale system that uses blockchain technology to store data, and it is the reason that the technology gained its popularity.

Bitcoin and other cryptocurrencies use blockchain technology. According to its fundamental principles, the blockchain is defined as a system that allows transactions between the parties to be recorded without any interference of a central authority (Beck, 2018). Blockchain is a list formed by adding the records called blocks one after the other. Each block contains a code which makes it possible to establish a link with the previous block, a timestamp, and information about the corresponding transaction. Thus, the blockchain is defined as a distributed ledger (Chen, 2019).

Adding the blocks behind each other like a chain ensures that the data is kept in a proper form and prevents manipulation. Blockchain is not managed from a single server; on the contrary, all data is stored by a network of computers called nodes. Every new node in the network enhances decentralization and strengthens the consensus mechanism (Beck, 2018).

In blockchain technology, the same information is kept at different nodes, and if a consensus is achieved between these nodes, a new record will be added to the chain. Under the working principle of blockchain technology, new information can be added to the existing chain, but it is not allowed to change the previously created records/blocks. Storing related information of transactions on different nodes allows the system to function as a distributed ledger. In the system of blockchain, there are miners that add newly formed records to the chain, as well as the nodes that keep all records. Miners ensure that transactions are verified and added to the chain in accordance with predetermined rules. They must decrypt the last created block in order to add a new block to the chain, and such a process needs computers with high processing power. Once decrypted, the miner will announce the solution and show the "Proof of Work"; after the solution is approved by other users on the network, the new records will be added to the chain (Böhme et al., 2015). Miners earn crypto money for their services (Ali et al., 2014).

The blockchain is open source and thus provides a high level of transparency. In addition, the blocks are encrypted to protect the records against possible retrospective manipulations. Being independent of any central authority, blockchain's transparency and openness and its resilience to manipulation and other frauds have attracted considerable interest in blockchain technology both in academic and practical terms. Blockchain, which can be used in many different fields, is shown among the technologies that will profoundly affect both the business world and societies in the coming periods (Webb, 2015).

Although blockchain was created much earlier (Haber & Stornetta, 1991), it gained popularity with Bitcoin, the first cryptocurrency, and its use has accelerated with increasing interest. Due to its unique and innovative features, blockchain technology is being used not only in the field of cryptocurrency but also in different fields, such as health, supply chain, energy, finance, and even music.

It is essential to keep records of transactions carried out for any organization, whether for businesses, multinational corporations, or governments. Keeping the records of past transactions is vital for organizations for their strategic planning. While these records are necessary for the proper and consistent operations within the organization, they also provide insight for the shareholders and stakeholders about how the organization performs. Bringing together records kept by different departments and individuals within organizations in the main ledger is a time-consuming and laborious operation and prone to errors (Iansiti & Lakhani, 2017). However, blockchain technology records each transaction in real time and controls it with records from different databases to ensure its accuracy. When any new records are added, all other copies are updated simultaneously.

Blockchain is an innovative technology that can allow governments to keep records at a lower cost and more consistently and quickly in many official areas, such as transfer of property rights, birth certificates, marriage certificates, business licenses, vehicle registrations, education certificates, and even voting in elections (Ølnes, Ubacht, & Janssen, 2017).

For Bitcoin, blockchain technology allows only the previous records to be stored, while, with the help of some computer programs called "smart contracts" included in the codes of blockchain, this technology can be used for different purposes. In that way, these smart contracts in blockchain technology have already been used in different areas such as supply chain, real estate market, and personal health data tracking. Some of the advantages of smart contracts are as follows: It enables bilateral agreements without the need for lawyers or brokers; related documents and data are stored as encrypted registries in the distributed ledger; there is no loss of data because of many copies of records stored by different nodes; it saves time with the help of automated programs for repetitive tasks; it reduces cost due to elimination of intermediary agents; and it is less prone to errors (Aste, Tasca, & Matteo, 2017).

There are also other technologies that have similar working principles to blockchain technology but have some technical differences. Some of the popular ones are Tangle (IoTA), Hasgraph (Hedera), Lattice (Nano), and Holochain (HoloFuel). These alternatives differentiate themselves from blockchain technology in some areas such as increased processing speed, reduced transaction costs, and enhanced security.

Bitcoin and cryptocurrencies

For thousands of years, humankind has used precious metals such as gold and silver, banknotes backed by gold, or fiat money as means of exchange. However, these kinds of money have some inherent challenges such as the difficulty of transport, risk of theft, need for trust to a central authority, and inflation because of excessive money supply. It is claimed that cryptocurrencies that are not administered by any state or central authority such as Bitcoin, which operate within the framework of specific mathematical rules, cover the negative aspects of these aforementioned currencies (Alstyne, 2014; Hütten & Thiemann, 2017).

The concept of cryptocurrency came into the literature with Bitcoin, and Bitcoin came into our lives with Satoshi Nakamoto's nine-page article published in 2008. Cryptocurrencies, a kind of digital money, theoretically show some features of the concept of money. After the popularity of Bitcoin, different cryptocurrencies emerged. Today there are thousands of them traded on cryptocurrency exchange platforms. While many of them do not bring any innovation, the cryptocurrencies that somehow contribute to the system gain value and importance.

Table 9.1 shows the top ten currencies with the highest market value. Bitcoin, surely, is the most popular one with the highest transaction volume among these cryptocurrencies. Although Bitcoin is called a cryptocurrency, Nakamoto (2008) described Bitcoin as "a system for electronic transactions without relying on trust" in his article. Blockchain technology enables peer-to-peer money transfer without the need for any intermediary institutions.

The most innovative feature of Bitcoin is that it functions as a monetary system outside a central authority. This feature gives a significant level of anonymity to the transactions. In order to ensure anonymity during the transfer of money,

Table 9.1 Cryptocurrencies with highest market value

Cryptocurrency	*Market Cap ($)*	*Price ($)*	*Circulating Supply*
Bitcoin	131,881,980,370	7.276	18,125,412 BTC
Ethereum	13,797,403,441	126.52	109,049,577 ETH
XRP	8,273,943,378	0.190998	43,319,477,613 XRP
Tether	4,141,085,876	1.01	4,108,044,456 USDT
Bitcoin Cash	3,668,880,002	201.70	18,189,950 BCH
Litecoin	2,613,946,107	41.02	63,726,269 LTC
EOS	2,445,045,074	2.58	946,148,059 EOS
Binance Coin	2,065,890,798	13.28	155,536,713 BNB
Bitcoin SV	1,631,139,315	90.28	18,068,415 BSV
Tezos	957,647,485	1.38	694,191,974 XTZ

Source: coinmarketcap.com (27.12.2019)

personal information is not specified in the transactions, and public keys indicate the origin and destination of the transaction. In order to complete the transactions, private keys that represent unique electronic wallets which are stored on personal computers of users or the websites created for this purpose are also required (Ober, Katzenbeisser, & Hamacher, 2013).

While the central banks and some other government agencies can have some degree of authority on the currency in circulation through monetary policies, no government or central authority has an impact on the Bitcoin supply. Instead of a central authority, the Bitcoin supply is determined by the network of miners according to mathematical algorithms within the framework of specific cryptography rules (Angel & McCabe, 2015). The amount of Bitcoin produced and the rate of increase is publicly available information. The miners achieve produce a new Bitcoin by earning Bitcoin for their services. The amount of Bitcoin obtained for the services of miners decreases with time within a certain ratio. A total of 21 million Bitcoins can be produced, and the total supply is expected to be reached by 2140. Although the total amount of Bitcoin is fixed, it is also possible for a sufficient number of miners to come together and increase the maximum amount by reaching a consensus (Böhme et al., 2015).

The first Bitcoins were produced in 2009, and they were traded on Mt. Gox, an online platform where game cards are exchanged. The first shopping with Bitcoin is considered to be two pizzas for 10,000 Bitcoins. Later, due to the anonymity of Bitcoin, it became the active currency of websites such as Silk Road, where illegal purchases (drugs and arms, etc.) were taking place. The arrest of the owner of Silk Road and the closure of the website in 2013 increased Bitcoin's recognition and popularity (Yermack, 2015).

Two main factors have played a role in Bitcoin's recognition. The first of these is that technology enthusiasts use Bitcoin for online shopping, and they believe that the value of Bitcoin will scale up by the increase in commercial transactions over the internet. The other is that the decentralized structure of Bitcoin is parallel to the ideas of those who do not trust the global financial system and seek an alternative system (Yermack, 2015). Notably, the emergence of Bitcoin after the 2008–2009 financial crisis[1] has helped it gain importance in this context.

Despite the innovations it brings, its popularity and high transaction volumes, there are some issues for the acceptance level of Bitcoin in daily life. One of the most important of these challenges is the fact that it is not commonly used in the purchase of products and services in real life today. Some leading companies, such as Microsoft, Overstock, and Expedia, as well as many businesses, accept trades with Bitcoin. However, most of Bitcoin's transaction volume belongs to speculative investments (Weber, 2014). For example, 90 percent of the transactions of Bitcoin as of 2019 were for investment and speculative purposes (Elevenews, 2019).

Another challenge is how people can get Bitcoin. The only way to get Bitcoin for any person is to buy Bitcoin using the money in circulation unless he or she is mining with a computer with high computing power.

Bitcoin's fluctuating price is also a problem. One of the conditions why a currency can be used as a means of exchange in purchases is to have a certain level of stability. In this context, another reason why Bitcoin cannot be used in daily life is its highly fluctuating structure (Weber, 2015). On a daily basis and even within minutes, the value of Bitcoin against other currencies can vary greatly. Therefore, product and service providers who want to trade with Bitcoin are required to make regular adjustments to their prices. Also, the fact that Bitcoin is at a level indicated in thousands of dollars (around 7,200 dollars as of December 2019) in daily transactions causes a $5 coffee to be expressed as 0.00069543 BTC. To overcome this situation, the Satoshi unit is used as one hundred-millionth of a Bitcoin.

There are other cryptocurrencies alternative to Bitcoin, known as “altcoin”. Although they are similar to Bitcoin in general structure, these alternative cryptocurrencies differ from Bitcoin in some methodical and technical ways. Some of these differences are reducing the amount of processing capacity and energy required to add new blocks to blockchain, increasing confidentiality, and using different smart contracts.

The first alternative to Bitcoin is the cryptocurrency called as Namecoin. Namecoin was launched in April 2011 based on the same “proof-of-work” algorithm as Bitcoin. So, similar to Bitcoin, a total of 21 million Namecoin will be produced, and this cryptocurrency aims to provide privacy to individuals when purchasing the domains of websites (Namecoin, 2019). Another notable alternative, Ethereum, which comes in second after Bitcoin in terms of market value, was launched in 2014. Ethereum, like Bitcoin, is based on blockchain technology but differs in terms of purpose and scope. The blockchain on which Bitcoin is based only monitors the transactions between peers, while Ethereum blockchain technology also runs programs called as smart contracts. As mentioned earlier, not only money but also content and document sharing can be done with smart contracts, and due to that feature, there are many cryptocurrencies such as Binance Coin that use the Ethereum structure (Buterin, 2014). Also, plans are in the works to launch a cryptocurrency called Libra in 2020 under the leadership of Facebook and with the backing of some multinational institutions such as Mastercard, Visa, eBay, Uber, and Vodafone (LibraAssociation, 2019).

Reactions of states to cryptocurrency, and Bitcoin in particular, are varied and still cautious. Some countries allow the use of cryptocurrencies and pass relevant legislation, while it is prohibited to use such money in others. Today, the most appropriate laws on cryptocurrencies exist in Switzerland. The Swiss-based ECUREX GmbH cryptocurrency exchange operates in full compliance with the Swiss Banking Act (Chornous et al., 2019). Although most of the developed countries, such as European Union countries, the United States, Russia, and Japan, have not introduced legal regulations specific to cryptocurrencies, the transactions made by individuals and businesses with cryptocurrencies are considered legal. In countries such as China, India, and the United Arab Emirates, cryptocurrencies are legally accepted, but some legal limitations have been imposed. In Canada, for example, in April 2018, the Bank of Montreal banned customers from buying cryptocurrencies using their credit or debit cards. In China, many cryptocurrency exchanges and platforms were banned with some regulations in 2017. In addition, many companies engaged in Bitcoin mining were closed in January 2018. On the other hand, in some countries such as Pakistan, Algeria, and Bolivia, the use and possession of Bitcoin and other cryptocurrencies is wholly prohibited (cryptonews, 2019). Venezuela is the first country to create a state-backed cryptocurrency (Petro). Some countries such as Russia, Japan, Estonia, and Dubai are also preparing to issue their own national state-backed cryptocurrency.

The fact that cryptocurrency is a new concept and people have little knowledge about the subject makes this area open to fraud. Fake wallets, phishing, pumping, and dumping the value of cryptocurrencies by big players called as whales and internet groups, fraudulent ICOs,[2] and hacking are examples for the methods used for fraud. Hacking of cryptocurrency exchanges such as Binance, GateHub, and Bitrue and scams with cryptocurrency such as Onecoin, Pincoin, and Bitconnect are just a few cases of many fraud incidents. The total amount of fraud committed with cryptocurrencies only in 2019 is considered to be 4.4 billion dollars (Ricca, 2019).

Reflections towards cryptocurrencies in the Islamic world

Cryptocurrencies, particularly Bitcoin, have attracted the attention of people from various economic levels, religions, and age groups in many different regions of the world and have entered their agenda in different ways. Undoubtedly, one of the factors behind this is the expression of "currency, coin or money" in the name of this innovation and excessive fluctuations in their prices. In addition, different segments of society have recently been paying attention to cryptocurrencies because of the influence of the media. Besides individuals, states also follow developments carefully in order to understand the possible threats and examine the opportunities the cryptocurrencies can offer. According to people's priorities and interests, cryptocurrencies and the blockchain technology behind them can be evaluated through various perspectives, such as an innovation that will change the world financial system or a pure scam.

While cryptocurrencies concern people from different religions and beliefs,[3] Shariah's perspective towards them is taken into consideration by Muslims to use, invest, or produce the cryptocurrencies. In other words, for the majority of Muslims who evaluate the issues from a religious perspective and take an approach according to it, the views of Islamic scholars towards cryptocurrencies is vital. For instance, for some people, cryptocurrencies are an excellent investment opportunity with high return, while others consider them as a waste of energy due to the mining process. From this point of view, for a Muslim, the evaluation of cryptocurrencies in the perspective of Islam and its verdict will determine the attitude towards them.

Islam encompasses every aspect of human life, and everyday commercial relations are among the most essential. In this sense, cryptocurrency is also a new phenomenon for Muslims as for the whole world. However, it is also crucial for Muslims to consider whether trading, investing, or mining cryptocurrencies is permissible in Islam. For this reason, Islamic scholars have been engaged in an effort to respond to the questions they receive for this phenomenon about their status from the *fiqh* perspective such as permissible (*mubah*) or forbidden (*haram*). Many of the answers were given by the well-known and respected shariah scholars who have in-depth knowledge on *fiqh* and a vital position in their social environment, and whose explanations could be accepted as reference for a wide range of people. Also, interpretations have been made by institutional religious authorities in different countries.

Personal fatawa

Due to the complexity of the underlying blockchain system and the launch of thousands of altcoins, the verdict (*fatwa;* plural *fatawa*) given by the relevant Islamic scholars or institutions may change over time. For this reason, the chronological evaluation of *fatawa* is essential. Because the level of understanding both the nature of cryptocurrencies and the blockchain technology increases, the verdicts given in the early periods may be revised. Bitcoin is the reference point for the majority of *fatawa* for cryptocurrency. With the increase in Bitcoin prices and the creation of new alternative cryptocurrencies after 2017, evaluations from the perspective of shariah have been made for all cryptocurrencies.

One of the first assessments on Bitcoin came from Professor Monzer Kahf, who is a prominent scholar in Islamic economics. At the beginning of 2014, in his reply to a question about Bitcoin, he first mentioned about whether Bitcoin could be considered as money or not. He stated: "it is a unit of account for those who accept it". However, he emphasized that the fluctuations in prices may lower confidence among its users. From the shariah perspective, Kahf argued that "like any other currency, it is money within its community and exchanging it with other currencies is definitely subject, in my opinion, to same conditions of exchanging currencies" (Kahf, 2017, p. 44). These conditions are to deliver both currencies at the time of exchange and no speculations on currencies.

Kahf made his first assessment in 2014 from the perspective that "a community could accept anything in itself as money".[4] However, in December 2017, his approach changed about Bitcoin and other cryptocurrencies. Kahf stated that "a currency requires a great deal of regulations in order to protect all the economic units; this requires a government" (Kahf, 2017, p. 1). In this sense, since the government does not back Bitcoin and other cryptocurrencies as a legal tender, it cannot be regarded as money from the shariah point of view. However, he asserted that if the government issues cryptocurrencies, it can be accepted as money.

He also discussed whether Bitcoin and other cryptocurrencies are an asset and referred to the view of OIC Fiqh Academy on indexes and options, and concluded that "Bitcoin and other cryptocurrencies are much lesser of assets than options and indexes as they are purely virtual and represent ownership of nothing!" He argued that Bitcoin and other cryptocurrencies are not money because of not being recognized by legal authority (government) as a legal tender, and they are not an asset. Therefore, he asserted that it is not permissible to own, buy, sell, or trade Bitcoin and other cryptocurrencies by referring to the OIC Fiqh Academy's view on options (where trading with options and indices is forbidden). Apart from his position on Bitcoin, Kahf is positive about blockchain technology, and he stated that it had opened a new dimension for digitalization and the future is moving in this direction.

In December 2017, another opinion was given by Professor Ali Muhyealdin Al-Quradaghi, Secretary-General of the International Union of Muslim Scholars. He evaluated cryptocurrencies, particularly Bitcoin, on a television program (Al Jazeera, 2017) and asserted that he did not recommend trading with them for several reasons. The first reason is that, unlike paper money, there is no official authority/state behind the cryptocurrencies, and the system is based entirely on cryptology. Another reason is the use of Bitcoin for illegal activities such as money laundering. The main emphasis of Al-Quradaghi is on the absence of a particular legal authority that regulates and supervises Bitcoin. In his statement, however, Al-Quradaghi argued that the world financial system would soon be entirely digital or electronic, and therefore the Islamic world should keep up with this development. So he calls upon the Islamic scholars in the world to convene and make a decision on the permissibility of cryptocurrencies (Al Jazeera, 2017).

In January 2018, Al-Quradaghi made a new statement about cryptocurrencies on the same television program and asserted that "at this stage" it is not permissible to buy, sell, and trade Bitcoin and similar cryptocurrencies (Al Jazeera, 2018). The main reason for this is that, like Kahf's second opinion, there is no authority behind the cryptocurrency. However, Al-Quradaghi's view cannot be said to have an approach that completely closes the door to cryptocurrencies. He proposed three alternative ways to make this kind of currency suitable for Islam: a state's adoption of any cryptocurrency as its primary or secondary currency; the issuance of cryptocurrencies by Islamic banks so that they are regulated; issuing cryptocurrency through a joint-stock company in which developers and investors are partners (Al-Quradaghi, 2018). The main purpose of these three options is to create a structure that will be addressed in case of any problem, and legal regulations can be made through these institutional structures. He argued that the cryptocurrencies are not money since they do not fulfil the functions of money, which are medium of exchange, store of value, and standard of deferred payment (Al-Quradaghi, 2018). Besides, he added, cryptocurrencies could not be considered as an asset because they do not have an intrinsic value (Adam, 2019).

One of the scholars who made a clear statement that cryptocurrencies are not permissible is Haitham Al-Haddad, a member of the Islamic Council of Europe. In his explanation announced in January 2018, Haddad compared cryptocurrency and paper money and highlighted the differences between them. Accordingly, the essential difference is the approval and regulation of the states behind the paper money. In this sense, he argued that the cryptocurrency is not money in any way and is completely created out of nothing. He stressed that in case of any problems (such as hacking, prohibition) it would vanish entirely because there is no authority or asset behind it. For all these reasons, he very clearly concluded that producing, selling, and buying cryptocurrencies and generating income from price movements of them is forbidden (*haram*). In addition, he added that although the paper money also does not have any assets behind it, the use of paper money is compulsory because the state forces it. Therefore he stated that the same would be the case if the state switches from paper money to cryptocurrency (Al-Haddad, 2018).

Another statement was made by Datuk Mohd Daud Bakar, the chairman of the Bank Negara Malaysia's Shariah Advisory Council.[5] His explanation differs from that of his predecessors and can be considered as one of the most moderate views on cryptocurrency. Elaborating on the benefits of blockchain technology, especially cryptocurrencies, he expresses his perspective explicitly by stating that "I am a man of Shariah, and I see ways to preserve Shariah within digital currencies, especially because digital currencies are a phenomenon that will happen, whether we like it or not". He pointed out that the *fatawa* given for Bitcoin and other cryptocurrencies as *haram* are based on the excessive uncertainty (*gharar*) caused by the fluctuations in their prices. Moreover, he argued that from this point of view, every risky transaction should be called *haram*. According to him, the reason behind their opinions is that scholars misunderstand the difference between risk and uncertainty (Pikri, 2018).

Professor Bakar, unlike other scholars, emphasized the blockchain technology on which the cryptocurrencies are built and indicated the applications that blockchain can be beneficial for Islamic finance. He asserted that

> For example, if we pay zakat through Bitcoin—if this is allowed by *fatwa*—then we can see exactly how the money is spent. Another example is the BR1M allowances. We can observe exactly where the money is spent, whether in schoolbooks, etc.
>
> (Pikri, 2018)

He also stressed Dubai's attempt to issue its cryptocurrency and proposed that Malaysia also can adopt its own cryptocurrency.

On the other hand, many Islamic scholars from different countries have expressed their opinion about Bitcoin and cryptocurrencies, and most of them have seen them as impermissible.[6] The main reasons are the lack of state support, so they are not legal tender, excessive uncertainty due to the speculative fluctuations in prices (*gharar*), and their usage for illegal activities.

Fatawa *by institutions*

Although most of the scholars mentioned have crucial positions in some committees, their evaluations can be considered as personal opinions. There are, however, several *fatawa* issued by institutions where experts with different qualifications come together to form their opinion. One of the first views about cryptocurrencies has come from Turkey's Directorate of Religious Affairs (*Diyanet*). There are two statements given for the questions about cryptocurrencies. In the first statement shared in November 2017, *Diyanet* stated that

> The purchase and selling of digital currencies is not appropriate according to religion *at this point* due to the fact that they are open to speculation in terms

of value and they can easily be used mostly in illegal deeds such as money laundering. They are also far from state auditing and supervision.

(HurriyetDailyNews, 2017; emphasis added)

A few months after this announcement, *Diyanet* issued a new statement and declared that the instruments, to be accepted as money, should not inherit these characteristics: Excessive uncertainty (*gharar*), being used as a tool of deception, and cause for unjust enrichment (Din İşleri Yüksek Kurulu Başkanlığı, 2017). Accordingly, *Diyanet* evaluated the available cryptocurrencies from these perspectives and concluded that they have severe uncertainties in their nature, possess a high level of risk of deception, and cause unjust and unjustified enrichment similar to a Ponzi scheme. Therefore, *Diyanet* concluded that usage of cryptocurrency is not permissible.

Another *fatwa* came from the Egyptian Mufti Shawki Allam. Allam's *fatwa* can be regarded as an institutional view since he is officially the head of the highest state institution for religious affairs. It was also stated that the *fatwa* was formed as a result of consultations with experts in the field of economics. In the *fatwa* published at the beginning of 2018, the Mufti stated that Bitcoin trading was not permissible (ahramonline, 2018). Their justifications are that cryptocurrencies are not seen as a tool of exchange by the state, they are not subject to any supervision, and they are used for money laundering. It is emphasized that the trade of cryptocurrency is gambling, and it is forbidden (*haram*) in this respect. Allam also referred to the risk posed by cryptocurrency for Egypt's economy by saying that "due to the exchange rate risk and the high-profit potential, they undermine Egypt's ability to protect and stabilise its own currency".

In the previously mentioned personal views about cryptocurrencies, Mohd Daud Bakar had the most moderate approach among them. A Shariah White Paper was prepared about Ether, the utility token of the Ethereum platform, in cooperation with the Ethereum Foundation and Amanie Advisors, of which he is the founder and a member of the Shariah Advisory Board. On 29 April 2019, Bakar and three shariah scholars stated that Ether is a shariah-compliant valuable asset or *mal* that is traded only in the Ethereum ecosystem and is necessary to ensure the continuity of smart contracts in the system (Amanie&Ethereum, 2019). It was emphasized that Ether was not designed as currency and therefore would not be regarded as money in Islamic terms. The committee decided that Ether, considered a shariah-compliant asset, could be bought, sold, or held by Muslims to join the Ethereum blockchain and take advantage of the opportunities offered by this technology (Amanie&Ethereum, 2019, p. 29). However, they emphasized that "The smart contract must not be involved in any of the prohibited sectors, and also the nature of smart contract must be free from any of the major prohibitions in Islam in terms of subject matter and investment activities" (Amanie&Ethereum, 2019). This *fatwa* about Ether will undoubtedly open new debates, both particularly in the academic field in the Islamic world and the legitimacy of cryptocurrency in general.

Cryptocurrency initiatives in Islamic countries

Evaluations on the cryptocurrencies from the shariah point of view have not yet come to an end, and the debate in this area seems to continue. However, there are some initiatives to create cryptocurrencies as a payment system on the state level. Leaders of the Muslim countries have also been voicing the need to create a cryptocurrency to be used in trade among Islamic countries and in particular to reduce the dependence on the dollar. Iranian President Hassan Rouhani proposed to create a Muslim cryptocurrency which is used among Islamic countries, and in this way has stated that they will be successful against the dollar in the Kuala Lumpur Summit where leaders of Turkey, Qatar, Indonesia, and Malaysia attended (NG, 2019).

Dubai has started to work on issuing its own cryptocurrency. In 2017, they declared that they would benefit from blockchain technology in the process of digitalization of the domestic economy and adopted a comprehensive strategy (Government of Dubai, 2017). In this perspective, they have made efforts to create the cryptocurrency called EmCash, but it has not been issued yet (O'Connell, 2019). In other Islamic countries, there are efforts to introduce central bank cryptocurrencies. For instance, Turkey has set the goal that "blockchain-based digital central bank money will be put into practice" in the 11th Development Plan (2019–2023) (SBB, 2019, p. 42).

Although there is no declaration about shariah compliancy for the central bank cryptocurrencies, there are also private initiatives outside the state that issue shariah-compliant cryptocurrencies. One of the examples is OneGram, which was announced to be the world's first shariah-compliant cryptocurrency in 2017 with its ICO in Dubai. Unlike other cryptocurrencies, OneGram states that each OneGram has at least one gram of gold behind it and is therefore protected against price fluctuations. They also emphasize that it has an intrinsic value due to its gold-based structure. OneGram has a shariah advisor and transfers 2.5 percent of the proceeds to the OneGram Foundation as a social responsibility (OneGram, 2019).

Evaluation of cryptocurrencies in terms of Islamic economics

In the previous sections, cryptocurrencies, blockchain technology, and the evaluation of these concepts in terms of Islamic law were mentioned with sharing the relevant *fatawa*. We can summarize the *fiqh* issues about blockchain and cryptocurrencies as follows:

1. Whether the cryptocurrencies function as a currency, and whether they would be able to do that in the future;
2. What can be used as a currency in Islamic law and the basic characteristics of the currency;
3. Whether the cryptocurrencies have internal value, and from this point of view, whether they can be accepted as a good or an asset;
4. Related to the previous item, what constitutes value in Islamic law;
5. Evaluation of the lack of supervision, authority, and regulation;

6 Criticism in terms of risk, *gharar*, volatility, speculation, and manipulation;
7 The possibility that they cause Ponzi scheme structures;
8 Ease of abuse, especially due to user anonymity;
9 Examination of the sectors in which cryptocurrencies are used from the Islamic point of view;
10 Energy waste (*israf*) due to mining processes;
11 Taxation issues, including *zakat*; and
12 Examining cryptocurrencies individually by considering their different characteristics.

This list summarizes the most important issues related to blockchain technology and especially cryptocurrency from the perspective of *fiqh*. In this section, blockchain and cryptocurrencies will be briefly examined and evaluated in terms of the Islamic economy, which has started to be formed since the first half of the twentieth century. Here, what is meant by the Islamic economy is, in the simplest terms, an Islamic perspective on economic issues.

Cryptocurrencies as currency

The most significant feature of cryptocurrencies for the Islamic economy is their acceptance and use as a currency. The importance of money can be derived from the hadith, which is about a conversation between Prophet Muhammad (pbuh) and Bilal al-Habashi.[7] According to that hadith, two main features of the money are general acceptance and being a medium of exchange. In addition, as Kalender (2019) summarizes, it can be inferred from things used as money in Islamic societies throughout history that money should have the following characteristics: Rarity, fungibility, transportability, stackability, durability, and value stability.[8] Of these features, general acceptance, being a medium of exchange, transportability, and durability are not yet fully applicable to cryptocurrencies. Furthermore, transportability and durability are contrary to the virtual structure of the cryptocurrencies. Also, the first two features appear to be difficult for cryptocurrencies to be fully realizes in the future because cryptocurrencies can be gained by two methods: Miners generate and acquire cryptocurrency, and the rest buy crypto money by available currencies. Considering that not everyone can be a data miner, the only way for most of the people to get crypto money is to buy from exchange platforms. With the accumulation of cryptocurrencies in the hands of everyone after a certain period, it is also possible that the transactions will be carried out in these cryptocurrencies and traditional money will be withdrawn. However, even then, because cryptocurrencies have a specific upper production limit, it might be an issue whether this upper limit will meet the money demand.

The relationship between cryptocurrencies and the real economy

Another critical issue for the Islamic economy is that to what extent cryptocurrencies may reflect real production. Today, one of the criticisms in terms of both the heterodox and Islamic economic views is that the amount of money and money equivalents in the world economy is much higher than the amount of real production. For example, according to the World Bank (2019), the total nominal gross national product (GNP) of 193 countries in the world was 86.6 trillion dollars as of 2019, while the total amount of money, including not only physical but non-physical money, was higher than $90.4 trillion even as of 2015 (Chang, 2017). If derivative products and crypto money are added, the figure increases to a quadrillion. The main reason for this is the creation of money through transactions via loans and leverages.

At this point, even if cryptocurrency will be considered as a currency, it is vital to have a close link to production. Cryptocurrency is a type of money that is not something tangible. However, the cryptocurrency is based on the decryption of the current business transactions in the virtual record. This means that a certain amount of cryptocurrency is produced based on each real transaction in the world. Therefore, it can be expected that there will be a direct relationship between cryptocurrency and real production. However, empirical studies on this relationship are especially necessary.

Cryptocurrency technology

It is possible to see some statements suggesting that Islam in general and the Islamic economy in particular regard technology as neutral. The first question to be asked at this point is whether this is the case. Second, in terms of an Islamic economy, a technology used in finance must be evaluated in these respects: interest (*riba*), speculation, manipulation, deception, excessive uncertainty (*gharar*), and incompatibility with *maqasid* (objectives of shariah) (Muneeza & Mustapha, 2019), because even if the technology is not developed directly to cause them, it may cause these problems in real life.

Although it is known as cryptocurrency technology, blockchain technology has much more extensive use. Therefore, apart from the cryptocurrency, it can be beneficial for the Islamic economy in terms of disclosure, transparency, and confidence-building. As described in the previous sections, blockchain technology provides a system in which the reliability of previous records is rechecked continuously at each step within a particular network structure.

One area in which these benefits of blockchain can be observed is smart contracts. For example, the contracts used in Islamic finance can be based on that technology. Apart from this, peer-to-peer structures can be used for Islamic crowdfunding platforms. Therefore, it is crucial to examine the opportunities in this area.

Cryptocurrency, balance, and justice

One of the main features of blockchain technology and cryptocurrency is that they are not under the control of a central authority. According to the widely accepted view, the process, management, regulation, and supervision are self-solved with the help of a network. First of all, it should be examined whether this is the case or not, and the potential problems and irregularities against this argument should be considered.

Second, the issue needs to be addressed from a more theoretical perspective. The defence of the market economy was based on a similar logic. Accordingly, without the need for any external authority, the "invisible hand" of the market would provide balance and justice. However, various events—such as the First and Second World Wars and the 2008 Financial Crisis—have shown that this is not so simple. Obviously, a digital technology-dependent system is not the same as the market economy. Nevertheless, "the theory of a self-regulating virtual market environment" can have similar negative consequences in practice, as the market economy in the theoretical construct of neoclassical economics leads to serious negativity. Therefore, how balance and justice can be achieved within such a structure must be discussed.

Conclusion and discussion

Digitalization, which has started to affect all areas of life, has the potential to transform economic and financial fields. However, "money" is one of the essential concepts that must be revolutionized for such a transformation to take place, because money is at the centre of the daily lives of people from almost all segments of society and "the state" lies at the basis of its legitimacy. Bitcoin that has a particular attention to the concept of anonymity initiated this challenge, but it has not yet received full acceptance for several reasons, such as its complex structure and price fluctuations that are open to manipulation and its use in illegal activities. Although Bitcoin gets much attention, when it comes to the billions of people who use money in their daily lives, it seems that it is actually of interest to a small segment of people. On the other hand, it should not be ignored that the emergence of different cryptocurrencies and the practical use of blockchain technology in various fields increases the acceptance rate of cryptocurrencies.

Although there the term "currency" is in their names, the debate about whether such currencies are money or not still continues. In this context, a definition of cryptocurrencies and the consensus on what they are will clarify many challenges—ranging from tax issues to the platforms on which they can be traded—and thus will increase the acceptance and use rate of cryptocurrencies in the society. However, at this stage, it is difficult to say that cryptocurrencies will change the world monetary system and eliminate the dominance of the dollar and other leading currencies. Although money is a matter of belief, as Niall Ferguson, the author of *The Rise of Money*, says, for the time being, that belief would be based on the existence of a state and the legality that it provides, not the idea of decentralization. Today, the state is the most powerful rule-maker and has the power to ban the production or use of alternative currencies. Already cryptocurrencies are currently completely prohibited in some countries.

In this sense, technology-oriented multinational companies are one of the most notable forces challenging governments. Such companies, which can be regarded as oligopolies in areas such as social media platforms, shopping sites, and search engines, serve billions of people worldwide. Notably, due to the close ties of the new generations with technology and the Internet, the impact of these companies is expanding. With new generations more inclined to technology, significant changes are inevitable in many areas, including money. Therefore, the possibility that cryptocurrencies will indeed function as "money" in the future should be discussed through these powerful companies as well as states. Therefore, the attitudes of companies such as Facebook and Amazon may determine the acceptance level of Bitcoin or other cryptocurrencies. Besides, other cryptocurrencies based on blockchain technology and the smart contracts they integrate into their systems lead to a significant transformation in different fields by reducing costs and sturdily maintaining records. Although they cannot perform a function as money, cryptocurrencies will continue to be the driving elements of digital transformation. It is also highly probable that states will take more practical steps towards digitizing their own paper money in the near future.

The first individual assessments were made from the perspective of Islamic economics in 2013–14 when the cryptocurrencies began to gain popularity under the leadership of Bitcoin and became an agenda of the states. At this point, the general approach was in the form of answers to individual questions asked to *fiqh* scholars about whether it is permissible to invest in cryptocurrencies or not. The answers focused on the lack of authority behind these currencies and the grievances and uncertainties that might arise, and the legitimacy of the money was discussed in this point of view. Moreover, the opinions expressed by the scholars are subject to Bitcoin, and other cryptocurrencies are just evaluated as "others". Bitcoin anonymity and its use for illegal businesses have been indicative of other cryptocurrencies, and the *fatawa* have been made by considering all of them as the same.

Recently, some changes have been observed in this approach. The most obvious examples of this are positive *fatawa* given to Stellar and Ether cryptocurrencies under certain conditions. However, there is no consensus on these *fatawa*. So, in order to have an *ijma'* (consensus) and to take substantial steps in the Islamic world in the future, it is evident that not only for Bitcoin but also the *fiqh* assessments for other leading cryptocurrencies should be made. Scholars such as Al-Quradaghi emphasize this necessity. Therefore, under the leadership of an institution such as the OIC Fiqh Academy, there is a need to bring together academics, shariah scholars, and practitioners from different fields of expertise in order to discuss the issue. This is important not only to provide a view for existing cryptocurrencies but also to set standards on which general principles the shariah-compliant digital currencies should follow in the future. Here, a definition for what cryptocurrency is (such as money, goods, securities) can contribute to the resolution of many uncertainties. However, rather than making quick decisions, the issue should be discussed from a wide range of perspectives; otherwise, as in the case of Bitcoin, opinions may change in time, and this affects reliability for the institutions and their decisions.

In the Muslim world, the approaches to blockchain, which is the technology behind cryptocurrencies, are generally positive, and it is emphasized that progress in this area can bring benefits in the field of Islamic finance. Therefore, blockchain technology can have significant impacts in many areas other than payment systems. In Islamic finance, asymmetric information problems can be prevented and costs can be reduced by integrating blockchain technology both on funds collection and financing processes of Islamic banks. Besides, as exemplified by Datuk Mohd Daud Bakar, in the social solidarity institutions that we can include in Islamic finance, blockchain technology can be used, for example, for transferring the *zakat* to the right places and keeping the records. Considering this technology solely on money hinders and diverges the Islamic world from generating new ideas on other possible benefits.

On the other hand, cryptocurrencies can be considered as a currency that Islamic countries can use among themselves. The aim is to break the dominance of the dollar, reduce sensitivity to external influences, and enable Islamic countries to determine monetary policies independently of the global system. The importance of such cooperation is better understood considering the Muslim population is more than 1.5 billion. In order to achieve this kind of cooperation, a strong political will as well as a realistic win-win relationship between Islamic countries is needed. In this context, the process of adoption of the single currency by the European Union countries stands as a good example. The rapid mobility offered by cryptocurrencies and the progress in this direction can contribute positively to the realization of Islamic cryptocurrency. Besides, concrete steps in this direction with the cooperation between several leading Islamic countries will provide substantial progress.

Notes

1 Economic crises can lead to different initiatives. For example, during the economic crisis in the 1930s, farmers in Denmark created their own money because they could not provide the funds they needed to operate their land and animals and had succeeded with their initiatives. However, the Danish government had banned this new money initiative (Ganzo, 2014). As a result, the farmers who realized that they could not have their own currency established the interest-free JAK Bank, which is based on the cooperative structure and is now considered as one of the best practices.

2 An initial coin offering is the public offering of a new cryptocurrency to finance projects in the blockchain area.

3 Some Christians have evaluated Bitcoin from the perspective of their own beliefs. For example, they consider the efforts to become rich by taking advantage of the extreme fluctuations in Bitcoin as greed (Netzly, 2018).

4 Similarly, Ferguson (2008, p. 29) asserts that "money is a matter of belief, even faith".

5 The speeches were done in Malay and were uploaded in social media on 30 November 2017 and 24 January 2018. The translation of the main points of the speech was shared in that website https://vulcanpost.com/632153/haram-cryptocurrency-syariah-advisory-council/. For the speech in Malay: www.facebook.com/100011958917862/videos/329487940793167/

6 Mahomed and Mohamad (2017) summarized the *fatawa* given from different countries through January 2018. In the paper, Mufti Taha Karaan, the Darul Iftaa Institution, and Mufti Siraj Desai from South Africa were among those whose view is that the cryptocurrencies are permissible. As a rationale, it has been suggested that cryptocurrencies should be regarded as an asset (*mal*) with the social concurrence and common usage (*ta'amul*), but they are not necessarily currency. However, the sources of the *fatawa* of the aforementioned scholars/institutions were not given by the authors, and therefore

the primary statements could not be reached and confirmed. On the other hand, Monzer Kahf was among those who gave a positive (permissible) opinion on cryptocurrencies. Only the first opinion of Kahf is given. However, he stated later on that it is forbidden to carry out any transaction with cryptocurrencies.

7 Abu Sa'id (ra) reported: Once Bilal brought (A good kind of) dates called Barni to The Prophet (pbuh) who asked him: "From where have you brought these?" Bilal replied: "I had some inferior type of dates of which I exchanged two *Sa*'s for one *Sa* of *Barni* dates in order that The Messenger of Allah (pbuh) would eat it." Thereupon The Prophet (pbuh) said: "Beware! This is definitely *riba*! Don't do so, but if you want to buy (a better kind of) dates sell the inferior dates in a separate bargain and then buy that (better kind)" (Sahih Muslim, 2005, 96-(1594)).

8 These features are undoubtedly not set in stone. Some new ones may be included in this list, while some may lose their influence over time. However, it cannot be considered a coincidence that the things used as money in the world throughout history contain more or less these features. Therefore, they can undoubtedly be considered as guidelines for understanding the meaning of currency.

References

Adam, F. (2019). Fatawa Analysis of Bitcoin. In M. M. Billah (Ed.), *Halal Cryptocurrency Management* (pp. 133–47). Cham, Switzerland: Palgrave Macmillan.

ahramonline. (2018). Bitcoin Trading Is Unlawful Pursuant to Islamic Sharia, Says Egypt's Grand Mufti. Retrieved December 21, 2019, from http://english.ahram.org.eg/NewsContent/3/12/286399/Business/Economy/Bitcoin-trading-is-unlawful-pursuant-to-Islamic-Sh.aspx

Al-Haddad, H. (2018). Fatwa on Bitcoin & Other Cryptocurrencies. Retrieved from www.islam21c.com/islamic-law/fatwa-bitcoin-cryptocurrencies/

Ali, R., Barrdear, J., Clews, R., & Southgate, J. (2014). The Economics of Digital Currencies. *Bank of England Quarterly Bulletin*, *Q3*(1), 38–47. Retrieved from https://papers.ssrn.com/sol3/papers.cfm?abstract_id=2499418

Al Jazeera. (2017). بها بالتداول أنصح لا ولكن البتكوين بتحريم فتوى أصدر لم: داغي القره علي . د. Retrieved December 21, 2019, from www.youtube.com/watch?v=VJXuO7vc_CQ&t=5s

Al Jazeera. (2018). الإلكترونية بالعملات التعامل حكم .. المال فقه-YouTube. Retrieved December 21, 2020, from www.youtube.com/watch?time_continue=439&v=Azq9myczgJY&feature=emb_logo

Al-Quradaghi, A. (2018). داغي لقره ا الدين محيى علي الدكتور الأستاذ لفضيلة الرسمي الموقع. Retrieved December 21, 2019, from www.qaradaghi.com/Details.aspx?ID=3790

Alstyne, M. V. (2014). Why Bitcoin Has Value. *Communications of the ACM*, *57*(5), 30–2. https://doi.org/10.1145/2594288

Amanie&Ethereum. (2019). Shariah White Paper on Ether. Retrieved from https://amanieadvisors.com/shariah-white-paper-on-ethereum/

Angel, J. J., & McCabe, D. (2015). The Ethics of Payments: Paper, Plastic, or Bitcoin? *Journal of Business Ethics*, *132*(3), 603–11. https://doi.org/10.1007/s10551-014-2354-x

Aste, T., Tasca, P., & Matteo, T. Di. (2017). Blockchain Technologies: The Foreseeable Impact on Society and Industry. *Computer*, September, 18–28. Retrieved from https://ieeexplore.ieee.org/stamp/stamp.jsp?arnumber=8048633

Beck, R. (2018). Beyond Bitcoin: The Rise of Blockchain World. *Computer*, *51*(2), 54–8.

Böhme, R., Christin, N., Edelman, B., & Moore, T. (2015). Bitcoin: Economics, Technology, and Governance. *Journal of Economic Perspectives*, *29*(2), 213–38.

Buterin, V. (2014). A Next-Generation Smart Contract and Decentralized Application Platform. Retrieved from http://blockchainlab.com/pdf/Ethereum_white_paper-a_next_generation_smart_contract_and_decentralized_application_platform-vitalik-buterin.pdf

Chang, S. (2017). Here's All the Money in the World, in One Chart. Retrieved December 12, 2019, from www.marketwatch.com/story/this-is-how-much-money-exists-in-the-entire-world-in-one-chart-2015-12-18

Chen, E. (2019). Implementing the Blockchain Technology in the Financial Services Industry. In K.-C. Li, X. Chen, H. Jiang, & E. Bertino (Eds.), *Essentials of Blockchain Technology* (pp. 257–71). New York: CRC Press.

Chornous, Y., Denysenko, S., Hrudnytskyi, V., Turkot, O., & Sikorskyi, O. (2019). Legal Regulation of Cryptocurrency Turnover in Ukraine and the EU. *Journal of Legal, Ethical and Regulatory Issues*, *22*(Special Issue 2), 1–6.

coinmarketcap.com. (2019). Cryptocurrency Market Capitalizations | CoinMarketCap. Retrieved December 27, 2019, from https://coinmarketcap.com/

cryptonews. (2019). Countries Where Bitcoin Is Banned or Legal in 2019. Retrieved December 21, 2019, from https://cryptonews.com/guides/countries-in-which-bitcoin-is-banned-or-legal.htm

Din İşleri Yüksek Kurulu Başkanlığı. (2017). Dijital kripto paraların kullanımının dini hükmü nedir? Retrieved December 21, 2019, from https://kurul.diyanet.gov.tr/Karar-Mutalaa-Cevap/38212/dijital-kripto-paralarin-kullaniminin-dini-hukmu-nedir-

Elevenews. (2019). 90% of Bitcoin Usage Is Speculation: 10% Transactions, Says Luno CEO.

Ferguson, N. (2008). *The Ascent of Money: A Financial History of the World*. London: Penguin.

Ganzo, M. (2014). Ethical Banking. In F. M. Atbani & C. Trullols (Eds.), *Social Impact Finance* (pp. 17–20). London: Palgrave Macmillan.

Government of Dubai. (2017). Dubai Economy Launches Partnership to Expedite emCash. Retrieved December 21, 2019, from www.dubaided.ae/English/MediaCenter/Pages/PressReleasesDetails.aspx?ItemId=233

Haber, S., & Stornetta, W. S. (1991). How to Time-Stamp a Digital Document. In A. J. Menezes & S. A. Vanstone (Eds.), *Advances in Cryptology-CRYPTO '90. CRYPTO 1990. Lecture Notes in Computer Science* (vol. 537, pp. C. 537, 437–55). Berlin, Heidelberg: Springer.

HurriyetDailyNews. (2017). Turkey's Top Religious Body Declares Bitcoin 'Inappropriate': Latest News. Retrieved December 21, 2019, from www.hurriyetdailynews.com/turkeys-top-religious-body-declares-bitcoin-inappropriate-123243

Hütten, M., & Thiemann, M. (2017). Moneys at the Margins: From Political Experiment to Cashles Societies. In M. Campbell-Verduyn (Ed.), *Bitcoin and Beyond* (pp. 25–47). Routledge. https://doi.org/10.4324/9781315211909-2

Iansiti, M., & Lakhani, K. R. (2017). The Truth about Blockchain. *Harvard Business Review*, January–February. Retrieved from https://enterprisersproject.com/sites/default/files/the_truth_about_blockchain.pdf

Kahf, M. (2017). Fatawa Money, Currencies, Gold, Sarf 2000–2017. Retrieved from http://monzer.kahf.com/fatawa/FATAWA_CURRENCIES_GOLD_COMMODITIES.pdf

Kalender, F. (2019). Dinde Kripto Para Nedir? Caiz Midir? Retrieved December 1, 2019, from https://darusselam.com/fikih/dinde-kripto-para-nedir-caiz-midir.html

LibraAssociation. (2019). Libra Whitepaper: An Introduction to Libra. Retrieved from https://libra.org/en-US/wp-content/uploads/sites/23/2019/06/LibraWhitePaper_en_US.pdf

Mahomed, Z., & Mohamad, S. (2017). Crypto Mania: The Shariah Verdict. *CIAWM Bulletin*, 33–6.

Muneeza, A., & Mustapha, Z. (2019). Blockchain and Its Sharia Compliant Structure. In Mohd Ma'sum Billah (Ed.), *Halal Cryptocurrency Management*. Switzerland: Palgrave Macmillan.

Nakamoto, S. (2008). Bitcoin: A Peer-to-Peer Electronic Cash System. Retrieved from https://bitcoin.org/bitcoin.pdf

Namecoin. (2019). Namecoin. Retrieved December 20, 2019, from www.namecoin.org/

Netzly, R. (2018). Should Christians Invest in Bitcoin?: Inspire Investing. Retrieved December 21, 2019, from www.inspireinvesting.com/2018/01/12/should-christians-invest-in-bitcoin/

NG, E. (2019). Iran Leader Urges Deeper Muslim Links to Fight US 'Hegemony'. Retrieved December 21, 2019, from https://apnews.com/b8bab8c75cff1580d28e03c7536a25f8

O'Connell, J. (2019). Municipal Crypto Spreading Around the World, From California to Dubai. Retrieved December 21, 2019, from https://cointelegraph.com/news/municipal-crypto-spreading-around-the-world-from-california-to-dubai

Ober, M., Katzenbeisser, S., & Hamacher, K. (2013). Structure and Anonymity of the Bitcoin Transaction Graph. *Future Internet*, *5*(2), 237–50. https://doi.org/10.3390/fi5020237

Ølnes, S., Ubacht, J., & Janssen, M. (2017). Blockchain in Government: Benefits and Implications of Distributed Ledger Technology for Information Sharing. *Government Information Quarterly*, *34*(3), 355–64. https://doi.org/10.1016/J.GIQ.2017.09.007

OneGram. (2019). OneGram: In Gold We Trust. Retrieved December 21, 2019, from https://onegram.org/

Pikri, E. (2018). Is Cryptocurrency Haram? The Chairmain Of BNM's Shariah Advisory Council Says No. Retrieved December 12, 2019, from https://vulcanpost.com/632153/haram-cryptocurrency-syariah-advisory-council/

Ricca, C. (2019). Year in Review: Biggest Cryptocurrency Scams of 2019 | Currency.com. Retrieved December 27, 2019, from https://currency.com/news/2019/12/27/biggest-cryptocurrency-scams-of-2019

Sahih Muslim. (2005). *The Authentic Hadith of Muslim*, Dal Al-Kotob Al-Ilmiyah, Beirut-Lebanon.

SBB. (2019). *On Birinci Kalkınma Planı (2019–2023)*. Retrieved from www.sbb.gov.tr/wp-content/uploads/2019/07/OnbirinciKalkinmaPlani.pdf

Webb, A. (2015). 8 Tech Trends to Watch in 2016. *Harvard Business Review*. Retrieved from https://hbr.org/2015/12/8-tech-trends-to-watch-in-2016

Weber, B. (2014). Can Bitcoin Compete with Money? *Journal of Peer Production*, *4*, 1–6. Retrieved from https://papers.ssrn.com/sol3/papers.cfm?abstract_id=2483867

Weber, B. (2015). Bitcoin and the Legitimacy Crisis of Money. *Cambridge Journal of Economics*, *40*(1), 17–41. https://doi.org/10.1093/cje/beu067

World Bank. (2019). Gross World Product. Retrieved December 1, 2019, from http://statisticstimes.com/economy/gross-world-product.php

Yermack, D. (2015). Is Bitcoin a Real Currency? An Economic Appraisal. In *Handbook of Digital Currency* (pp. 31–43). https://doi.org/10.1016/B978-0-12-802117-0.00002-3

10 Contemporary debates in Islamic monetary economics

A retrospective look

Ahsan Shafiq

Introduction

In our contemporary times, financial markets have grown, banking giants have swelled, internationalization has reduced the borders, and complex derivates have enshrouded money markets. Yet what this whole modern financialization has brought, more than anything else, are frequent market crashes, market giants crumpling, banking institutions toppling, bailouts, and bankruptcies at the level of countries. People are lost in the labyrinths of an economic enigma that hardly anyone knows the way out of. Despite the high hopes towards the end of each recession to become the last of its kind, it always is followed by another; following every big crisis, central banks and governments step in, artificial ignitions to economy turn into reckless speculative activity, bullish but unsustainable, hence beating the trumpets of another Minsky moment and market collapse. The complex international financial landscape exacerbates the repercussions of this game even more. The effect which would have otherwise caused a domestic recession travels through the arteries of the international system, causing an economic catastrophe wherever it reaches.

The credit-based economies and perpetual debt structures have grown into a vicious web which the world's financial structure has fallen prey to. Rowbotham (1998) goes to the extent of equating a mortgage with the "Grip of Death", that is, a death pledge, since its growth is an insidious form of personal indebtedness which places householders into a position of complete dependence with respect to the financial system. This growth of debt-based economy relative to national income takes individuals into a state of "debt slavery". Debts are issue and reissued, speculative stories drive irrational markets, hikes in asset prices turn into asset bubbles which, once popped, take economy after economy into recession. Once this chronic indebtedness propels itself into a lack of demand, asset prices fall, markets collapse, and countries are plagued with huge layoffs and mass unemployment. To some, like the Nobel Prize-winning economist Joseph Stiglitz, the most recent of these crises was the most damaging of the several concurrent crises—of food, water, energy, and sustainability—that are tightly interrelated (Stiglitz, 2010).

The repercussions, as if are not enough themselves, are that the lenders of last resort pull up their gears, blowing up the sizes of their balance sheets in the name of labour market recovery and combatting deflation danger. Interestingly, advocates of quantitative easing (like Fed's ex-chief Bernanke) claim such policies to be successful even if the evidence suggests non-appearance of any strong economic expansion (Bernanke, 2015). The policy does hardly anything beyond creating a systemic risk with its monetary manipulations,[1] and when originating from the dominant currency, the risk spreads all over the world.

The inherent existence of the aforementioned problems in the financial system is widely accepted, but what precisely needs to be fixed has become the subject of enormous controversy. Diametrically opposite views on the one hand suggest the fractional reserve structure of modern banking to be at the bottom of all financial catastrophes, while others attribute it to the irrational exuberance of flooding liquidity to financial markets in times of cantankerous downturns. Yet there are others that draw an analogy between the contemporary role of banks and the creation of credit out of thin air.

Islamic economics, which dived in the pool through its peculiar financial institutions hardly forty years ago, is yet midway. The nihility of fallibilities of conventional banking institutions and their traditional instruments, including mortgaged-backed securities (MBS), collateralized debt obligations (CDOs), and credit default swaps (CDSs), which are believed to be responsible for the crisis, left the Islamic banking industry relatively immune to the subprime crisis (Wood, 2009; Warde, 2012; Alqahtani and Mayes, 2017). This promising performance is fragmentary. Use of dubious instruments and departure from their actual aim of replacing the dominant debt-based system have reduced Islamic banks to financial institutions with Islamic addendums merely cloning their conventional counterparts.

Since the aforementioned in one way or other are related to the creation and supply of credit in the economy, the true conception of Islam's monetary theory is of vital importance. Unfortunately, this field too is brimming with diverse opinions ranging from gold dinar and silver dirham to banking based on full reserves. Interestingly, that is not all; finally, there also are voices in favour of a fiat currency that is backed up by an efficient economy and just system. To them, moving to a gold standard or commodity-based currency is like adopting an obsolete system and abandoning a modern one, travelling back in time.

Deficit financing and quantitative easing

An idiosyncratic pattern has been observed lately in the global economy. Every big crisis is followed by a tsunami of credit by central banks seeking to inflate the economies out of debt with an explosion of bank liquidity and credit—which means yet more debt (Figure 10.1) (Hudson, 2010). All central banks in general and the Fed in particular purchase existing government bonds to pump money into the financial system in order to stimulate spending, especially in situations when interest rates fail to work.[2]

The deluge of quantitative easing since the credit crunch of 2007–08 has driven up the asset holdings of the world's central banks from $6 trillion in 2007

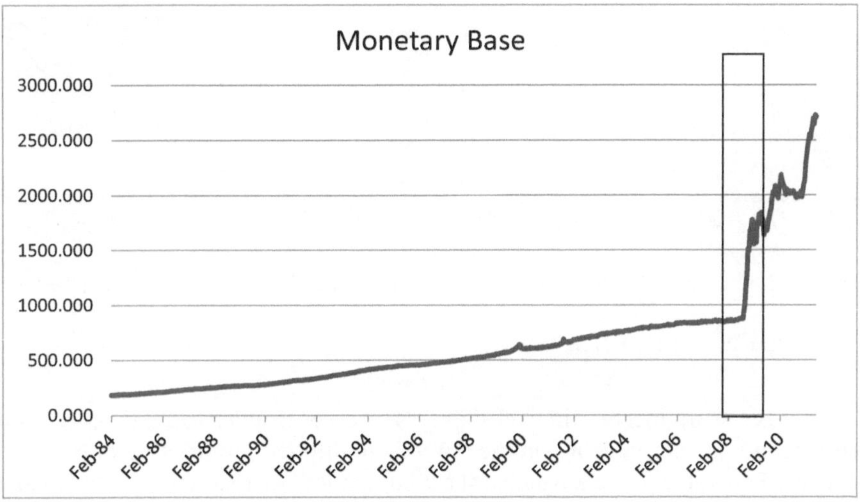

Figure 10.1 Adjusted monetary base (BASE) (billions of dollars)

Note: Shaded areas indicate US recessions.

Source: Federal Reserve Bank of St. Louis

to $21.3 trillion in 2019 (Lund et al., 2018 June). Just from 2008 to 2015, the US Fed bought bonds with an approximate worth of $3.7 trillion. The Federal Reserve expanded its balance sheet, with monetary base as share of GDP rising from 7 percent to 23 percent between 2007 and 2014[3] (Brown, 2015). The United Kingdom also injected $550 billion into its economy from 2009 to 2012, and the European Union pumped in $600 billion of new money post-crisis through 2017.[4] More recently, the European Central Bank (ECB) has kicked off a mammoth $820 billion QE program. On top of this, the ECB under its Pandemic Asset Purchase Program has plans to buy millions in government, corporate, and agency bonds (ECB, 2020).

QE is little more than a financial boondoggle. Monetary expansion, quantitative easing, and a zero-interest rate policy are all inputs to the asset bubbles. Interestingly, the financial crises emanating from the bursting of asset bubbles are dealt with by a wilful expansion of the monetary supply in the name of corrective action, something that led to the creation of the bubble in the first place. Hence all these skewed incentives knitted in an institutionalized system not only let big bankers and corporate executives play their gamble but also allows them to walk off scot-free, tumbling down the house of cards. What follows always is a deep recession and economic crisis that destroys trillions of dollars worldwide.

Policy makers frequently rejoice that the reckless pumping of money through QE does not lead to hyperinflation, a claim that somewhat has been true. Interestingly, that does not prove the efficacy of quantitative easing policy. The real success of this corrective measure depends on the fact of whether this money finds way into the pocket of consumers. Should this not happen, the monetary expansion

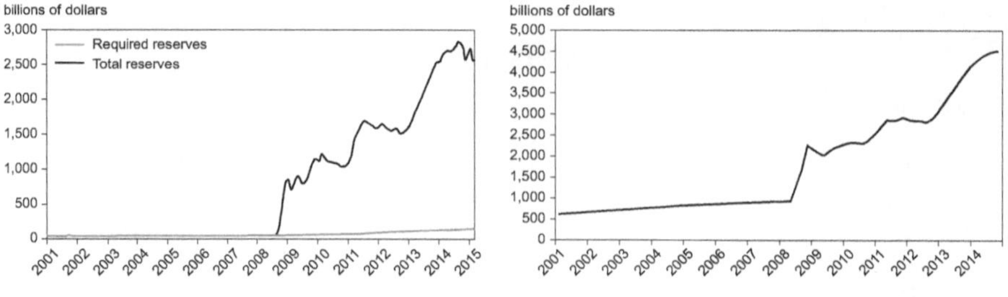

Figure 10.2 and *10.3* Comparison of Federal Reserve liabilities and bank reserves, 2001–15

Source: Federal Reserve Bank of St. Louis

only causes a sharp increase in banks' excess reserves (Figure 10.2.) coupled with a corresponding sharp decline in the "money multiplier", translating only into a rise in the Federal Reserve's balance sheet but not into increased money available to the public in the usual fashion (Cline, 2015).

The fatal financial gamble played to save a few big giants bites the economy from both ends; it either fans the flames of inflation or piles up the bank reserves, hence failing to invigorate spending, something it was put in place for. The virus does not stop spreading internationally. Instead of banks lending to local households and firms, cheap US keyboard credit flies abroad due to banks playing arbitrage gambles and glutting currency markets. Fed policy therefore floods the global economy with a glut of US dollar credit, depreciating the dollar and pushing up foreign currencies, resultantly destabilizing the global financial system.

Exorbitant privilege

The aforementioned paragraphs have discussed the repercussions of reckless injection of money into economies every few years. The problems exacerbated when these non-traditional policy interventions come from the Fed and QE ends up creating an excess of global liquidity, causing a massive acceleration of credit flows to emerging economies (Fratzscher et al., 2018). With the plunging exchange rate of dollar, money managers themselves lead a capital flight in order to buy foreign currencies and bonds, gold, and other raw materials, even entire companies, with cheap dollar credit. Since this capital does not take the form of tangible investment abroad, all it results in is an endless creation of debt and its multiplication by cloning: credit insurance, default swaps, and an array of computerized forward trades, a situation that compels many economists and policy makers to draw an analogy between the financial quests of today and the military quests of older times (Hudson, 2010).

What has been relatively less discussed in the literature is the hegemony of reserve and vehicle currencies that a French finance minister, Valery Giscard d'Estaing, termed as an "exorbitant privilege" of the United States because of its currency's role in the international monetary system (Gourinchas and Rey,

2007)—the fact that a large fraction of world's trade is invoiced in dollars; importers and exporters hold dollar assets to facilitate trade. Using this privilege, the United States could finance[5] its current account deficit by issuing dollar assets at a very low rate of interest. Studies using two-country models[6] have found that besides the issuance of paper instruments, there are several other privileges that the home country (the United States) enjoys. The foreign country (the rest of the world) pays an ongoing seigniorage equal to the product of their holdings of home bonds and the liquidity value of bonds (Canzoneri et al., 2013).[7] Additionally, the shifts in monetary policy emanating from the home country have a greater effect on inflation and output abroad compared to if the same actions had come from abroad. Guess what is more interesting: the United States can print money to buy back government debt at a discount. The apparent arrangement therefore makes it hardly distinct from the tactics of currency debasement used by the Byzantines and Romans. Hence, once the Fed has exhausted its monetary options, it can resort to printing money. This vicious cycle therefore led the current U.S. president, Donald Trump, to say that "this is the United States government . . . you never have to default because you print the money" (CRFB, 2016).

Hence, no matter how you approach these issues imbedded in the foundations of the concurrent financial system, all debates will always converge to the creation of money and its reckless printing and endless multiplication at the hands of interest-based fractional reserve banking. This is the point where the dynamics of the modern financial system come to a crossroads with the Islamic concept of money and its creation; hence this long prologue.

Fractional reserve banking and money out of thin air

The issues of money creation by central banks (or commercial banks) and fractional reserve banking are topics not new to economics literature. The issues have been dealt at length both in the conventional and Islamic studies related to economics and finance.[8]

Of the contemporary critiques on the role of banks in the ongoing financial system, what may be termed as a rather mild criticism is the literature that questions the role of banks in exponentially increasing the credit from deposits. The mechanics of this system rest upon the incidence of interest; hence from a given amount of deposits, many times multiple of it may be introduced into the system as money, that is, fractional reserve banking. This happens when banks issue a multiple of their reserves in the form of derivate deposits by lending to the public. Banks are required to maintain reserves which are only a fraction of their deposits; hence, this multiple expansion process works. The excess reserves are therefore used by banks to increase earning assets, that is, loans and investments (Federal reserve bank of Chicago, 2009).

A stronger criticism has also surfaced for some years now. Some theorists have claimed to have found convincing evidence which proves that banks do not wait for the central banks to issue a monetary base. They work counterclockwise by first making loans and creating derivative deposits and, to make matters worse, rush to the central bank to cover their reserves positions that, as a lender of last resort, it is forced to oblige (Moore, 2001). Hence, every time a loan is made, the supply of money increases. Alternatively, the banks are creating money out of thin air.

How does this alchemy run? McLeay et al. (2014) claim that most money takes the form of bank deposits; however, the way these deposits are created is often misunderstood. The concept of money multiplies is far from factual. What banks instead do is simultaneously create a matching deposit in the borrower's bank account while making a loan to him, thereby creating new money. Hence the deposits are not created from savings of households but from the lending itself.

The concept of money and solution proposals

Money in the Islamic perspective

Early Muslim scholars considered money to be a medium of exchange, a standard of value and a unit of account, but rejected its function as a store of value. Ibn e Taymiyyah[9] is reported to have recognized the two functions of money as an instrument of exchange and measure of value. He also opposed the trading of money because it accrued to deviating money from its real purpose. In other words, money is not a commodity and has no value in itself. It instead is simply an expression of value. Money can only be exchanged for money when this exchange is simultaneous and involves no delays. However, it cannot be sold for a value higher than its nominal value; neither can it be hired (since that opens room for interest). Ibn Khaldun in his contribution to the theory of money does not regard money as a real form of wealth but a vehicle through which wealth can be acquired. Hence, in Islam, money is only an instrument of transfer and carries no additional charge or price that is associated with its usage. This probably is the reason many Islamic economists believe that in the Islamic perspective, money is demanded only as medium of exchange and has no value of itself. The demand of money for speculative purposes or to gain risk-free return on short-term lending will therefore be absent and a money market will not exist. The best currency for today therefore can be a fiat currency backed up by an efficient economy and a just system.

In contrast, the opinions of some classical scholars including Ghazali have made people believe that God has created gold and silver to be used as money. Yet there are others who think that any medium that satisfies the objectives of the *Shari'ah* (*Maqasid al-Shari'ah*)[10] qualifies to be used as money. Therefore, anything (representing money) that contributes towards the attainment of the *Maqasid al-Shari'ah* can be termed as "Islamic" and anything that takes away from them "un-Islamic".

Gold dinar and silver dirham

Resting upon the viewpoint of some classical scholars, some Muslim economists have externalized the Islamic theory of money as the theory of coinage in the form of *dinar* and the *dirham*. To them, the Islamic theory of money is grounded in the theory of value, which is akin to the classical theory of value (Abdullah, 2016).

Ghazali and Ibn e Khaldun,[11] the most notable names from this strand, claim that Allah made gold and silver to be used as money. According to this school, in the last 1,400 years, only gold and silver have been the best performing forms of money, followed by copper, while the paper currency (fiat) money has performed the worst in terms of maintaining its function of storing value. Fiat currency has lost about 98 percent of its value since the 1970s.

There are some other economists who do not claim gold and silver to be ordained from Allah as legal money but assert that bimetallism is free from almost all ills that economies face due to fiat money, including rampant inflation, credit crunches, and recessions. Hence, gold and silver coinage should not be supported for *Shari'ah* binding but instead for its practical superiority over all other currencies that have ever been used.

Unfortunately, these too are claims that are little too tall. Using frequent references from the history of bimetallism, Çizakça (2010) has analysed in great detail the risks attached to such money. At the outset, he asserts that central banks in the presence of fiat currency have a greater innate ability to achieve the Islamic ideal of a zero interest rate than is possible in the alternative system of bimetallism.[12] Though (in bimetallism) government can try to reach zero interest rate by adjusting macroeconomic variables under its control, yet it may be impossible, because the intrinsic value of coinage is not determined by the central bank but the global demand and supply of the metal contained in the coin. Additionally, the coins will have a positive rate of interest because their circulation in the economy would be affected in the long run by fluctuations in prices of precious metals in the world markets. Furthermore, in the almost --a borderless world today, an inflow of gold into a country will cause inflation and an outflow depression (Çizakça, 2010). Hence, even historic references contradict the claims of this school because money supply, even under bimetallism, faced frequent supply fluctuations, either because of the discovery of these precious metals or government's deliberate debasement.

There is yet more to say about the *dinarits* whose claims are grounded in their apparent apprehension that gold and silver have been created by God to be used as money. The rebuttal of this conjecture came from the second righteous Caliph Umar ibn al Khattab himself, when introducing a new currency became a formidable task that impinged upon international currency arrangements that had been in place for centuries. When he expressed the intention of minting money from camel skins, his advisers expressed the fear of annihilation of baby camels; hence, he gave up the idea.[13] Nonetheless, his conception of money, as something not necessarily based on bullion, was ahead of his time.[14] This is why some authors have gone to the extent of expressing plaudits for Caliph Umar for contemplating the issue of "banknotes" in the form of camel hide dirhams (Koehler, 2014; Mackintosh-Smith, 2019). It is therefore logical to apprehend that the Holy Prophet (pbuh) endorsed the Roman gold and silver coins of his time as commodities but not legal tender, as they were in the Roman empire.[15] It is needless to delve further into this issue; a pertinent quote from Muhammad Nejatullah Siddiqi would serve the purpose, who, while responding to Masudul Alam Choudhury's credence for bimetallism, elucidated:

> Dr. Choudhury is free to support his stand by reason as well as empirical evidence, but he better avoid involving God in this matter. For God has already spoken to man for the last time, and gold standard is not there in what He said!
> (Siddiqi, 2014)

Full reserve banking

In the fractional reserve system that is currently under practice across the globe, banks create a multiple of reserves initially issued by the central bank that form the monetary base. To many, this structure of a fractional reserve system is the backdrop against which most of the problems of the contemporary financial system have emerged. In addition, the application of fractional reserves has weakened the grip of the central banks on the money supply, as most of the money supply is issued by banks in multiples of the monetary base. It has also allowed banks to gain wealth at the expense of the public as they lend money to the public at a rate of interest. Moreover, the use of the required reserve ratio as a tool of monetary policy appears to be counterproductive, as any change in the ratio would produce multiple changes in the money supply, threatening monetary policy to be a source of instability. Even if we disapprove of the credit creation theory of banking and approve of the fractional reserve and financial intermediation theories; according to this strand, the idiosyncrasies of the system themselves are pivotal to much of the financial problems we are facing today.

The problems of fractional reserve banking are not peculiar to the Muslim countries; the criticism has equally come from the West. The extensive debate over fractional reserve banking (FRB) has spanned decades and includes volleys from many contributors. The common solution proposed to the problem of swings in the volume of commercial bank credit is by imposing a 100 percent reserve requirement on all bank liabilities. Several Islamic economists have joined this call and have raised their voice for the application of full reserves in order to provide the central bank with absolute power to control the money supply, to prevent the wealth redistribution in favour of banks' shareholders, and to do away with a tool of monetary policy that mostly leads to instability (Al-Jarhi, 1981, 1983, 2016).[16] The proponents of this idea believe that such a system would pose a lesser risk to the depositors and would be safe from frequent bank runs. Furthermore, the absence of interest would make it impossible for banks to generate profit from interest on loans. Hence, in terms of conforming with the principles of *Shari'ah* and safeguarding the faith and wealth of individuals, full reserve banking helps in attainment of *Maqasid al-Shari'ah*. Summing up, the 100 percent reserve requirement is supported on three grounds. Firstly, it will overcome the instability of the fractional reserves system, which is caused by fluctuations in supply of money that originate when switching high powered money to deposit money and vice versa. Secondly, when the money supply changes, either because of deposit creation or substitution between deposits and cash, maintaining the existing stock of real balances or adding to it becomes more costly. Thirdly, the benefits of the process of money creation should accrue to the whole society, which can be best achieved through a 100 percent reserve system (Siddiqui, 2008).

Easier said than done; if a bank holds all deposits intact and becomes a 100 percent reserve storage or safety deposit bank, to call such a business a bank itself is something of a misnomer, since such a bank will make no loans. Mises believes that unsustainable booms are witnessed when newly created money enters the loan market and distorts interest rate before other prices in the economy adjust. In principle, the process has an equal probability of occurring in a setting with commodity money or 100 percent reserve banking. The criticism has come from within the Islamic economics fraternity as well (Murphy, 2019). According to Chapra, some proponents have glossed over the question of how the expenses of commercial banks will be met should there be a 100 percent reserve bank. Will they depend entirely on service charges, or will they be subsidized partly by the state? (Chapra, 1984). This school therefore recognizes the problems of the contemporary system of credit creation yet proposes to solve them within the framework of fractional reserve banking. In their view, if proper checks and balances are put in place on the creation of credit by commercial banks, the process of money creation even through the fractional reserve system will not be unstable.

Islamic banking: a journey long started yet midway

Islamic economics dived in the pool through its peculiar financial institutions hardly forty years ago. A multibillion-dollar Islamic finance market has emerged across the globe, reconstituting the architecture of the world's financial market. The sector has grown at an accelerated pace, and year on year, new banks are emerging, financial institutions are being set up, and newer *Shari'ah*-compliant modes of finance are being developed. The total assets of Islamic finance industry world have exceeded $ 2.5 trillion (Shafiq, 2020). The presence has been felt across the industry, with footprints being witnessed in all sectors including banking, stock exchanges, insurance, and non-banking institutions.

The largely known credit crunch witnessed in the first decade of this century unleashed some interesting revelations for this industry. While it led to financial giants melting down, stock markets collapsing, millions losing jobs, businesses facing bankruptcies, and banks themselves crashing, yet this recession only marginally brushed the gigantic Islamic finance industry that was growing at a pace equal to its parallel conventional sector and hence revealed its resilience to the shocks. The nihility of fallibilities related to conventional banking institutions and their traditional instruments, including mortgaged-backed securities (MBS), collateralized debt obligation (CDO), and credit default swaps (CDSs), which are believed to be responsible for the crisis, therefore left the Islamic banking industry relatively immune to the subprime crisis (Wood, 2009; Warde, 2012; Alqahtani and Mayes, 2017).

Unfortunately, the performance of Islamic banking on ground is not all promising. What makes Islamic banking distinct from the conventional sector, at least in theory, is its profit-and-loss sharing (PLS) paradigm. In practice, however, Islamic banks all over the world, instead of moving towards PLS banking, have been relying more on debt-like financing on their assets side. Islamic banking in this sense has failed in using profit and loss sharing modes of finance at a scale that would necessitate any meaningful change in the monetary policy and its tools.

This probably is because the field has been taken over by financial and banking experts who are generally working under an environment of competition with conventional banks and are aiming at maximizing profits with minimum exposure to business risks. This has been a principal cause of their heavy reliance on the use of debt-like financing techniques, albeit seeking approval of the same from their respective *Shari'ah* boards. The PLS modes have dropped out of sight, while the dubious ones (like *Tawarruq*) are widely used.

The phenomenal growth in the number of Islamic banks all over the world, therefore, is not a result of their use of PLS structures but instead rooted in the Islamic resurgence worldwide. There however is a feeling among the masses that the sector has not covered any considerable distance towards attaining *Maqasid al-Shari'ah*, including poverty alleviation and equitable distribution of income and wealth. The movement was launched to usher in a financial system that would help remove the inequity and inefficiency perpetrated by the dominant system based on debt, yet it fell prey to it. It is our duty to not endorse a process that could someday take us back to the same system. There is a pertinent need to step back on track, which is only possible through an innovative recourse by switching to sharing-based modes and asset-based financing. Alternatively, this performance is fragmentary, and use of dubious instruments and departure from their actual aim of replacing the dominant debt-based system would reduce Islamic banks to financing institutions with Islamic addendums merely cloning their conventional counterparts.

Further discussion

The policy makers in the world today are ready to gamble global prosperity on a set of theoretical propositions and innovatory tools as pioneered under their own chosen brand of economics. Though the financial system today is marred with diseases including fractional reserves, moral failure, poor governance, easy credit, imprudent lending, excessive debt and leverage, and regulation and supervision failure, what lay at the epicentre of these problems are the issues of debt and interest. In today's economies, debts are issued and reissued, speculative stories drive irrational markets, and hikes in asset prices turn into asset bubbles which, once popped, take economies after economies into recession.[17] Once this chronic indebtedness propels into a lack of demand, asset prices fall, markets collapse, and countries are plagued with huge layoffs and mass unemployment.

Interest, which should have had no role in the creation of money and money management, is embedded in the bedrock of the modern financial system. Had it not been for interest, the world and its financial system would have been safe from financial gambles like the expansion of keyboard credit and quantitative easing, all of which are played to save a few big giants at the cost of millions of individuals whose economic welfare is put at risk.

The fragilities of the contemporary fractional reserve system and the risks attached to the reckless use of debt instruments as well as interest as tools for money creation and management are crystal clear. Additionally, changing the international financial system is by no means easy. We clearly need to consider the cards we can play, which certainly are limited. Crudely, the United States wants to inflate the rest of the world, while the latter is trying to deflate the United States. The United States must win, since it has infinite ammunition, that is, there is no limit to the dollars the Federal Reserve can create. What needs to be discussed is the terms of the world's surrender (Hudson, 2010).

The performance of Islamic banks has also shown that they have little option in the mutter of credit creation: their methods and precautions could of course be different. As Hasan (2011) notes, the real question in fact is on the control side, since it still requires contemplation about what would or could replace the bank rate as control weapon in the hands of the central bank.

An overhaul is impossible. The requirement now is to keep Islamic financial institutions away from dodgy modes that resemble the debt-ridden financial arrangements which have played havoc with the economy of man. Interest is at the epicentre of money's creation and extinction today. Here, too, the pioneers have blazed the trail and have devised instruments that replace interest by sharing in the kit of tools needed for expanding or shrinking the supply of money. They propose that the central bank will buy financial papers from the state that promise a rate of return linked to the growth of the national economy, paying it with newly created money. The need of the day is to start putting things into practice and realize that unless the plague that has diseased the whole financial landscape is completely removed from our financial institutions, every step we take will take us further from our destination.

The realm is large, and a lot has yet to be done. The need of the day is to withdraw from labyrinths of utopian debate of what could replace the world's financial order. Instead, like the work of a reductionist, each ideal should be reduced down to small doable and realistic targets, so that with each step taken, another ring enters the chain and it keeps becoming longer, yet intact. For example, instead of calling for a gold standard or full reserves, one may ask—despite the same fractional reserve system everywhere—why some countries provide more justice in term of price and financial stability than others (and other similar questions). Every time we solve one question, the clarity of our overall scheme will improve until we reach the end, where it finally blossoms into the ideal financial system of Islam that is our ultimate aim.

Conclusion

The credit-based economies and perpetual debt structures drenched in interest have grown into a vicious web which the world's financial structure has fallen prey to. Debts are issued and reissued, speculative stories drive irrational markets, and hikes in asset prices turn into asset bubbles which, once popped, take economies after economies into recession. Once this chronic indebtedness propels us into a lack of demand, asset prices fall, markets collapse, and countries are plagued with huge layoffs and mass unemployment. Downhill from there, the world has lately hopped on the bandwagon of the financial boondoggle called quantitative easing. Apparently, the irrational exuberance of flooding liquidity to financial markets in times of cantankerous downturns through fractional reserve structure of modern banking coupled with debt[18] that has penetrated all corners of financial relations and monetary management appears to be at the bottom of all financial catastrophes. The rebuttal of self-apprehensions like gold and silver as Islamic money has come from Caliph Umar himself, while we are moving towards a money with no corporeal existence. The performance of Islamic banks has been fragmentary, and the use of dodgy instruments along with departure from their actual aim of replacing the dominant debt-based system has reduced them to institutions with Islamic addendums merely cloning their conventional counterparts. The need is there, yet changing the international financial system is by no means easy. Meaningful small steps would serve better than aimless quantum leaps. The role of debt or credit in financing is not new. No money can manage itself, and money must be managed by humans; hence, the utmost criteria for its selection would be its efficiency and fairness. There is real need for new money in a world characterized by an increasing population and expanding market. The actual challenge is to discover a proper mix and link money creation in the monetary system to real wealth generation. Islamic banks need to distance themselves from dubious modes that resemble the debt-ridden arrangements of interest-based financial institutions. The realm is large, and a lot has yet to be done. The need of the day is to withdraw from utopian debates and switch to pragmatic steps; each, once taken, would add another ring to the chain. Every time we solve one labyrinth, the clarity of our system will improve until we reach the end, where it finally blossoms into the ideal financial system of Islam that we today are arguing about.

> "There is a light at the end of the tunnel, but the way out is through".
>
> —David Allen

Notes

1 "Powerful global asset price inflation" of the mid-1920s was "fuelled by the monetary disequilibrium created by the Benjamin Strong Fed" (Brown, 2015).
2 Central banks tend to follow this policy of reducing short-term interest rates to cope with the threat of deflation and recession. However, an alternative policy is required in situations where aggregate demand fails to respond to even lower rates.
3 See Figure 10.1.
4 Interestingly, this happened despite a prohibition of using quantitative easing in EU law.
5 Historical evidence tells that the United States has financed most of its recent current account deficits by issuing dollar-denominated debt; hence foreign official holdings of U.S. treasuries have grown dramatically in the last few decades.
6 Where one country represents the United States whereas the other represents the rest of the world.
7 Foreign holding of U.S. treasuries has reached a record high of $7.0666 trillion (Chavez-Dreyfuss, Reuters, 2020).
8 It is beyond the scope of this study to approve or disapprove either of the diametrically opposing opinions present on the topic.

9 Ibn e Taymiyyah opined that money is a matter of convenience, and so is the commodity (or non-commodity), whatever people find suitable to use as money (Siddiqi, 2014).

10 Some argue that this includes the protection of wealth (*hafiz al-mal*) by retaining its store of value function of money.

11 M. Nejatullah Siddiqi reflects upon this issue in an interesting way. According to him, Ibn Khaldun was an empiricist and wrote what he observed, in the language of his times, stating observed facts as eternal truths. Had he been living today, "Ibn Khaldun today would have said, Lo! God created computers to usher in electronic money!" (Siddiqi, 2006).

12 Japan and several other countries have successfully driven down rates close to zero.

13 He instead introduced copper coins, withdrawing his initial proposal.

14 Paper money came into circulation in China some 150 years later.

15 Years later Islamic dinars circulated throughout Europe, the era that French historian Maurice Lombard has referred to as "1'âge du dinar et de la suprématie économique du monde musulman" (Koehler, 2014).

16 A number of eminent Islamic economists have proposed their models of full reserve banking with some differences in their modus operandi; a discussion on the nuances of these is beyond the scope of our study. For the detailed dynamics of these models and their analyses, see: Kahf (1978), Al-Jarhi (1981, 1983), Iqbal and Khan (1981), Choudhury (1997, 2004) and Siddiqui (2008).

17 Economists therefore draw an analogy between carbon dioxide and debt pollution (Hudson, 2010).

18 Both emanating from incidence of interest in the system.

References

Abdullah, A. (2016). *The Islamic Currency*. Kuala Lumpur: International Council of Islamic Finance Educators (ICIFE).

Al-Jarhi, M. (1981, June). Towards an Islamic Monetary and Financial System: Structure and Implementation. *The Arabic Publications Series 5*. King Abdulaziz University, Jeddah, KSA. Retrieved from http://iei.kau.edu.sa/Files/121/Files/149853_48-Al-Jarhi.pdf

Al-Jarhi, M. (1983). A Monetary and Financial Structure for an Interest-Free Monetary Economy: Institutions, Mechanism and Policy. In Z. Ahmad, M. Iqbal, and M.F. Khan (eds.), *Money and Banking in Islam*. Jeddah: Center for Research in Islamic Economics; Islamabad: Institute of Policy Studies (IPS).

Al-Jarhi, M. (2016). The Nature of Money in Modern Economy: Implications and Consequences (MPRA Paper No. 72238). Munich Personal RePEc Archive.

Alqahtani, F., and Mayes, D.G. (2017). The Global Financial Crisis and Islamic Banking: The Direct Exposure to the Crisis. *Banks and Bank Systems*, *12*(3), 100–12. doi:10.21511/bbs.12(3).2017.08

Bernanke, B. (2015, March 30). Why Are Interest Rates So Low? *Ben Bernanke's Blog*, Brookings Institution.

Brown, B. (2015). *A Global Monetary Plague: Asset Price Inflation and Federal Reserve Quantitative Easing*. New York: Palgrave Macmillan.

Canzoneri, M., Cumby, R., Diba, B., and López-Salido, D. (2013). Key Currency Status: An Exorbitant Privilege and an Extraordinary Risk. *Journal of International Money and Finance*, *37*, 371–93. doi:10.1016/j.jimonfin.2013.06.006

Chapra, M.U. (1984). A Review of the Islamic Economy: Analytical Study of the Functioning of the Islamic Economic System: Plainfield, Indiana: The Muslim Students' Association of the United States and Canada by Monzer Kahf. *Journal of Research in Islamic Economics*, *1*(2), 81–3.

Chavez-Dreyfuss, G. (2020, April 16). UPDATE 1-Foreign Holdings of U.S. Treasuries Hit Record High-Data. *Reuters*. Retrieved from www.reuters.com/article/usa-treasury-securities/update-1-foreign-holdings-of-u-s-treasuries-hit-record-high-data-idUSL2N2C32BY

Choudhury, M.A. (1997). *Money in Islam: A Study in Islamic Political Economy*. London: Routledge.

Choudhury, M.A. (2004). Micro Money and Real Economic Relationship in the 100 Percent Reserve Requirement Monetary System. *Review of Islamic Economics*, *8*(15), 35–54.

Cline, W.R. (2015). Quantity Theory of Money Redux? Will Inflation Be the Legacy of Quantitative Easing? *National Institute Economic Review, 234*, R15–26.

CRFB. (2016, May 16). Donald Trump's Treasury Buyback Plan. *Committee for a Responsible Federal Budget*. Retrieved from www.crfb.org/blogs/donald-trumps-treasury-buyback-plan

Çizakça, M. (2010). The Case against the Islamic Gold Dinar. MPRA Paper No. 26645. Munich Personal RePEc Archive, Munich.

ECB. (2020, March 18). ECB Announces €750 Billion Pandemic Emergency Purchase Programme (PEPP). Retrieved from www.ecb.europa.eu/press/pr/date/2020/html/ecb.pr200318_1~3949d6f266.en.html

Federal Reserve Bank of Chicago. (2009). *Modern Money Mechanics a Workbook on Bank Reserves and Deposit Expansion*. Chicago: Federal Reserve Bank of Chicago.

Fratzscher, M., Lo duca, M., and Straub, R. (2018, February). On the International Spillovers of US Quantitative Easing. *The Economic Journal*, *128*, 330–77. doi:10.1111/ecoj.12435

Gourinchas, P., and Rey, H. (2007). From World Banker to World Venture Capitalist: Exorbitant Privilege. In R. Clarida (ed.), *G7 Current Account Imbalances, Sustainability and Adjustment*. Chicago: University of Chicago Press.

Hasan, Z. (2011). Money Creation and Control from Islamic Perspective. MPRA Paper No. 28366. Munich Personal RePEc Archive, Munich.

Hudson, M. (2010). *US "Quantitative Easing" Is Fracturing the Global Economy*. Working Paper No. 639. Berlin: Levy Economics Institute of Bard College.

Iqbal, M., and Khan, M.F. (1981). *A Survey of Issues and a Programme for Research in Monetary and Fiscal Economies of Islam*. International Center for Research in Islamic Economics, King Abdul Aziz University, Jeddah and Institute of Policy Studies, Islamabad.

Kahf, M. (1978). *The Islamic Economy: Analytical Study of the Functioning of the Islamic Economic System*. Plainfield, Indiana: The Muslim Students' Association of the United States and Canada.

Koehler, B. (2014). *Early Islam and the Birth of Capitalism*. London: Lexington Books.

Lund, S., Woetzel, J., Windhagen, E., Dobbs, R., and Goldshtein, D. (2018, June). *Rising Corporate Debt Peril or Promise?* (Discussion Paper). Amsterdam: McKinsey Global Institute (MGI), Multiple offices.

Mackintosh-Smith, T. (2019). *Arabs: A 3,000-Year History of Peoples, Tribes and Empires*. Yale, UK: Yale University Press.

McLeay, M., Radia, A., and Thomas, R. (2014). Money Creation in a Modern Economy. *Quarterly Bulletin, Q1*. Bank of England's Monetary Analysis Directorate.

Moore, B.J. (2001). Some Reflections on Endogenous Money. In L.P. Rochon and M. Vernengo (eds.), *Credit, Interest Rates and the Open Economy: Essays on Horizontalism* (pp. 11–30). Cheltenham: Edward Elgar.

Murphy, R.P. (2019). More Than Quibbles: Problems with the Theory and History of Fractional Reserve Free Banking. *The Quarterly Journal of Austrian Economics*, *22*(1), 3–25.

Rowbotham, M. (1998). *The Grip of Death, a Study of Modern Money, Debt Slavery and Destructive Economics*. Charlbury, UK: Jon Carpenter Publishing.

Shafiq, A. (2020). Tekafül Ve Tasarrufa Dayali Finans. In A. Shafiq (ed.), *Türkiye'de Islam Iktisadi-2019*. Istanbul: ILKE.

Siddiqi, M.N. (2006). A Discussion with Professor Siddiqi. M.N. Siddiqi & Kreatoc Ltd. Retrieved from www.islamic-finance.com/item141_f.htm

Siddiqi, M.N. (2014). Man and Money. In M.A. Choudhury (ed.), *Socio-Cybernetic Study of God and the World System*. Hershey: IGI Global.

Siddiqui, S.A. (2008). An Evaluation of Research on Monetary Policy and Stability of the Islamic Economic System. *Proceedings of the Seventh International Conference on Islamic Economics & Finance*, Jeddah, 1–3 April.

Stiglitz, J.E. (2010). *The Stiglitz Report: Reforming the International Monetary and Financial Systems in the Wake of the Global Crisis*. United Nations.

Warde, I. (2012). Status of the Global Islamic Finance Industry. In D.M. Eisenberg and C.R. Nethercott (eds.), *Islamic Finance: Law and Practice*. Oxford, UK: Oxford University Press.

Wood, A. (2009). Islamic Finance Escapes Worst of Crisis. *Financial Times*. Retrieved from https:// www.ft.com/content/28e16ac6-5341-11de-be08-00144feabdc0?nclick_check=1

Index

Note: Page numbers in *italic* indicate a figure and page numbers in **bold** indicate a table on the corresponding page. Page numbers followed by "n" indicate a note.